T0325309

ADVANCE PRAISE FOR *FIXING FOOD*

"Dr. Williams offers a scathing—and justified—indictment of the FDA, the nation's most powerful regulatory agency. From his decades of experience as a senior food regulator there, he provides numerous examples of bureaucrats making decisions about the U.S. food supply that protect their own jobs, reputations,and budgets, rather than public health."
—Henry I. Miller, M.S., M.D., Former Founding Director of the FDA's Office of Biotechnology

"The FDA does very little to keep our food safe or address obesity or the other evolving dietary challenges Americans face. Instead, the 'food bureaucrats' are extremely good at issuing and enforcing regulations that restrict trade, drive consumer costs up, and advance the FDA's power and budget with your tax dollars. Richard Williams' brilliant exposé, taken from his long and distinguished career fighting the good fight within the FDA, is brilliant, insightful, and poignant. At times, it's laugh-out-loud funny, but you feel guilty laughing because the bureaucratic stupidity at work affects real people—us.
—Ret. Brigadier General Dale Waters, USAF and Military Executive and Director for Military Support and Operations, National Geospatial-Intelligence Agency.

"In *Fixing Food,* Richard Williams has provided something truly unusual. Taking us inside the FDA bureaucracy, where he worked as an economist for decades, he's given us a well-written, often entertaining, highly informative account of both meaningful and meaningless efforts tomake our food safer and better.Whether you are an economist, policy nerd, politician, or just a good old consumer who wantsto know more, if you start reading, I am betting you won't stop till you finish the last chapter."
—Bruce Yandle, Dean Emeritus, College of Business & Behavioral Science, Clemson University and former Executive Director, U.S. Federal Trade Commission

"Williams' engaging account of life as an FDA insider provides a startling perspective on how government bureaucracy undermines the safety, affordability, and variety of food we eat."
—Professor Jayson Lusk, Distinguished Professor, Department Head of Agricultural Economics, Purdue University

"This is an eye-opening account of efforts to bring risk analysis and economics into federal food safety regulation. Told by a veteran insider of the FDA, the book is a must read for anyone interested in food safety or the federal rulemaking process."
—The Honorable John Graham, Former Administrator of the Office of Information and Regulatory Affairs, Office of Management and Budget; former Dean of the Indiana University O'Neill School of Public Health and founder of the Harvard Center for Risk Analysis

"The Food and Drug Administration, established in 1906, was the first federal regulatory agency devoted to health and safety. So why, after more than a century, have foodborne illnesses-per-capita remained unchanged and has obesity increased? In *Fixing Food: An FDA Insider Unravels the Myths and the Solutions,* Richard Williams addresses those questions with a tell-all account of the dysfunction and misaligned incentives of the agency where he worked for almost three decades. With amusing anecdotes and war stories of battles he lost and won, Williams reveals the bureaucratic infighting, political maneuvering, and interest group influence that he concludes undermine food policies today. He then offers a path forward, abandoning the tired approaches of the last century and embracing new technologies and practices that can usher in a healthier future."
—Susan E. Dudley, Director, The George Washington University Regulatory Studies Center, Distinguished Professor of Practice, Trachtenberg School of Public Policy & Public Administration

FIXING FOOD

AN FDA INSIDER UNRAVELS THE MYTHS AND THE SOLUTIONS

RICHARD A. WILLIAMS, Ph.D.

A POST HILL PRESS BOOK
ISBN: 978-1-63758-012-7
ISBN (eBook): 978-1-63758-013-4

Fixing Food:
An FDA Insider Unravels the Myths and the Solutions
© 2021 by Richard A. Williams, Ph.D.
All Rights Reserved

Post Hill Press
New York • Nashville
posthillpress.com

Published in the United States of America
1 2 3 4 5 6 7 8 9 10

This book is dedicated to my loving wife, Christine Clements, who has been my backbone helping me to keep going, and my son, Tripp Williams, who always gives me new ideas. This book is based on my notes and memories from my time at the Food and Drug Administration and reflects events as such. With the exception of very senior people and those who requested to be in the book, all names have been changed.

TABLE OF CONTENTS

Acknowledgments

Thanks to Sarah Precourt for helping me with my website and weekly posts; Michelle Katz for her help with Twitter; Tim Noonan (consultant and president of Heritage Histories) who was an early help with creating the book and the book proposal; Michelle Mercurio (Story Brand Marketing) who helped with my brand and was an enthusiastic supporter helping me to keep my flagging spirits up; Katherine Taylor (editor); Debra Wolf (editor); Deb Ewing, editor and artist, who inspired me; Kyle Clements (reviewer), Jenifer Abi-Najm (reviewer), Katharine May Ghani (reviewer), David Zorn (reviewer), Arlington Writers Group (chapter reviews), and, particularly, Dale Waters who gave the book a thoroughly edited review; the Pendemics (chapter reviews); Karen Chase of the James River Writers, for referring me to Lisa Hagan, my agent, who believed in the project and managed to find a publisher who was willing to take this on; Debra Englander (Consulting editor) and Heather King (Production Editor); and Post Hill Press for publishing it.

Prologue

WE WANTED TO BE HEROES, part of something big and good that would make our lives meaningful. By the time I started at the FDA in 1980, it was mostly show over substance.

The decline of the Food and Drug Administration started in the late twentieth century, when we had no obvious solutions to make food safer or to help people make healthier choices. When we couldn't think of any fresh ideas, we had to focus on our survival. No one strategized or had top-level planning meetings about survival. It was more of an evolution. We had to maintain the illusion that we were still the protectors, that people could depend on us to safeguard the family dinner.

The show wasn't to entertain; it was to make the public trust us. We even convinced ourselves that we should be trusted.

But that was later. Early on, and well before I got there, we were heroes.

The FDA was created over one hundred years ago, when an unknown writer named Upton Sinclair published *The Jungle* to alert the public about what "industrial masters were doing to their victims," the migrant workers in Chicago's meat plants. It was the beginning of mechanization in the United States, and Sinclair was concerned with rapid production lines, long working hours, and unsafe conditions. He later admitted that his 1906 book had failed, as "he aimed at the public's heart and by accident hit it in the stomach."[1]

Sinclair wrote, "The meat would be shoveled into carts, and the man who did the shoveling would not trouble to lift out a rat even when he saw one—there were things that went into the sausage in comparison with which a poisoned rat was a tidbit." The book caused a major public-health scandal, something that had never affected the young American nation before.

Sinclair wasn't the only one. Harvey Wiley, a chemist in the Department of Agriculture in the 1880s and 1890s, was passionate about testing foods for contaminants and had tried unsuccessfully to get bills through Congress. When the bills failed, he took a budget of $5,000 and formed a squad of twelve young volunteers. All were men without families from the US Department of Agriculture's (USDA) Bureau of Chemistry and Georgetown Medical College. They became known as the "Poison Squad." Wiley deliberately fed them chemicals at high enough doses to make them sick. One Christmas meal included turkey, turnips, cranberry sauce, and borax. Borax, once used as a food preservative, can cause vomiting and respiratory illness when taken in exceedingly high doses. Wiley published his results in *Good Housekeeping* magazine; he became known as one of the first consumer crusaders and was nicknamed "Old Borax."

Between Sinclair's and Wiley's alarming publications, President Teddy Roosevelt felt pressure to involve the federal government in food safety. He didn't trust either Sinclair or Wiley; the former was a known socialist, and the latter, in President Roosevelt's mind, a publicity seeker. He observed of Sinclair's book: "I wish he had left out the ridiculous socialist rant at the end[2]…betraying the pathetic belief" in socialism to solve social problems.[3]

But President Roosevelt, along with many food manufacturers, was concerned about food purity. Despite his misgivings, two factors influenced him. First, he recalled that while he served in Cuba during the Spanish American War, hundreds of American troops had died from eating rotten meat from America's meat packers.[4]

What really got to President Roosevelt was whisky. There were two methods of making whisky: distilled grain (straight whisky) and rectified (later known as "blended whisky"). Straight whisky is distilled and aged in barrels, while rectified is distilled twice and then blended with aged whisky for coloring and flavoring. When Wiley demonstrated to President Roosevelt how rectified whisky could be turned into ten-year-old scotch, the president said, "If a man can't get a good drink of whisky when he comes home from work, then there ought to be a law to see that he does."[5]

Just to make sure the food safety reports were accurate, President Roosevelt sent his own agents into the meat plants and had them report directly back to him. That report, known as the Neill-Reynolds report, was described in the *Chicago Daily Tribune* on June 5, 1906:

> *Meats intended for canning purposes are thrown into heaps on filthy floors.... We saw meat shoveled from filthy wooden floors, piled on tables rarely washed, pushed from room to room in rotten box cars, in all of which process it was in the way of gathering dirt, splinters, floor filth, and the expectoration of tuberculous and other diseased workers.[6]*

That was enough for President Roosevelt to create America's first public health agency, the Food and Drug Administration.

The FDA had tremendous successes in the early years, cleaning up plants and preventing obvious poisons from being added to food. While those problems are still with us in small measure today, they are no longer the biggest problems with food. Our current problems lie in nutrition and ubiquitous foodborne pathogens in every arena of food production.

The biggest food-safety solution, although not immediately adopted by the FDA, was the discovery in 1864 by Louis Pasteur that tiny microbes in food could cause disease, and that you could kill them with heat. Pasteurization, the application of heat, is still the best preventive technology for making food safe.

In the early part of the twentieth century, milk was responsible for 25 percent of all food and waterborne diseases. When the FDA required pasteurization, that problem was all but eliminated.[1,7] In 1973, the FDA required commercial sterilization for canned products and reduced botulism outbreaks by 33 percent.

Nearly forty years later, on March 14, 2009, President Barack Obama declared, "There are certain things that only a government can do. And one

---

1 Unfortunately, besides pasteurization, some milk producers also used formaldehyde as a preservative.

of those is ensuring that the foods we eat are safe and don't cause us harm." Andrew C. von Eschenbach, a Republican who was commissioner of the FDA in 2007, said, "Nothing good in creating a healthier America through food and medical products will come to pass without the involvement of the FDA." On its website today, the FDA states, "Today, as in the past, FDA strives above all else to safeguard the health and well-being of the American people."

In 1980, when I joined the FDA, I believed those things.

PART I:
THE BUREAUCRAT YEARS

WHEN I FIRST JOINED FDA, I had a lot to learn about being a successful bureaucrat. Ultimately, I succeeded, but only after making every conceivable mistake.

During my twenty-seven years at FDA, we handled huge issues like infant formula, seafood, and fruit-juice safety, as well as nutrition issues including obesity and implementing the Nutrition Labeling and Education Act.

All of this had to be done while controlling the influences over FDA to ensure to that our budgets continued to grow, our regulatory scope continued to increase, and we limited the interference in our decisions from congress, the courts, and the executive branch. We also needed to manage the press, the industry, the activists, and academics.

Early on, my first boss told me that regulations were just to show we were doing something. We didn't have to accomplish anything.

Chapter 1:
WELCOME TO THE FDA, YOU'RE FIRED

"I WOULD NEVER DO THAT. I'm not an economic prostitute!"

The old man with wild white hair and an untucked shirt turned a shade of purple.

"You will absolutely do it, or you're fired."

His aide standing next to him started to say, "I think what Mr. Ronk means…"

"I know exactly what he means," I cut him off.

Ronk said, "You are going to be leaving this agency."

I should have left it there, but I retorted, "You can't fire me, I'm a federal employee."

Turns out I was wrong about that. A federal employee *can* be fired in the first year without any particular reason, but that didn't end up happening to me. In October 1980, I'd only been in the Food and Drug Administration for four months when I attended a two-day orientation that resulted in that exchange.

I'd been working on my second assignment: an economic analysis of a regulation for the Bureau of Foods, as it was known then. Now known as the Center for Food Safety and Applied Nutrition, or CFSAN, it is one of six product centers including drugs, medical devices, biologics, veterinary medicine, and tobacco. They regulate twenty cents out of every dollar Americans spend.

My job was to do cost-benefit analyses of our regulations. My current assignment was about the primary component of men's hair dye, lead acetate. It was then and is still used to "progressively take the gray out of your hair." The concern was that it might cause skin cancer. Even though I was finishing my dissertation for a PhD in economics from Virginia Tech, I didn't know much about how to do a cost-benefit analysis. It wasn't in my graduate program.

I'd come to the FDA almost by accident. After leaving Virginia Tech, a large university in Blacksburg surrounded by the mountains of southwest Virginia, I worked as a professor at Washington and Lee (W&L) University in Lexington for a year. During that year, I interviewed with twenty colleges and agencies at an economist job fair in a Chicago hotel in the middle of a blustery winter. I accepted a permanent job as a professor at Fairleigh Dickinson University in Teaneck, New Jersey. That job seemed like everything I wanted in a university life: a college in a small town where I would teach and write for a living, or what economist Thorstein Veblen called the "Leisure of the Theory Class."

I left W&L at the semester's end in June 1980 and came home to McLean, Virginia, for the summer. The last thing I expected was a phone call from my chairman at Virginia Tech, Nicolaus Tideman. Nic was a Harvard-educated economist with a red pirate beard, black-rimmed glasses, and a high-pitched voice. Besides being my chairman, we'd become friends during my two years in Blacksburg.

"Hi, Richard," he said. "Congratulations on your job with Fairleigh Dickinson."

"Thanks."

"I know you interviewed with the FDA and I am curious why you didn't choose them?"

Without stopping to wonder how he knew that, I said, "I really hadn't ever considered working for the government. I just interviewed as many places as I could."

Nic continued, in his usual contemplative tone, "Perhaps you should reconsider. I don't think there are a lot of economists like you in the government and it may be that you could do some good there. At the very least, you could get some interesting stories to tell your classes."

He started me thinking. One of the classes I taught at W&L was government and business. If I was going to continue to teach those kinds of classes, it might help to spend a year or two seeing how the government worked. If Fairleigh Dickinson wouldn't be too upset, I would call the FDA and accept.

The people at Fairleigh Dickinson were gracious; they wished me well. I would leave college life behind for a while and go to the most powerful city in the world.

So, on a Monday in July 1980, I stood in front of the Bureau of Foods. It was a large, gray, rectangular building within sight of the Capitol at 2nd and C Street Southeast. I walked through the glass doors and turned to the right toward the personnel office. There were no guards, no one to show any identification. That came later after bank robbers had run through an Office of Management and Budget (OMB) building with police firing after them.

No one welcomed me. I was just told to take a seat and handed a stack of forms to fill out. After filling out paperwork for several hours, Larry Buckley showed up. He was the FDA staffer who had interviewed me in Chicago.

"You made it!" he exclaimed.

"Yep, where do I sit?"

He took me to the sixth floor and led me into a small windowless office with two desks. Mine faced the door and had a bookcase next to it with the FDA's section of the *Code of Federal Regulations*. The *Code*, if stacked end to end, would be twenty-seven feet tall.

I said hello to my new roommate, who introduced himself as Harold Winston. He was a tall, good looking, thin black man with a minimal beard who said he also worked in "management."

Larry said hello to Harold and turned back to me. "I'll be back to get you around eleven o'clock for lunch." He left, and I spent the next two hours browsing the *Code*. It was some of the most boring reading I could imagine.

I turned around to Harold's desk. Like most men in government back then, he wore a short-sleeved collared shirt, this one yellow, with a brown tie. He looked as though he should have a deep bass voice with his large angular head, but when he spoke, it was high-pitched and frequently rose a few notes higher when he giggled.

He stood up and came over to shake my hand and welcome me to FDA. I found out later that Harold had been a hometown black radical activist in

DC in the '60s along with Mayor Marion Barry. He was now a management worker in the FDA, content in a life shared with Jesus and the bureaucracy.

We became friends the first day. Harold constantly tried to figure out what I was doing there, an economist in a science organization. More important to him, however, was to convert me.

Our morning conversations went like this:

"Rich, I think today is the day you should let Jesus into your heart."

"Harold, I think today is the day you should let beer into your gut."

That always got a high-pitched snort.

My first job was an economic analysis written by an FDA chemist about leaking polychlorinated biphenyls (PCBs) in electrical transformers in food plants. Apparently, one had leaked and some got into the food. I had suggested on the top of the analysis that, rather than replace the transformers, they should just put a six-inch concrete wall around them. If the transformers leaked, it would be easy to spot before the PCBs went anywhere, and they could fix them. Since this would save money by not having to replace the transformers, I thought it was a neat idea. If anyone ever read it, they didn't tell me.

Within my first three months, I was assigned to write the economic analysis of the lead-acetate decision. There was no internet back then, but we had an excellent library that would get us any article or book we needed. I requested books about cost-benefit analysis and papers on lead and toxicology (the science of poisons).

One of the first things I found out was that the Romans made lead acetate by dipping lead combs in vinegar and, when combed, tiny bits of the acetate were deposited on their hair, slowly coloring it. They also boiled grape juice in lead pots that produced lead acetate. They used the resulting liquid to sweeten wine, not realizing it was toxic.

As I was reading this I wondered, *Why is this even an issue if it causes cancer? Why should it be allowed on the market?*

But I wasn't asked to make that decision; I was only asked to estimate the benefits and costs of banning it from the market. My next question was, How likely is it to give someone skin cancer?

I read the findings from animal studies. Animal studies are done with rodents (rats or mice) given massive doses of potential poisons. It took me months to understand how the studies worked and how you extrapolated results from rodents to people, but I came to understand that there was a very low chance of anyone getting cancer from using lead acetate to color their hair. That meant that the benefits of banning lead acetate were small.

Next, I had to figure out what the cost would be if we banned it. Here, the economic cost resulted from forcing men (this is primarily a man's product) to use their second-best choice for coloring their hair. There didn't seem to be any other products that colored hair slowly. I assumed men used this stuff because they didn't want people to realize that they were dying their hair. If there weren't any suitable substitutes, then the cost of a ban would be high.

That's the essence of cost-benefit analysis. Look at a decision and compare the benefits, in this case, a ban, with the costs. For example, the Consumer Product Safety Commission banned lawn darts. These were heavy darts that kids threw in the air; one of them embedded in a child's chest and killed him.[8] Benefits, preventing the death of children, were high compared to the cost of losing one toy where there are many substitutes.

They were charged with deciding which water projects, like dams, were allowed to go forward. Prior to using cost-benefit analysis, decisions were ad hoc and often contentious. They were rejecting more than half of the proposals, angering politicians on the losing end of their pet projects.

By the 1920s, the Corps required that projects must have benefits in excess of costs. Cost-benefit analysis wasn't created by economists in an ivory tower; it was created by engineers to help the Corps and Congress solve political fights.

They were charged with deciding which water projects, like dams, were allowed to go forward. Prior to using cost-benefit analysis, decisions were ad hoc and often contentious. They were rejecting more than half of the proposals, angering politicians on the losing end of their pet projects. By the 1920s, the Corps required that projects must have benefits in excess of costs. Cost-benefit analysis wasn't created by economists in an ivory tower; it was created by engineers to help the Corps and Congress solve political fights.

See the "History of Cost Benefit Analysis" from the Chicago Chapter of the American Statistical Association, https://community.amstat.org/zthechicagochapterold/calendar/pastevents/20052006/may52006conference/downloadpresentationshistoryofcostbenefitanalysis.

I ended up with an analysis showing small benefits from a ban, because the dye was unlikely to cause cancer, but large costs because there were no suitable substitutes. I turned in my analysis and forgot about it.

Several days later, one of the young female staffers from the center director's office found me sitting at my desk. I'd met her but had forgotten her name. She stood in my doorway and I looked up.

"Hi Richard, how's it going?"

"Fine."

"They've read your analysis, but they need two analyses, not one."

"I don't know what other analysis you're talking about."

"Well, they haven't decided whether to ban that stuff yet, so they need one that supports a ban, and one that doesn't."

I just stared at her, letting that sink in. She didn't understand that I was very close to finishing my dissertation and would soon be a *professional PhD economist* and was not about to compromise my integrity by honoring this request.

"Please let *them* know that *they* will only get *one* analysis, the one I've already sent in."

Her face collapsed.

"But…," she started.

"One analysis, and they have it."

In my naïve mind, that was the correct, professional response.

"Okay, I'll tell them." She turned on her heel and walked away.

A few weeks later, I was sitting in the FDA orientation class on the first floor with about twenty-five new FDA inductees. Most of the other new employees were in their twenties and thirties. Although none of us knew each other, we were excited and talking to the people next to us about our new jobs. The first few speakers welcomed us and talked about what the FDA did and what the Bureau of Foods regulated.

Then we were excused for lunch for an hour and a half. I went out to lunch with Larry and had several beers.

When we sat back down after lunch, we were introduced to Richard J. Ronk, the deputy center director. He was the sloppiest man I had ever seen. He was fat, with gray and white hair flying everywhere, and his shirt was tucked in front and hanging out the back. I found out later that he gave a nutrition talk in Atlanta one time (weighing in at 250 pounds) and some lady got up and said, "You people from Food and Drug…. You're all nutritional disgraces."[9] One of my scientific colleagues described him as a science imposter. He bullied people to cover up the fact that he didn't know what he was talking about.

Ronk started and everyone quieted down immediately to hear from the first senior manager we'd encountered. He talked about what we (FDA) did and how we, the new recruits, would fit in. He kept emphasizing following orders and even ended with: "Keep your nose clean and to the grindstone and you won't get into trouble."

I sat there thinking, *Wait, this is a science organization, but he sounds like an army sergeant.*

With a few beers in me, I got more and more upset with Ronk. I began to think he was just like whoever had told me to do two analyses that came to opposite conclusions.

At the break, I marched up to the front of the classroom with Larry trailing me. I asked Ronk if he believed I should have followed that order.

His face flushed red, and he shouted, "That instruction came from me!"

"I would never do that. I'm not an economic prostitute!"

The old man with wild white hair and untucked shirt turned a shade of purple.

"You will absolutely do it, or you're fired."

His aide standing next to him started to say, "I think what Mr. Ronk means…"

"I know exactly what he means," I cut him off.

Ronk said, "You are going to be leaving this agency."

I should have left it there, but I retorted, "You can't fire me, I'm a federal employee."

Of course, I had no idea if that was true, and of course it wasn't.

I understood that he had just fired me.

Larry, who said nothing during this whole exchange, turned to me. "You blew it."

I later realized that he meant I had drawn unwanted attention.

I came into work the next day waiting for someone with a bunch of paperwork to escort me out of the building. I didn't see any reason to work, so I just sat there and read. No one came.

No one came the next day, or the next.

The next few weeks, as I walked down the halls, people ducked into doorways rather than acknowledge me. A leper would have gotten a warmer reception.

Larry told me later he had a dream where we were both in a foxhole and we had a machine gun to fend off invaders—Ronk and the other managers. I accepted it at the time, two lonely economists under fire, but later realized it was only me against them. I should have known that when Larry didn't speak up for me.

You're wondering what happened, right? Nothing. Nothing ever happened. The issue just faded away. He could have fired me, but didn't.

No one ever told me, but the FDA ended up not banning lead acetate.[10]

Not long after that, my office director retired. Taylor Quinn was a small, bald man, and I'd heard he had an encyclopedic knowledge of food-and-drug law.

I didn't really know him well, but on his last day, he asked me to come and see him. I walked into his office not having any idea what to expect but wondering if he would fire me, or at least chew me out.

I knocked on his door and saw him packing.

"Come on in," he said in a Louisiana lilt.

I came in and sat in front of his desk, waiting for it.

"Williams, you did the right thing, standing up to Ronk the way you did. Not everyone in this agency will do that. So, here's what I want to tell you: you just keep doing that kind of thing, keep standing up for what you think is right, and you'll be OK."

I was so overwhelmed, I could only squeeze out, "Thank you, sir and good luck on your retirement."

The Ronk encounter was far from the last time anyone told me to change an economic analysis. I may have been right to stand up to Ronk, but I was a long, long way from understanding the business of working in the FDA.

Chapter 2:
ONLY EVERY OTHER THING GIVES YOU CANCER

"WE THINK THIS IS A WIN for consumers," said Erik Olson of the Natural Resources Defense Council (NRDC) on October 6, 2018.[11] NRDC and others forced the FDA to ban seven food additives because rodent tests showed they could cause cancer. NRDC had written, "The U.S. Food and Drug Administration and current chemical-safety laws don't protect people from risky chemicals and additives." If it was such a big win, why, the day before, did the FDA publicly apologize for banning them, even though tests showed that the additives caused cancer? In fact, why would an agency ever apologize for taking cancer-causing substances off the market?

Fortunately for activists like Erik, a scare story always beats out one that says, "Nothing to see here, folks, return to your homes." Besides, who cares if we ban a few food additives, anyway?

Well, we all should. For a start, food additives have been enormously valuable in feeding the planet.[12] They increase shelf life, keep food fresh, prevent spoilage, and reduce the number of harmful microbes in foods. They can replace vitamins and minerals lost when food is processed, and they make food both look and taste better. Unless scientific experts already know they are safe, mostly from many years of use, they must be pre-approved by the FDA after undergoing a battery of safety tests.

Even if they are valuable, if food or color additives cause cancer, they should not be in our food supply. Who's right: Erik and his allies, or the FDA scientists who apologized because they didn't think they were preventing any cancers?

We started down the path of trying to understand what causes cancer back in the 1930s. One of the earliest scientists investigating cancer was Hermann J. Muller, an American geneticist, who dosed fruit flies with high levels of radiation. From this experiment, Muller concluded that radiation caused cancer—any amount of radiation, no matter how small.

It was assumed that if radiation is bad at low doses, then the same must be true for chemicals. In 1958, that theory led Congressman James Delaney to propose a law (commonly known as the Delaney Clause) that said that no chemical that causes cancer in man or animals will be allowed in the food supply. In the 1970s, the Environmental Protection Agency (EPA) went with this theory and announced that for their regulations, any amount of a chemical shown to cause cancer at high doses was also likely to cause cancer at low doses. That theory is the key to unraveling the mystery.

EPA's theory found a champion with President Richard Nixon in 1971, who, realizing that people feared what was then called "The Big C," started a war on cancer. Congress joined the war with a $1.6 billion cancer "moonshot."[13] Ten years later, in 1981, the Delaney Clause was responsible for Ken Harvey walking into my office.

He said, "There's a guy you don't know yet, a toxicologist named Dave Brandt."

Ken was a thirty-year-old mathematical statistician with thinning brown hair and a round Charlie Brown face. He had the abstract air of someone so lost in thought they would walk off a pier in a fugue. I'd met him briefly the year before when I asked him a question about lead acetate.

"Dave and I have been working on this risk paper about Delaney. We know that Delaney doesn't work, and we've figured out a way that the FDA doesn't have to ban everything that comes up in an animal test as a 'carcinogen.' We'd like you to review it."

"That sounds cool, but why me?"

I was still new and didn't know much about carcinogens or risk assessment.

"Because you're an economist and we used economics in the paper."

"When do you need comments back?"

"How about a week from today?"

I took the paper and read it right after Ken left my office. It had lots of equations in it, but it didn't take me too long to figure out what they were doing. At the time the Delaney Clause passed, scientists could detect a chemical in food in one part per million.

That's like being able to find a drop of a chemical in a ten-gallon bucket of water.

By 1980, it was well below one part per trillion.

That's like being able to find a drop of chemical in a lake.

If the method is sensitive enough, it means you can find a chemical that is classified as a carcinogen in almost any food. Most people at the FDA knew about the "sensitivity of method" problem by the '80s. The other related problem that accompanies the sensitivity issue is that too many chemicals are classified as carcinogens because of the way we test for them.

Toward the end of the '80s, the secretary of the Department of Health and Human Services (DHHS) told the world that a popular color additive, Red No. 3, had to be banned even though the risk was "extremely small." Red No. 3 was used in fruit-cocktail cherries at the time, and the rat test group ingested the human equivalent of 724,700 cans of fruit cocktail every year for their life (1,945 cans per day).[14] Nevertheless, Sidney Wolfe, head of the Public Citizen's Health Research Group, said, "It's really very simple. It causes cancer. We should get rid of it."

Ken and Dave were reacting to both the sensitivity and the high-dose problem. Giving high doses to animals to indict low doses in humans was also the problem when the FDA was considering banning the most common artificial sweetener used in the mid-'70s, saccharine.

When the FDA threatened to ban saccharine, consumers went crazy and wrote 50,000 letters to the agency. I started at FDA just after the letters came in and was curious about them. I read hundreds of them and I still remember quotes from three of the letters:

- "I am coming to Washington and I am going to shoot every bureaucrat I see." (*How would he know who we were*?)

- "Thank you for banning this substance that has been killing my brethren. Signed, the Rats of America."

- "How can feeding rats the equivalent amount of saccharin in eight hundred cans of soda a day have anything to do whatsoever with me drinking two Tabs a day?"

If we applied this principle to every food or color additive tested, we would end up banning a lot of additives that would never give anyone cancer. Ken and Dave had written a draft paper that said if the costs of banning a product exceeded the benefits (i.e., it wasn't very risky), then we shouldn't *call* it a "carcinogen." If we didn't call it a carcinogen, we wouldn't be forced under Delaney to ban it. They'd created a cost-benefit test for calling a chemical a carcinogen.

They made one mistake—they gave it to one of the agency's lawyers. The attorney immediately sent it to the FDA general counsel's office (the head lawyer), who sent word down that Ken and Dave had to recall every draft and shred them. The general counsel thought we could get in trouble for trying to thwart Congress, which, in fairness, Ken and Dave were trying to do. I forgot to shred it, but I lost it over the years.

We know a lot more now. If enforced literally, the Delaney Clause could make us ban well over half of the food we eat. We can handle small doses of just about anything and, to see why, I ask you to step back to pre-human days.

When life emerged on earth 3.5 billion years ago, it emerged as bacteria in a toxic atmosphere bombarded by high levels of ionizing radiation and nasty chemicals. Around 2.2 million years after bacteria came along, humans emerged. Throughout this period, bacteria and all larger life forms adapted to high levels of both chemicals and radiation. Had we not adapted, life would have ceased to exist. In fact, all levels of the body—molecular, cellular, and whole organisms—have a host of mechanisms that repel and repair assaults on our DNA at various stages before they can cause cancer. What this means is that we don't typically get cancer from low doses our bodies have learned through evolution to handle. We could get it from the high doses fed to rats and mice, but it doesn't make sense to apply those findings to low doses that are typical of most exposures. To make the point even sharper, when animals get cancer at extremely high doses, the way it happens internally—that is, the biological *mechanism*—is different than what typically happens when humans get cancer from low dose exposures.[15]

The Center for Science in the Public Interest went after the FDA for another "cancer" problem—urethane, accusing the FDA of failure to warn the public about it. Urethane, otherwise known as ethyl carbamate, is created in wine and liquor when they are fermented or distilled. The risk for cancer is low, and no one in the FDA wanted to tell manufacturers of aged bourbon to pour it out. Eventually, wine and liquor manufacturers agreed to do everything they could to keep the levels extremely low.

But while we were concerned about losing a twenty-year-old bourbon, no one cared that much about losing a few lipstick colors. Even though the colors in lipsticks are approved before they go into commerce (premarket approval), meaning we were not required to do cost-benefit analysis, the center director asked me to analyze them anyway.

I started with a draft proposal to ban a red color and asked Ken about the probability of getting cancer from the tiny amount of lipstick absorbed through the lips. He looked over the studies and thought it was very unlikely. There is a negligible amount of color in lipstick compared to the oils and waxes (accounting for 95 percent).[16] Some colors are derived chemically, and some are from nature like Carmine red, made from boiling down cactus beetles (Beetlejuice?). Even then, only a tiny amount of color is absorbed.

The problem that complying with the Delaney Clause imposes is, to approve an additive, you must be able to say that it is *not* a carcinogen. You can't really prove it, certainly not with animal tests. In fact, it doesn't mean anything whether the test group of animals gets more cancers than the controls, because the animal dose is so much higher than what humans get.

I wrote a cost-benefit analysis of the lipstick rule, suggesting that the benefits of preventing cancer were virtually zero, while the costs were the loss of that color for women. I emphasized that this was only one of many that we were banning.

I sent my analysis to Gary Donaldson, the rule writer in our Office of Food and Color Additives. After he'd had it for a day, I went to talk with him about it.

Gary started, "Come on, Williams, these things aren't even food additives. At least some of those are useful."

"That doesn't mean there isn't a cost if we ban a color additive."

"What possible cost can there be to banning a lipstick color, for God's sake?"

"Women care."

"Nonsense, women only need one lipstick color, and that's red."

I looked at Gary, thinking, *Only a man would say that.*

Besides food additives, people worry a lot about whether pesticides are giving us cancer. Bruce Ames, the inventor of one of the most famous tests for carcinogens, found that both synthetic and natural pesticides have about the same possibility of being carcinogenic and that 99.99 percent (by weight) of all the pesticides we are exposed to occur in plants naturally.[217] Every plant on earth has natural pesticides and, if we tested them at high enough doses, half of them would either kill the test animal or give it cancer (or both).

Today, a lot of media take their cancer cues from the International Agency for Research on Cancer (IARC), a division of the World Health Organization (WHO). Unlike our regulatory agencies, IARC didn't stop at 50 percent of all substances causing cancer. They've looked at close to one thousand substances and concluded that all but one (a substance found in toothbrush bristles), have the potential to cause cancer.

---

2   The Ames test for carcinogenicity uses a bacterium to see if a chemical can cause a mutation in DNA.

CHEERIOS, NATURE VALLEY CEREALS CONTAIN ROUNDUP INGREDIENT, STUDY FINDS

This kind of scary headline works although most people don't know what it means. I use the same technique when introducing risk analysis in college classes. I walk in with a test tube and tell the class it contains a mixture of water and arsenic. I ask for volunteers to drink it so that the class can see what happens. I even go along the aisle holding it next to them to watch them recoil. Inevitably, no one volunteers, so I drink it. Then I tell them, truthfully, that it came from their hall water fountain. This is how I begin the explanation of why it is so important that they understand that dose makes the poison.

A friend of mine from the FDA, Clark Carrington, now retired, is an excellent toxicologist. In his book, *The Science-Policy Shell Game & the Probability of Truth,* he makes the dose/response point by using federal standards for finding a safe dose of water. If water were a new ingredient in food, it would have to go through the food additive petition process, meaning the government would have to declare it safe before it could be used.

They would feed rodents, say rats, a very large dose of water, enough so that half of the rats that got the water would die (called the LD50, or lethal dose that kills half of the test group). Studies have shown the dose would be 9 percent of the rat's body weight or, for humans, about a gallon and half all at once. The rats die because the kidneys cannot keep up (a problem called hyponatremia).

Once you have the LD50, you divide by safety factors, usually factors of 10. In this case, they would be:

10—because humans are more sensitive than rats, and

10—because humans have much more response variability than rats.

Combining those two factors, we divide the high dose (LD50) by 100 (10 x 10).

Since Clark did the math for us, the answer is that the "safe" dose of water for people would be 200 grams or about 8 ounces of water a day. Any more than that and you are at risk.

Since watermelon is about 92 percent water, a study finding might say:

"Watermelon found to contain water, study finds!"

Chapter 3:
NAZI BABY KILLER

ONE OF THE MOST serious foods FDA regulates is infant formula. There are only two choices to feed babies: breastfeeding, recommended for most babies, and infant formula. Whether infant formula or breast milk is used, each is the sole source of nutrition for babies up to about four months of age.

Congress passed the Infant Formula Act in 1980 and amended it again in 1986. The original act passed because, in 1978, one manufacturer of infant formula[3] didn't add enough salt to their product. It led to 22,000 infants having chloride deficiency, critical for brain development.[18] It also led to a recall of 8.5 million cans of formula; 24,000 letters from FDA to doctors; letters to wholesalers, hospitals, food markets, drugstores, and food brokers; a criminal investigation; a House and Senate investigation; a violation of an existing law (section 402 of the Food Drug and Cosmetic Act); and over $3 billion worth of lawsuits that continued well into the 1980s. It was a serious problem, and both laws gave the FDA new authority over the contents and production of infant formula.[4]

---

3   Syntex made Neo-Mull-Soy and Cho-Free.

4   The 1980 act gave the FDA the authority to establish nutritional, quality control, record-keeping, notification, and recall requirements necessary to ensure that infant formula is safe and will promote healthy development.

The 1986 amendment, passed in the Reagan Administration, resulted from two formulas missing vitamin B6. That amendment required good manufacturing processes, regular audits, notifications to the FDA, testing every batch, record retention, and specific nutrient quality control.[19]

I was the economist assigned to write an economic analysis of the regulations that would implement both laws in 1986. What I didn't know at the time was if you criticize anything that has to do with regulating baby products, you're put in the same category as puppy beaters.

How did we get infant formula, anyway? Liebig's Infant Food was the first infant formula, invented right after the Civil War to replace wet nurses. Wet nurses were on their way out (some had been slaves) and had all but disappeared by 1900.[20]

The most common problem with infant formula is that some babies can't tolerate milk. If they can't, we call them "lactose intolerant." The only way to know this is to feed them milk-based formula. Congress couldn't do anything about that because it was just a matter of switching from one formula to another (like soy). Instead, they focused on production methods and required the FDA to monitor and test all batches for missing ingredients or contamination. In fact, both the FDA and the industry said that nutrient shortfalls were exceedingly rare events, and the FDA already had the authority it needed (section 402) to prevent this from happening again.[5] Congress, on the other hand, reasoned that the law would prevent babies "from ever being threatened by defective baby formula."

Who could argue with what seemed like a little preventive regulation? The FDA couldn't; once Congress passes a law, it's the president's job to enforce it and the FDA, as a member of the executive branch, is charged by the president to enforce the laws created by Congress.

Gary Donaldson (of the lipstick fame) was assigned to write the regulation, and he dutifully began to produce comprehensive rules for how to manufacture formula. Gary was middle-aged, white, and seemed like an easygoing fellow. Like most FDA regulation writers, he stretched the law as far as possible. In this case, it was to require lots of new record keeping, la-

---

5   One thing the law didn't address was people buying cheaper formula in a loss leader like K-Mart and then reselling it. Former FDA attorney Phil Derfler talks about this in his oral history.

beling, and reports to the FDA. Meanwhile, I was responsible for estimating the benefits and costs of his new regulation.

As I usually did, I began with the potential benefits of making safer baby formula. The first thing I found was that the FDA kept a tight rein on who could produce it. There were only five companies making formula at the time, and when people wrote in to tell the FDA they were thinking about getting into the business, we sent them a polite letter back telling them, "Please don't." That way, we could inspect the few plants more frequently.

The infant-formula industry is profitable, in part because mothers both here and abroad have been convinced that their babies deserve formula. In 1970, only 25 percent of babies were getting formula. But by 1989, advertising helped to increase the percentage to 52 percent, so that nearly every other baby was using it.[21]

To learn more about the industry, I went to one of the researchers in our consumer studies group, Joyce, who'd been conducting surveys of infant formula. Joyce was also dedicated to getting more mothers to breastfeed. She was the consummate mother; listening to her felt like listening to a mom with a gentle, guiding voice to keep a small boy on the right track in life.

She told me there were only a few firms in the industry and suggested I investigate what was going on in the Federal Trade Commission (FTC). I called over there and an economist at the FTC told me they were investigating those firms for colluding to fix prices for government-supplied formula. By 1986, because of the high prices, the state WIC (USDA's Women and Infant Children) programs were running out of money to serve needy families.[22]

I asked Joyce what the consequences of higher-priced formula were for consumers, particularly those who, for whatever reason, were not getting it free from the government.

"Rich, it's a huge problem. Most poorer women buy the powdered infant formula that you mix with water."

"Why is that a problem?" I asked.

"Because as the prices have gone up, there is evidence that they try to make it last by watering it down."

"That makes sense. Is it a serious problem?"

"You don't understand," she said, "this milk is a baby's *sole* source of nutrition and when you water it down, babies will have nutrient deficiencies.

Nutrient deficiencies cause really serious problems that affect their growth and development."

"That was the problem the law was supposed to address, right?"

"No, this causes deficiencies in all nutrients. It's much more serious than just missing something like sodium."

"Have you talked to anyone about this?"

"No, because no one takes me seriously here; I'm just the 'breastfeeding' lady."

I asked Joyce to write it down for me. I took her analysis and wrote it up in an interoffice memorandum that I sent to Gary, his boss, and mine. I outlined the new record keeping and monitoring requirements and the likely costs of each. I explained that, using existing authority, we were already carefully monitoring the few firms making formula and that there would be minimal benefits from these new regulatory requirements. I concluded by explaining how this would cause health issues for babies from poor families. The new requirements would add costs to production that would be passed on to consumers in the form of higher prices. Higher prices, in turn, would adversely affect infants in less affluent homes whose parents had to buy the formula.

This was a form of analysis I'd only recently been exposed to: risk/risk analysis. The theory says that whenever you try to reduce risk in one area, you may raise a risk in another area. I compared it to the kids' game Whac-A-Mole. Every time you whack a pop-up mole, another pops up elsewhere. We see the same thing happening when we ban pesticides; we get a replacement that is also risky. Most people, especially people in health regulatory agencies, don't like to think about these things because it just confuses the decision with harder choices.[6]

---

6   But even back in Wiley's day, they understood risk/risk trade-offs. Wiley recounted the testimony given when Congress was considering whether FDA should allow preservatives in foods. Victor Vaughan, a scientist, testified: "Experiments have shown that boric acid in large amounts disturbs digestion and interrupts good health, but they have not shown that boric acid in the small quantities which would be used as a preservative…has any effect on the animal body." After Vaughan's testimony, Robert Eccles testified that because benzoic acid was useful to kill harmful microbes, the use of preservatives in North Dakota and Berlin, Germany, was stopped. He said, "The deaths were nearly three times as many as there were during the same period as the year before." Wiley argued in his book that he was originally against adding benzoic acid but later believed that it would be all right to add

I ended my memo on infant formula with two suggestions:

1. We minimize the requirements to keep the increases in prices as small as possible and,

2. We ask the president to go back to Congress and reconsider the law based on this information.

I felt surprisingly good about the memo. I thought it was professionally researched, well written, and was exactly the job that economists were supposed to do to make regulations better. Had I asked anyone who had been at the FDA longer than me before sending out this memo, I probably would have found a better way to make my point than just throwing a memo out there.

The day after the memo went out, a red-faced Gary threw open my door and marched in clutching my memo in his fist.

"What are you, some kind of Nazi baby killer?"

I was stunned, to say the least, but I quickly recovered.

"Did you read the memo?"

He ignored that and screamed some more about how much good his regulation was going to do for the babies of the United States. He accused me of using economic *gobbledygook* (his word) to derail his vitally important regulation.

There wasn't a lot more conversation. He turned and marched out of my office and slammed the door. Another enemy. I could have written a book, *How to Make Enemies and Influence No One*.

To me, there is a happy ending to the story. The regulation was derailed. The program office said they weren't dropping it; they were just getting to more important regulations. The final rule took twenty-eight years and was finally published in 2014. There were still high testing costs but, perhaps having learned their lesson, the FDA declined to do an economic analysis, saying that the rule was "insignificant."[23] Barbara Tuchman, who wrote *The March of Folly,* might have described the success of the memorandum as "folly delayed."[24]

---

benzoic acid for use in preserving food because that would be "the less of two evils." From Harvey Wiley's 1929 book, The History of a Crime Against the Food Law.

Chapter 4:
NUTRITION MORONS

"AN ALMOND DOESN'T LACTATE, I will confess. And so, the question becomes, have we been enforcing the wrong standard of identity? The answer is probably not," said Commissioner Scott Gottlieb at the Politico Pro Summit on July 17, 2018. "The challenge for us is, as a regulatory agency, if I want to change our regulatory posture with respect to how we're enforcing the existing standards of identity, I can't just do it unilaterally."

Should almond- or other plant-based beverages be allowed to be called "milk," given the fact that they don't lactate, that is, secrete milk? Another way of stating this more precisely is, will consumers be confused if a milk made from almonds is called "almond milk"? Would they think it is from a cow named Almond? Are the people assigned to work on problems like this being punished by the FDA?

Gottlieb went on to explain that to make a change would require responding to public comments and creating draft guidance.

"That's going to take time. It's not going to take two years, but it's probably going to take something close to a year to get done," he said. "But that's what we intend to do." After two years, in August 2020, they still hadn't figured it out. Of course, almond milk has a lot of competition in alternative milks from foods like coconut, rice, cashews, walnuts, quinoa, oats, and flax.

Standards of identity, or simply, food standards, have been creating controversies since 1938, when they were first established by law. I came across food standards in 1980, when I was sitting in the food-standards division director's office.

"Rich, you just don't understand dinner parties."

When Shirley Walsh said that, I realized I'd never been to a dinner party. I was sitting in her office looking at her government gunmetal gray desk, and I could see the US Capitol behind her on the hill. Next to the window were matching gray bookshelves with *Federal Register* issues and food technology books. There were piles of paper on her desk creating a musty old paper smell. Most of them appeared to be pending regulations from who knows when.

Shirley was about fifty and at the time was one of only three women directors in the bureau. I thought of her as being German, although I had no idea whether or not that was true.

"Dinner parties" was Shirley's way of explaining to me why we had to make sure that all canned pear halves are approximately the same size.

"Rich, suppose you're sitting at a dinner table and you look at the pear salad in front of the person next to you and you see that her pear is bigger than yours."

I hadn't the faintest idea what was in a pear salad, and she could see my confusion.

"A pear salad is a slice of pear on a piece of lettuce with cottage cheese and a cherry on top of it. You can see how upset someone would be if they got a smaller pear slice than the person next to them."

I remember thinking, *We use the authority of the federal government to ensure that dinner parties go smoothly?*

How did we get here? Canned and packaged foods that were ready-to-cook emerged in the 1920s and freed women from long hours in the kitchen. But as mothers turned to packaged foods, two problems emerged: manufacturers were adding things to foods that didn't belong, like sawdust, and they were making up their own recipes. In response, to ensure that moms would not be surprised when they opened a food package, Congress passed a law declaring that food recipes should remain "like mother used to make."[7] The result was federal recipes for processed foods.

As historian Rachel Laudan says, "That we can talk about 'a cake made from scratch' when the butter, sugar, and flour that go into it are highly processed shows how we have lost awareness of the energy that formerly went into food preparation."[25] Back in the '30s, you didn't go to a store for a birthday cake; you started with flour, butter, and sugar, and you cranked out your homemade masterpiece. Soccer balls and Disney characters came later.

Food standards were also a gift for food manufacturers. No one wants to compete against better quality if they can get the government to block potential competitors with better recipes.

President Franklin Roosevelt signed the bill in 1938 that would "promote honesty and fair dealing in the interests of consumers" by requiring standardized recipes. For food, that meant sticking with "The Old Deal." FDA first standardized catsup and eliminated benzoate of soda because Harvey Wiley thought it was unnecessary. By 1905, Wiley had partnered with Henry Heinz to sell preservative-free catsup, and homemade catsup disappeared.[26] Next, they ensured that jelly should be half fruit and half sugar.

Then the courts got into it. The Supreme Court allowed an imitation jam despite the FDA arguing that moms didn't make imitation anything. They also heard a statistician testify that there shouldn't be an additive to make bread feel soft when squeezed. But for major legal food battles, nothing beat peanut butter. It took ten years of combat for the courts to say that peanut butter must consist of 90 percent peanuts and 10 percent additives.[27]

Today, about 45 percent of all foods are standardized; the rest are not.[28] Catsup is standardized; salsa is not. Guess which one has thousands of varieties to appeal to every taste?

By the late '80s, I wondered if consumers really cared about fifty-year-old recipes. I decided that I would use some of our contract money to study standards. I didn't buy Shirley's argument about pear jealousy.

---

7   In fact, along with washing machines and dishwashers, packaged food played a significant role in freeing women to work outside the home. Why not a national holiday for processed food that freed up half the population from making food from scratch?

I also knew that newer food- and color-additive rules kept the poisons and sawdust out of food, and by the 1980s, I guessed that moms didn't really know original recipes anymore.

Shirley Walsh had been replaced by Fred Shank as the food-standards director. Fred would later become the center director. I needed his signature to get the contract started, and this was to be my first meeting with him. It probably couldn't have gone worse.

He'd asked for a meeting in his office to discuss my request for proposal. Fred looked like an NFL center, at five foot eight with a barrel chest.

My view was we didn't need federal recipes, and if you sold a food that consumers didn't like, they wouldn't buy it again. I was ready to put out the contract that included a technical economic appendix on the economics of consumer choice. I knew there was very little interest in food issues among economists, so part of the reason for the appendix was to get economists interested.

I found Fred sitting at his desk facing the door. His desk was devoid of paper and he had neat bookshelves behind him. He looked up, scowling.

"Hi, I'm Richard Williams."

Fred said, "I know who you are, Williams."

Oh, that's how this meeting is going to be.

"What's this proposal all about? Why do you want to open up food standards?"

I presumed by "open up," he meant *study* them.

I replied, "I guess I wonder why we are spending time and money on food standards when we have serious food safety issues."

In my research, I found that in 1977 the FDA had spent zero dollars creating or enforcing food standards, and I thought that made sense. Interestingly, two years later, the FDA held a hearing on food labeling, and 41 percent of the people who talked about food standards said that we should eliminate them.[29]

Fred ignored my question and said, "What's this appendix all about? I can't understand a goddamn word of it."

That's when I said something stupid to the director of the food-standards division. "I didn't write it so that *you* could understand it."

Fred glared at me, stood up, walked around his desk, and faced the wall. He had his hands at his sides and began banging his head against the wall.

I stood there watching him.

Finally, he stopped, still looking at the wall and said, "Get... outta...my...office."

Another day, another enemy.

Interestingly, when the contractor sent me a finished report, most people said they liked food standards; in effect, it said that even though they didn't know what the recipe was, they wanted the same thing every time.

Still, I continued to investigate. Bottled water has an interesting "recipe." The standard requires manufacturers to distinguish between "bore hole" and "spring hole" water.

Bottled water "manufacturers" who get their water out of a spring (spring hole), meaning one of the zillion places water just bubbles up out of the ground, decided that they didn't want those who *drilled* for water (bore hole) to be marketed the same way as spring water. Perhaps this is one of those things that makes some people feel superior, bragging that they only buy water that springs naturally from the ground. Maybe they would argue that this way Gaia, Mother Earth, hasn't been violated to obtain her water.

There is absolutely no difference in how water comes out of the earth, but the food-standards scientists at the FDA are always happy to help an old constituency. For those waters that don't come from a natural spring, perhaps they can class it up by calling them *Eau du Robinet*. Penn and Teller, two comedy magicians, once asked diners at a gourmet restaurant to rate several brands of bottled water. The customers talked about the different waters having "hardness," "freshness," "crispness," or "purity," and were adamant that all were superior to tap water. Then the comedians informed them that all of the bottled water came from the garden hose outside.[30] The truth is that about 30 percent of bottled water comes right from the tap, and one of the most famous brands of this pure water comes from a tap in London's East End.

The FDA enforces standards diligently. A Massachusetts bakery that wanted everyone to love its granola bars listed "love" as an ingredient. No doubt FDA labs tested them and were unable to detect the "love ingredient" and sent a strongly worded cease-and-desist letter.[31]

In the '90s, FDA nutritionists made the case that we needed to update food standards to allow food manufacturers to lower the fat content of standardized foods. They understood that making people use the name "imitation" for ice cream with a lower percentage than 14 percent butterfat might not be the best nutrition policy.

But there was still concern that we were wasting time on trying to improve standards, so the FDA did what bureaucracies are famous for: we formed a committee. The head of the committee turned out to be Ed Stevens, my office director.

Ed was an attorney who had risen rapidly in the FDA. When he spoke, it was like summer thunder, which would have been great in courtroom dramas. I'd already had problems with Ed, who could never seem to understand how insulting he was. For example, when food company lawyers would come in and talk to him about the cost of regulations, I was never invited. When I asked him about it, he told me that these were "high-level meetings," and I wasn't "important" enough to attend.

Ten of us were assigned to the committee, including Shirley Walsh, a lifelong food-standards person. At the outset, Ed asked that we go around the room and give our opinion on what we should do about standards. Shirley started and said that she didn't see any need for changes, with the exception of a few nutritional changes for high-fat products. I was next. I said I thought we could just do away with them, that they really didn't help consumers, and that they were there just to protect incumbent firms.

As I finished, I turned to Shirley and saw she was upset.

I said, "Really, Shirley, we have definitions for canned pineapple, for God's sake."

She said, "We have eleven."

"Eleven what?"

"You don't know the eleven optional styles of pack for canned pineapples?"

"You're kidding, right?"

She began, tearfully, "Well, there are sliced, cubed, minced…" and eight more I confess I still can't remember.[8]

---

8   For example, Title 21, CFR 145.180 (vii) *Chunks*—consisting of short, thick pieces cut from thick slices and/or from peeled cored pineapple and predominantly more than 13 mil-

Ed chewed me out later for making her cry, but I already felt bad about it. Our committee got nowhere.

But the committee had to do something, as standards were now a national issue. George H.W. Bush, as Ronald Reagan's vice president, had been tasked to review the need for standards, and when he became president, he made it one of Commissioner David Kessler's issues. I had already met Dr. Kessler before we got into the standards issue.

I briefed newly appointed Commissioner Kessler on the economic executive order shortly after he joined the FDA.

I asked the FDA chief economist for the other FDA centers to join me in briefing Commissioner Kessler. Our mission was to convince him that economic analysis could help him make decisions that worked well for consumers. If they were significant regulations—defined as costing over $100 million—or politically controversial, or just regulations that OMB decided they wanted to review, the analyses were mandatory.

It was just the three of us in Commissioner Kessler's gigantic office, and I did most of the talking. I knew that this was a guy who was now nationally famous, in part for completing his law and medical degrees at the same time.

I started by thanking him for seeing us, but he just looked at me. He sat there and stared at each of us without saying a word.

I talked to him about the importance of economic analysis and how he was supposed to use the results to inform his decisions. In fact, OMB expected him to read or be briefed on our analysis of options before he decided. That is what the president's executive order required of him. When I finished, Commissioner Kessler finally spoke.

Because he hadn't objected during my few minutes of speech, I assumed that he was impressed. He paused a moment and looked at both of us.

"Let me get this straight," he said. "You guys do an analysis, but I still make the decisions about what we're going to do, right?"

"Right," we chimed in, together.

"No offense guys, but I don't really need you to make decisions."

We were stunned. But he wasn't wrong. He was the confirmed commissioner, and it was his prerogative to disregard our recommendations—

---

limeters (0.51 inch) in both thickness and width, and less than 38 millimeters (1.5 inches) in length and does not include large cubes.

no one, except the president, could force him to do otherwise. He had essentially banished us and our staffs to Siberia, and he was just beginning at the FDA. I couldn't have failed more completely, and I mumbled, "Thanks for your time," and walked out of the building.

Nevertheless, Commissioner Kessler asked Fred Shank to bring a few people, including me, to brief him on food standards.

I was ready and walked in with my notes.

I would start by telling him that only half of all foods have standardized recipes and tell him about catsup versus salsa.[9] I would tell him that we had additive rules that prevented manufacturers from adding any harmful chemicals or fillers to foods. I would tell him that markets take care of people who are disappointed with foods like fruit cocktail without enough cherries or string beans that have too much string. People wouldn't buy them a second time and they would go out of business. Manufacturers would try new recipes, like New Coke, and if they didn't sell, they would go back to their old recipes. I would tell him that we have 250 million Americans and nearly that number of unique tastes in food. These standards insulated existing manufacturers from competition, and they were a waste of FDA resources that could be better spent on food safety and nutrition.

Finally, I would tell him that protecting consumers from recipe changes is treating them like morons.

We sat around the large table in the commissioner's conference room. It was huge with a gigantic white board on one side and no windows anywhere. Besides Commissioner Kessler and several people from his staff, there were just Fred, Ed, a few people from the food-standards division, and me. By now, Fred knew that I was opposed to food standards and he probably had a fairly good idea of what I was planning to say.

Commissioner Kessler said, "Alright, we are here today to talk about food standards. As some of you may know, this is an issue that the president has an interest in. I have no particular feelings about it one way or another so I'm just here to listen to what you guys have to say. I want you to start with what would happen if we just got rid of these things."

9   Want to get into the business of making catsup? Make sure you buy a Bostwick Consistometer first to make sure that your flow is "not more than 14 centimeters in 30 seconds at 20 degrees," 21 CFR 155.194 (iii)(b). Amazon sells them for as little as $472.00.

I opened my mouth, but Fred jumped in first.

"It would be chaos," Fred said.

"Chaos?" Commissioner Kessler asked.

"Absolute chaos," Fred continued. "Manufacturers will start making food any way they want to, and no one will know what's in their food."

"So, you guys are in favor of keeping them, right?"

"Right," said Fred.

"Okay," said the Commissioner. "Thanks for coming."

He got up and walked out of the room.

Thirty years later, we would spend at least two years trying to figure out if almond milk should be allowed to be called milk.

I have inserted a sleep aid below.

CHAPTER 1—FOOD AND DRUG ADMINISTRATION DEPARTMENT OF HEALTH AND HUMAN SERVICES

SUBCHAPTER B—FOOD FOR HUMAN CONSUMPTION

PART 155—CANNED VEGETABLES

Subpart B—Requirements for Specific Standardized Canned Vegetables

Sec. 155.120 Canned green beans and canned wax beans.

"If strings have been removed for testing, as prescribed in paragraph (b)(2)(vi) of this section, test them as follows:

Fasten clamp, weighted to 250 g (8.8 oz.), to one end of the string, grasp the other end with the fingers (a cloth may be used to aid in holding the string), and lift gently. Count the string as tough if it supports the 250 g (8.8 oz.) weight for at least 5 seconds. If the string breaks before 5 seconds, test such parts into which it breaks as are 13 mm (1/2 in.) or more in length; and if any such part of the string supports the 250 g (8.8 oz.) weight for at least 5 seconds, count the string as tough. Divide the number of tough strings by the weight of the sample recorded in paragraph (b)(2)(v) of this section and multiply by 340 to obtain the number of tough strings per 340 g (12 oz.) drained weight.

(viii) Combine the deseeded pods with the trimmings reserved in paragraph (b)(2) (vi) of this section, and, if strings were tested as prescribed in paragraph (b)(2)(vii) of this section, add such strings broken or unbroken. Weigh and record weight of combined material. Transfer to the metal cup of a malted-milk stirrer and mash with a pestle. Wash material adhering to the pestle back into cup with 200 cc of boiling water. Bring mixture nearly to a boil, add 25 cc of 50 percent (by weight) sodium hydroxide solution and bring to a boil. (If foaming is excessive, 1 cc of capryl alcohol may be added.) Boil for 5 minutes, then stir for 5 minutes with a malted-milk stirrer capable of a no-load speed of at least 7,200 rpm. Use a rotor with two scalloped buttons shaped as shown in exhibit...." and so on.

Chapter 5:
POWERPHILES, DRONES, AND NERDS

"What's the use of having power if you can't abuse it?"
—Anonymous IRS agent

"Bureaucracy is the death of all sound work."
—Albert Einstein

I WAS WALKING TO my car in the basement of Federal Building #8 in Washington, DC, to go home when I saw the deputy commissioner for policy, Michael Taylor. I started talking to him about a labeling decision he'd made at a meeting that afternoon.

Rather than respond to my question about what I considered to be a dumb decision, he just said, "Your problem is that you don't see the 'Big Picture.'"

"What *is* the Big Picture?"

He just smiled enigmatically and walked to his car.

Mike was Tipper Gore's cousin, so presumably his big picture included something to do with the Democratic Party. Or maybe it was about growing the FDA. Who knows? I'd heard from other CFSANers that he used this expression often, but then left mysteriously. A few years after I retired, I found myself on a panel with Mike at Resources for the Future in DC.

Mike sat to my left on the stage and spoke just before me.

He started, "I'm going to get out of the weeds and start at the thirty-thousand-foot level."

He finished his talk, and I was next.

"I'm going to pull back to the sixty-thousand-foot level."

The audience laughed, but Mike glared at me.

No matter what he meant by the big picture, it was almost certainly about power in Washington. Mike was what I call a "powerphile." That means he loves power—for himself, but also for the agency. In between his stints in government, he'd written a tract that described his vision of the FDA becoming the apex of a vast network of federal, state, and local governments, all reporting to the FDA.[32] In return for providing data upward and submitting to the FDA's authority, the FDA would dole out cash to each of them. It wasn't too hard of a stretch for me to think he envisioned himself sitting on the FDA throne.

Except for Ronk, most of the people I had met early on in government were drones. Merriam-Webster defines the verb *drone* as "to pass, proceed, or act in a dull, drowsy, or indifferent manner." That describes the actions of drones, but the most proficient slug I encountered was Larry Buckley.

Larry had interviewed me for the FDA job during that freezing winter in Chicago. The interviews were in a large, carpeted basement room with fifty small tables adorned with placard numbers on each table. In the middle of twenty interviews, I met with Larry, the representative from the FDA. He was a small white man in his late twenties from the hills of Pennsylvania with a black beard and mustache.

He introduced himself and began asking me questions.

He asked me where I was in the dissertation process; I told him I'd spent a year working on it while teaching at Washington and Lee University, but I still needed a few months to finish it. He said that was fine. He continued, "Until now, the economic analyses have been done by a chemist, but I've been told that they will move me out of consumer studies. If you come to work with me, we will both be working on economic analysis, costs and benefits, and that kind of stuff."

Then he asked, "Have you ever read *Fear and Loathing in Las Vegas*?"

I had read Hunter S. Thompson's *tour de force* about a drinking-and-drug fueled trip to the Super Bowl for *Rolling Stone* magazine (although

Thompson never saw the Super Bowl). It was wildly popular among a certain set of people. Larry was that kind of people.

Without knowing why he'd asked, I replied, "You mean the Bible?"

I had seen Thompson on stage at Virginia Commonwealth University in Richmond, Virginia. He appeared to be happily on drugs.

Apparently, that was the answer Larry was looking for.

That's how I ended up in Federal Building #8 at 200 C Street Southwest, Washington, DC, on Monday morning in July 1980, when Larry returned at 11:00 a.m. as promised. I didn't yet know much about him other than the interview we'd had a few months earlier.

Now, at 11:00 a.m., he introduced me to the job he had in mind.

We left the FDA in his car and headed out of DC into Arlington, Virginia. He pulled into a strip-mall parking lot next to a Chinese restaurant, Szechuan Garden.

The hostess sat us, and the waitress came over and spoke to Larry. "So happy to see you today. The usual for you?"

He said, "Yes, and bring one for my friend too."

She appeared a minute later with two Budweisers.

Long before our lunch had arrived, he ordered the second round. We completed the fifth round about an hour and a half after the first, and we got back in his car. Instead of heading north over the Fourteenth Street Bridge into Washington, he went south on 395 toward Annandale.

When we pulled up in front of a small house, I followed him from the car into the front door. He went over to a television, turned it on, and said, "Wait here, I'll be right back." He marched upstairs.

By now we'd been gone over three hours and it was 2:00 p.m. After a few minutes, he came back downstairs dressed in old, grease-stained clothing.

"Look, I like to race cars and I need to go to the junkyard to find some parts. You have on nice clothes, so I know you won't want to go. Just wait here, you can watch TV. I'll be back in a while."

With that, he went out the door and closed it behind him. Daytime television is boring; I had nothing to read, so I lay down on his couch and, with a belly full of beer, fell asleep. The next thing I knew, he was waking me up.

"What time is it?" I asked.

Instead of replying directly, he said, "We'll be back in the office by five."

He drove back, and we went up to our floor.

Larry punched the time clock with a smile on his face. "Perfect, got a credit hour," he said. "See you tomorrow."

Not every lunch lasted this long, but they often went on for hours. Larry explained to me over these lunches that this was the way to "get over" on *the system*. At the end of the year, when he was getting his review, our boss told him he was inclined to stop letting him get credit hours because he was rarely in the office during those periods. Larry had violently objected to this and the director backed down.

When I pointed out to him that our boss was right, he said, "It's the principle of the thing."

One thing about drones is that they don't have to worry about being promoted. One example was Minnie, the FDA commissioner's secretary in Washington. Her boss normally worked in Rockville, Maryland, nearly twenty miles away. Apparently, when he decided to stop by on his way to Congress or to say hello to the center director, he wanted a secretary there. Most of Minnie's job was to "be there."

Minnie was a GS-13 when I worked with her (I was a GS-11). She seemed to know everyone, as she was constantly visiting people around the office. I once asked her about her job:

"How often does the commissioner come here?"

"Gosh, Rich, at the most, once a month."

"What do you do when he's not here?"

She just smiled.

I asked around. In fact, what Minnie did was to arrange trips for her friends, mostly to Atlantic City, to go gambling. In 2020, a GS-13 made an average of $116,000.

My officemate, Harold, was also a GS-13. Once, when I asked him what he did as a management analyst, he replied, "You know, this and that."

Harold was amazing. It was no accident that his desk faced the wall away from the door. One time I watched him and could see his head tilted down and his hand arm moving ever so slightly as he wrote. I decided not to say anything to him but leaned over him to see what he was doing. He was sound asleep but somehow his arm was moving as though he was writing. I never let on to anyone his secret of busy sleeping.

How did they get to be GS-13? My division director told me.

"I believe it is my job to get everyone promoted, regardless of what they do or what their ratings are."

Oddly enough, even though he knew Larry constantly cheated on his timecard, he kept promoting him.

One day, I finally told Larry that I couldn't go to lunch with him that day.

"I have to work on this analysis, it's due this week."

"What the f**k are you talking about?

"I want to get it in on time."

He turned and stomped off saying, "That is such bulls**t."

That was the day I actually started working at the FDA.

Larry, Minnie, and Harold were drones. Mike Taylor, on the other hand, was a powerphile. Ed Stevens, my longtime office director, was another powerphile. Like other powerphiles, Ed believed he was a master politician, even if he had never run for elective office. He also determined that one way to advance was to help the agency expand both the number and reach of our regulations.

I started working in Ed's office a few years into my life at the FDA. Not long after that, I gave a presentation on the Delaney Clause at a risk conference. I mentioned some problems with Delaney, particularly that as we were able to find lower and lower levels of chemicals that test carcinogenic at high doses, we would be much more likely to ban foods and additives (with very low levels of those chemicals) that were actually safe for consumption. For economics, this would mean the costs of a ban would vastly exceed the benefits. I'd taken a lot of this talk from the paper that Ken and Dave wrote, but did not address the legal issues.

There was a guy in the audience who worked at *Science,* the premiere science journal in the country. He asked me if I would like to write a brief article based on my talk for the magazine. Absolutely I would.

I wrote the article and, a few weeks later, during a routine meeting with my immediate boss, I mentioned the article.

It was a big mistake.

He said that his boss, Ed Stevens, needed to look at it before it went out. I objected. I said, "This is an article about economic analysis. Ed's a lawyer who doesn't know the first thing about economics." I was relying on the fact that this was early in the Reagan administration; most people still didn't know what economists were doing in health and safety agencies and couldn't knowledgeably edit what we were writing.

Despite my protest, the paper went to Ed and he called me into his office the next day. It was a repeat of my asking him about coming to meetings when costs were discussed.

"Rich, I can't let this paper go out."

"Why? They asked for it, they will print it, and it would mean a lot for me to be in *Science*."

"Frankly, you're not important enough to write an article like this."

I stared at him. *Was he kidding, was he right, or was he just an absolute bastard?* I didn't know.

It never went out.

Ed was part of the FDA management team that looked after each other. This was best illustrated by giving his deputy, Carl, a huge yearend bonus after a debacle in Canada. Carl was the senior member of our trade group sent to negotiate food safety and labeling rules as part of the US/Canada Free Trade Act. He was also slavishly loyal to Ed. Most of the staff couldn't understand why he was Ed's deputy instead of driving a dump truck. We all went out to dinner, and the Canadians started ordering wine. Carl was the only American left in the restaurant when he passed out, plunging his face into his remaining spaghetti dinner. The Canadians ended up carrying him to his hotel room. However, it was his turn that year for a senior manager cash bonus and Ed agreed to it.

I have fond memories of the fun follies of my old colleagues. Here are three of them.

Ed once walked into the commissioner's conference room only to find two relatively senior scientists going at it like lab rats on the conference table. Was there some symbolism there?

At the time, we had animal laboratories in the building. Two events were memorable. The first is marching two guys out of their labs in handcuffs for making methamphetamine in the labs. The second happened late one spring night as I was leaving the building. For some reason, the elevator stopped on the third floor. No was there except a sea of white bunny rabbits someone had freed from their little cages.

Just before Joe Levitt arrived as center director for CFSAN, Fred Shank decided to reorganize the center. He formed a new support office and chose as its head a GS-14 chemist, Ken Falci, to lead it. I wanted to get away from Ed, so I privately approached Ken and asked him about moving economics into his new office. He was enthusiastic about the idea even though he didn't know me or any of the economists.

When Joe asked me during the managers meeting where we should be, I suggested that the economics branch be moved out of the regulations office because analyzing regulations decided by the regulation's office director created a conflict for us. You can't very well say that a regulation has costs exceeding benefits if your boss is the one who made the decision.

During the break that day, Ed cornered me in the hallway.

He had that enormous smile on his face. "Rich, I think we work well together, and you should go back in there and tell Joe that you want to work for me."

I looked at him and knew two things: 1) that economics had become important, particularly after Reagan had become president; and, 2) that having economics to Ed meant he could control us and increase his personal power.

I told him, "I don't think so. I think we would be better off in an independent office."

The smile disappeared from his face, and he moved his huge face to within two inches of mine.

He said, "You're either with me or against me."

"Well, then, I guess I'm against you."

Ed would spend the entire rest of his career in the FDA getting even for that exchange. That's what powerphiles do.

One of my own hires ended up trying to do exactly that—get even with me for what she perceived as a slight. It is a story of a drone becoming a powerphile.

Here's what happened.

I'd hired Pat when her private-sector job in a cable company wasn't working out. She had an undergraduate degree when she was hired in 1987 as a GS-7.

She didn't work that hard the first few years, and I assumed she was going to be another drone, just trying to get by. One day, I was looking for her around 2:00 p.m., and I asked one of the other economists if they'd seen her after lunch. He suggested I go to the office of the guy she often ate lunch with.

I walked downstairs and opened the door to a small office with a card table, four foldout chairs, and Pat sitting with three other people, each holding a hand of cards. This apparently was the way they were planning on spending the afternoon. There was a pile of cards in the middle and I walked in, grabbed them, and told Pat it was time to get back to work.

While she glared at me, one of the guys said, "Hey man, those are my cards."

I stopped cold and looked at him. He looked away.

She got up silently and walked out.

She got engaged, and a year went by with almost no work being turned in. I had never done anything like this before, but I looked at her computer during lunch. Back then, there were no passwords for entry. Sure enough, there were a few work files from the last year but dozens of wedding files. She was due to get married soon, so I just dropped it.

There was a bureaucratic rule in the FDA that each group needed someone always available to answer the phone. The way Ken Falci put it to me was, if there is an important caller who wants something immediately from the economics team, there must be someone in charge ready to act on the request. That was a riot—no one would ever call and ask for an urgent economic analysis.

I imagined a joke scenario where the president of the United States called down to say, "Quick, I need an economic analysis of a food safety regulation, am I speaking to the person in charge?"

Pat had been there longest, so the first time I went on a brief vacation, I went into her office and told her she would be acting for me while I was gone.

The second I told Pat she would be in charge, her entire body changed. It seemed to swell up like a hot air balloon, and her facial expression looked like Winston Churchill resolving to fight on beaches, in the air, in the pubs, in the toilet, or wherever. She didn't even sound like the sweet little Pat we'd hired; she sounded more like an army drill sergeant. She began immediately to *take charge.*

"OK, while you're gone, I'll have Mike prepare a memo and have Jeannie start on that new regulation." She paused as I looked at her in horror.

I said, "Don't *have* anyone *do* anything, just take a phone call if someone important calls."

Everyone on the team had long-term assignments and didn't need any additional assignments, particularly for the few days I would be out.

She looked deflated, as though she couldn't wait until I left so she could tell the first staffer she saw to "stand at attention when you're talking to me." It didn't matter what I said. As the week wore on, she apparently became the Empress Ming. I assume she went home daily and got down on her knees and prayed to a small shrine dedicated to "having Richard killed tragically in a car accident." The obvious implication would be they would select her to be in charge permanently.

But I continued to promote Pat because eventually she did good analyses—not great, but good. It also helped that she got along with the regulation writers. But when it came time for a promotion to GS-13, I balked because that is supposed to be a senior economist (a minimum of a master's degree, if not a PhD, in economics) and she had zero formal training in economics. In fact, she had gone back to school while in the government to get a master's degree, but had chosen to get it in accounting.

This is probably where Pat got the most pissed off at me, and I don't think it ever went away. I told her that to be promoted to thirteen, she needed to write one professional paper. I wanted her to experience the mental rigor that a professional economist goes through when preparing a paper for publication. I even told her I would help. The fact is though, I was making her jump through hoops that, no doubt, she felt were unfair.

Looking back on it, given that she was doing a good job, I probably made a mistake. One guy at the Department of Commerce was a GS-13 economist, and his job was to answer mail.

You may be wondering what happened to her.

Pat never wrote the paper. She quit instead and went to FDA's parent organization, the Department of Health and Human Services (DHHS). She went into the planning group as a researcher. We gave her a going away party, and I suggested that she had been successful and was likely to be much more so. She smiled and said a few words, but I didn't realize at the time just how much resentment she was harboring.

It was only later, when I got a new boss, that she told me that Pat had called her and told her I was "out of control." She told me that if I thought Pat was my friend, I was very much mistaken.

"She's out to get you."

Pat also told one economist working for me that her goal was to come back to the FDA as my supervisor. If I had stayed in the government, she would probably have figured out some way to make that happen, and I guess I would do at least twenty pushups a day.

As of this writing, she is an associate deputy assistant secretary. I'm not making that title up.

What she did was smart, bureaucratically. She trashed me, which made her look like part of the senior-management team. She was playing a card, identifying herself as a (management) team player, as in, "We in the management [powerphile] club need to stick together to help each other with this kind of employee." As she brought with her all of the FDA's secrets to our parent organization (DHHS), she no doubt ingratiated herself with them. As I'd said in her going-away event, Pat would be successful. She had mastered the bureaucratic game, and the powerphile game, perfectly.

There are other ways to get ahead in the bureaucracy besides being a powerphile. Some people who work for the federal bureaucracy only want to retire on a comfortable pension with government-subsidized healthcare. Others are much more calculating and intend to do a lot better for themselves when they leave the government.

For the latter, there are very specific rules for what you can do to lobby the government after you leave. One thing that's allowed, and where ex-government regulators can make real money, is telling people how to comply with rules you have written. One ex-FDA employee wrote a rule on dietary supplements and then immediately quit to make a lot of money advising the industry how to comply with it.

There is one more group of government employees that exist between drones and powerphiles. In the FDA, they are the scientists—the nerds who don't have any power and aren't trying to rise as fast as they can. Most of the scientists working in the labs are happy just to be doing science. When they try to get involved in policy, they are mystified and depressed to find out that, like everything else in government, decisions are based on politics.

If they try to write about their laboratory experiments, particularly if it would affect a sensitive policy, they encounter the "subjects that must not be named." FDA keeps a running list of subjects that are controversial, and if you want to write about those, you have to get signatures all the way to the commissioner's office, which effectively means you can't write about them.

There are a lot of nerds in the FDA and, I suspect, all over govern-ment. They try to do their job well and are happy if promoted, but won't claw their way up.

Maybe there are more like me, not wanting to be a powerphile, a drone, or a nerd. I remember telling people that there was no reason to stab me in the back, because, by then, the scar tissue on my back was so thick that it wouldn't hurt.

A few years before I left the FDA, a senior nutritionist approached me after a meeting.

She started, "You know, Rich, everyone in this center, if not the agency, is afraid of you."

"Afraid? Of me?!"

"Yes, it's because you always say what you are thinking, and it doesn't matter what everyone else is thinking. It scares people because you're not afraid to tell the truth."

"Like, the king has no clothes."

"Exactly like that."

I was dumbfounded. At first, I thought, *I've arrived.* My very next thought was, *As what, a super bureaucrat?*

I guess even now I don't know how I fit in the bureaucratic hierarchy.

Chapter 6:
BUGS, BUDGETS, AND BLAME

In 1981, GSA found that employees in Federal Plaza in Manhattan were spending $3,000 a month calling Dial-a-Joke and similar recordings.
–New York Times, March 14, 1981

ONCE EVERY YEAR OR TWO, you hear a speech by some federal politician that threatens hiring freezes or budget cuts for regulatory agencies. These speeches bring out both defenders of individual agencies and defenders defending all agencies.

Whenever you hear these generic speeches about what the government does for you, listen for this one: "…and keeps our food safe."

For politicians, it's a good line to use because it is impossible for almost anyone to know whether it's really true or not, and it sounds good. It sounds like if we were to cut budgets for agencies like the FDA or USDA by a few bucks, children will die.

Carl Sagan once wrote, "One of the saddest lessons of history is this: If we've been bamboozled long enough, we tend to reject any evidence of the bamboozle. We're no longer interested in finding out the truth. The bamboozle has captured us. It's simply too painful to acknowledge, even to ourselves, that it has taken us. Once you give a charlatan power over you, you almost never get it back."[33]

I was introduced to how the FDA's annual budget worked in my first year there. It begins with agencies like the FDA telling the president what they need to get the job done for the next year; next, the president's OMB compiles the budget for the executive agencies and sends that to Congress, which does precisely what *they* want to do.[10] But agencies take the first step seriously.

I hadn't been at FDA very long when a pretty, dark-haired woman named Brenda from our management office approached my desk and asked me what I wanted.

"What do you mean, what do I want?"

"Well, what do you need to do your job better?"

I thought about it. This was before personal computers, and we had a small but efficient library a few floors down that would get me any article or book I requested.

"Nothing, really," I replied.

She rolled her eyes and gave me a slight withering look as if to say, "Rookie." She explained to me that everyone needs something, and if we don't ask, our budget doesn't increase. We also have to spend it every year or the money goes back to the treasury. When that happens, they cut our budget the following year.

She stood there and waited until I got creative.

"Well, I guess I could use a better calculator."

She mentioned one made by Texas Instruments and I said that would be great.

She continued, "And they have some attachments that have all sorts of mathematical functions."

"All right, I guess I could use some of those too."

She issued a clipped, "Thank you," and strode off to enforce the next Christmas gift.

Apparently, we were pikers when it came to the budgetary "big ask," but that all changed in 1996. That year, we started discussions with a USDA

---

10 There are fifteen executive-branch departments in the federal government, like the DHHS. Under those, there are eleven agencies, like the FDA in DHHS.

microbiologist, Jack Wilson, who would join us in 1998. At the time, he was a researcher in USDA's Agricultural Research Service and had been a deputy administrator in USDA's food agency, the Food Safety Inspection Service.

Jack was interested in coming to the FDA, but he thought we needed a bigger budget for what he wanted to do. He pointed out that USDA's food budget in 1995 was $683 million, compared to the FDA's food budget of $211 million.[34] The FDA got 30 percent of the food budget but regulated 80 percent of the food supply. In fact, it regulates everything except meat, poultry, and pasteurized eggs. Jack's advice: quit thinking small and ask for a lot more money with a much bigger program.

We did, and President Clinton got behind it. In 1997, he announced an enormous increase in our budget ($43 million) to address food safety, called the Food Safety Initiative.[35] Food safety does not refer to chemicals causing cancer or that are otherwise toxic; food safety refers specifically to microscopic bugs, including viruses, pathogens, and other harmful bacteria.

Kim Kardashian would have had a tough time competing with the ensuing spending spree.

Before we go any further with the spree, let's look at what we didn't do.

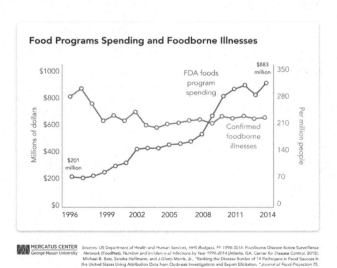

Food Programs Spending and Foodborne Illnesses

MERCATUS CENTER
George Mason University

Sources: US Department of Health and Human Services, HHS Budgets, FY 1998-2016; Foodborne Disease Active Surveillance Network (FoodNet), Number and incidence of infections by Year 1996-2014 (Atlanta, GA: Center for Disease Control, 2015); Michael B. Batz, Sandra Hoffmann, and J.Glenn Morris, Jr., "Ranking the Disease Burden of 14 Pathogens in Food Sources in the United States Using Attribution Data from Outbreak Investigations and Expert Elicitation." Journal of Food Protection 75, no. 7 (2012): 1278-91.
Produced by Richard Williams and Tyler Richards, October 29, 2015.

As you can see, after a bit of progress in bringing down a few pathogens, we didn't make much of a dent. A friend of mine from USDA wrote a paper where he concluded, "These data provide a lack of evidence for continuous reduction in illness due to bacterial pathogens commonly transmitted by food in the United States during 1996–2013."[36] Another study found similar results, "No correlation is recognizable between the FDA budgets and the disease statistics."[37] Still another paper looked at both USDA and FDA's food-safety programs and reported, "We cannot conclude from the reported cases that [FDA's regulatory] requirements have reduced disease incidence."[38]

It's not like we didn't have the money. Just for food safety, we doubled our funding to $440 million and added nearly one thousand new people.

More money and more people didn't help. We did not solve, and have not been solving, food-safety problems.

But we accomplished a few things with the Clinton cash bonus. First, everyone got a new personal computer. I remember going to my car in the basement one night and staring at the stacks of new computers that no one wanted because everyone already had one. Even better, every senior manager in the center got brand-new office furniture. We also handed out money to friendly academics who would write papers on practically anything that had to do with food safety.

Apparently, someone got wind of the party in Congress, because they started an investigation into our spending. Ed Stevens had his office redecorated with tasteful furniture. Debbie Marino, our food ambassador to the tonier towns in Europe, happened to be out of town when we heard about the investigation.

I was in a meeting with the senior directors when Debbie breezed in wearing a fashionable scarf and dress direct from the Champs-Élysées. A few people looked at her and smiled, knowing she was fresh meat.

The deputy director said, "Come on in and have a seat, Debbie. We're ready to begin."

I saw the look on her face, as in, *Why am I being singled out?*

The deputy, Mary Durrand, continued, "While you were gone, the House launched an investigation requiring us to account for every penny we've spent on the Food Safety Initiative. What's going on in your office?"

Debbie froze, as she had just seen the invoices for the yet-to-be-delivered expensive furniture.

"Oh, I didn't know, I mean, I thought it was OK...."

"No," Mary said, "it's not OK."

"But...," Debbie protested, "I mean, everyone else is...."

Mary just glared at her.

"OK, I'll cancel the order." By this time, her cheeks were the color of ripe apples.

Half of the office directors were smiling, enjoying her embarrassment. I knew that some of them already had their new furniture. The vast amount of money went to Jack Wilson's microbiologist buddies, but I never heard of any studies that helped with policy.

Thinking back on it, it's surprising that Congress never asked for a report on what we achieved with the extra cash, where we spent it, or what it achieved to make food safer.

In 2002, President George W. Bush's OMB "green eyeshade" geeks decided they were interested in agency results and told agencies that they were to list their previous years' accomplishments when they requested a new budget. Then they threw in a frightening statement.

If an agency could not show sufficient accomplishments, they would recommend *cutting their budget.* As Tevye said in *Fiddler on the Roof* about his daughter getting engaged without his permission, "Unheard of. Absurd!"

It was blasphemy, but at least the bean counters had the good sense to give the whole exercise a nice bureaucratic name, the Performance Assessment Rating Tool (PART). I liked to think that during the briefings to agencies the OMB staffers would end by saying, "What PART of this program don't you understand?"

PART was met with quiet, seething outrage by the agencies, although, at the same time, it was also widely regarded as a joke.

At the time, I was working on another project with the commissioner's office, specifically with his head of strategic programs, Catherine Copeland. She was a thin, blond dynamo who, once she started talking, would cover twenty subjects before she stopped ten minutes later. I admired her brains and enthusiasm.

The commissioner chose Catherine to manage FDA's response to PART, and just as she'd done with other programs, she jumped right into it. Because she knew me, she requested that I be CFSAN's representative.

Since everyone in CFSAN thought the entire thing was just another clueless presidential initiative that would go nowhere, no one objected to me representing the center.

The first meeting started off with Catherine summarizing the Government Performance and Results Modernization Act of 1993 (GPRA) and how that law had been largely ignored. She declared that this administration seemed determined to hold us accountable for results, and that we had to take it seriously. I looked around the room to see some slight smirks.

Personally, I thought PART was an excellent idea, so I was ready when she turned to me.

"Richard, what's the most important project CFSAN is working on right now?"

"It's trans fatty acids," I said. "We're trying to get it on food labels."

"OK, what's the goal, the public health goal, of doing that?"

"To reduce consumer's consumption of trans. It's bad for the heart."

As she had done with the other center representatives, she asked me, "OK, what would be a stretch goal for trans?"

I thought for a minute and said, "To reduce the overall consumption of trans by ten percent in a year. I have to check with CFSAN to make sure that works for everybody."

Catherine smiled and said, "Of course, get back to me as soon as you can."

The next day, I went to see our director in the Office of Nutrition, Hannah Becker. Hannah was in her forties, would periodically smile, and when she spoke, had a very silken, feminine voice. I told her what happened, and she said, "Rich, no one will pay the slightest attention to anything Catherine's doing, so I'm not worried about it."

A few days later, a report drifted out of OMB that EPA had refused to take the goal-setting exercise seriously, and OMB was going to recommend cutting their budget.

There are two ways to get the attention of agency managers: 1) set them on fire or 2) threaten to cut their budget. I got a call from Mary, asking me what was going on with Catherine's group. Mary was the most senior woman in our center, a lifetime employee devoted to her job. She was smart, a powerphile, and she did whatever it took or was asked of her.

"They asked me to set a goal for CFSAN and I told them that our most important project was trans."

"What was the goal?"

"That we would, following trans appearing on the label, reduce consumption by ten percent. That's supposed to be a stretch goal."

"OK, when is your next meeting?" I told her it was in two days and she said, "I'll get back to you tonight. We can't have that goal."

One distinction that OMB was making, resulting from work by Maurice McTigue and Jerry Ellig of the Mercatus Center at George Mason University, was to distinguish between outcome and output goals.[39] Both are different from inputs. For example, a Department of Education outcome goal would be to increase kid's reading levels by 10 percent. A regulation that mandated that goal is an output. Buying 10,000 books is an input. The point of outcome goals is that they are something that people actually value.

OMB wanted outcome goals.

I worked with Maurice after I went to work at George Mason University. As a former New Zealand minister of labor, Maurice loved GPRA and PART and started a project to see if US regulatory agencies were establishing goals and meeting them. By law, they are supposed to do both. Each year he gave out awards to the best agencies.

The project had been going on for nine years when we sponsored a meeting for congressional chiefs of staff in DC, and I got a chance to ask them how they felt about his project.

One chief explained it to me like this: "You guys just don't understand. Nobody, *nobody* cares whether regulatory agencies succeed at anything. We fund them because if they're handling it, we (in Congress) don't have to about worry it."

We stopped the project shortly after that.

But I still believed in holding agencies accountable for outcomes, although most of the FDA did not like this idea. Mary got back to me on her goal right before I left for home that night.

"Rich, as I told you, we don't want that goal. We can't be blamed if consumers don't reduce their consumption of trans."

"Don't we have a planned campaign to let people know, at the same time the regulation comes out, that trans fatty acids are not good for people?"

"Yeah, but we have no idea if it will work, and we can't risk our budget over that."

"OK, what do you want to put in its place?"

At the time, 13 percent of the American public was "aware of trans fatty acids," 7 percent thought they were good for you, and 6 percent thought they were bad for you.

Mary said, "We want to say that we will increase awareness by 10 percent of trans fatty acids in the food supply."

I immediately thought, *That's an output, and even at that, increasing total awareness by 1.3 percent hardly qualifies as a stretch goal.*

It didn't matter. Congress paid no attention to PART, so it died a natural death.

The FDA's budgets continued to rise, and they continued to deftly tap dance around being held accountable for anything.

Chapter 7:
BAMBOOZLING THE BARBARIANS

"If you can't dazzle them with brilliance, baffle them with bull."
- W. C. Fields

THE NUMBERS GAME

The FDA told Congress in their 2011 budget request that 48 million people get foodborne diseases each year.[1] That's about one in every six people. In 2008, it was noted that cases hadn't changed much.[2]

Now go back thirty-four years to 1986 and find that Centers for Disease Control (CDC) scientists were telling Congress that there were 76 million cases of foodborne diseases.[3] Did FDA policies reduce cases from 76 to 48 million cases through its policies?

No. The 76 million cases estimate actually came from a paper by FDA scientists. They never intended that number to be used for anything. They said that if you made enough wild assumptions, you would get that ridiculous number. The CDC finally caught on to what the paper actually said and changed it by applying more sophisticated estimation procedures, resulting in an estimate of 48 million.

That was the right number all along. The only thing that changed was that CDC had been overestimating the number of cases based on one paper.

1. "Surveillance for Foodborne Disease Outbreaks United States, 2011: Annual Report," Centers for Disease Control, https://www.cdc.gov/foodsafety/pdfs/foodborne-disease-outbreaks-annual-report-2011-508c.pdf

2. David G. Nyachuba, "Foodborne Illness: Is it on the Rise?," *Nutr Rev* 68, no. 5 (May 2010), p. 257–269.

3. Douglas L. Archer and John E. Kvenberg, "Incidence and Cost of Foodborne Diarrheal Disease in the United States," *Journal of Food Protection* 48, no. 10 (October 1985), p. 887–894.

THE FDA IS BOMBARDED by multiple groups trying to affect policies. These include Congress, large food companies, the president (primarily through OIRA, the Office of Information and Regulatory Affairs)[11], the courts, food activists, and to a much smaller extent, small firms and consumers. The FDA is like the master lion tamer in the circus, with whips to keep all the lions in line. It's more than just handling the overseers, panhandlers, and supplicants; it's maintaining the image.

My first boss, Leo Robinson, explained the image to me. Leo was a mathematical statistician in his early forties—tall, lean, a healthy shock of grey hair—and was, as my dad used to say, "so full of it his eyes were brown." He was married with a thirteen-year-old son who seemed to run away every other week, and after having him as my boss for a while, I wanted to join the kid. After I'd been in the FDA for a few months, he came to my office and introduced himself, offering to "give me a tour and tell me what the FDA was *really* about."

During our tour of the CFSAN building in southeast DC, Leo went to a lot of effort to show me the women, married or single, who were "hot and ready." Instead of commenting on the hotness quotient, I told him about my work on the hair-dye rule, and how, if we banned it, I didn't think it would prevent any cancers.

He stopped in a stairwell and looked back up at me.

---

11 This small office in the OMB, comprising about fifty employees, oversees the work of many thousands of employees making federal regulations. I have referred to them in Congressional testimony as "David vs. Godzilla."

"It's not necessary for us to *actually* protect anyone with a regulation. What we're trying to do is to stop people from attacking us."

"What? How do we do that?"

"Easy, we just have to *appear* to be doing something about a problem. You see, as long as we keep putting out regulations that address the things people are concerned about, they go away. The good part is, no one ever checks to see whether or not what we actually did *anything*."

What was I doing here?

Was Leo right? Did that work?

What about the fourth estate, the press? *Scientific American* had an opinion on that theory.

> *For example, the FDA assures the public that it is committed to transparency, but the documents show that, privately, the agency denies many reporters access—including ones from major outlets such as Fox News—and even deceives them with half-truths to handicap them in their pursuit of a story. At the same time, the FDA cultivates a coterie of journalists whom it keeps in line with threats. And the agency has made it a practice to demand total control over whom reporters can and can't talk to until after the news has broken, deaf to protests by journalistic associations and media ethicists and in violation of its own written policies.*[40]

You might think it would be harder to do this with Congress. I got to watch FDA's interaction with Congress in 1993 when we published the regulations and the regulatory impact analysis implementing the Nutrition Labeling and Education Act (NLEA).

The Senate held a hearing on our announcement to delay implementation of the rules for a year. The law allowed this, but some senators didn't like the idea of delaying this magnificent consumer benefit. In the economic analysis, we estimated the delay would save US consumers and producers $700 million by exempting tiny food companies and delaying implementation so that companies wouldn't have to order new labels until they ran out of the old ones.

The hearing was on June 9, 1992, with Mike Taylor, the then deputy commissioner for policy under Commissioner Kessler.[12] Mike was in charge of managing the NLEA.

Senator Metzenbaum started off the hearing by declaring, "There may be no end in sight for the current food labels that are at best confusing, and at worst, downright deceptive."

He continued to berate us and the president, "Why does the Bush administration want to deprive consumers of lifesaving nutrition information after the American people have demanded it as soon as possible?"

He finished with, "Do you solemnly swear to tell the truth, the whole truth, and nothing but the truth, so help you God?"

He started right in on Mike, saying he knew we didn't have justification for delaying the imposition of the food label. He questioned whether we were sure that the industry wouldn't have sufficient capacity to print the labels immediately.

> *Senator Metzenbaum: If it cannot be resolved, then is it the fact that you would recommend against an extension or delay in the implementation of the regulations, because absent that, you are going to have the hiatus where there are no regulations in effect?*
>
> *Mr. Taylor: We're going to carry this out in as coherent a way as we can, Senator Metzenbaum.*
>
> *Senator Metzenbaum: You're ducking.*

And so, it went until, in disgust, the senator gaveled the meeting to an end.

When it was over, Senator Metzenbaum descended from the stage and walked up to us. He was all smiles and told us what an impressive job we were doing. This was a real "welcome to Washington" moment for me.

He confided that he quietly sympathized with us, noting that the decision to delay was a "political decision." He had earlier blasted White House officials for this decision.

---

12   Read the transcript here: https://babel.hathitrust.org/cgi/pt?id=pst.000020349646;view=1up;seq=5.

Then he asked Mike, "You guys are going to go back there and do a big study on whether there is sufficient capacity to print these labels more quickly, right?"

Without a moment's hesitation, Mike said, "Yes sir, senator." We walked out.

Knowing that would be my job, I turned to Mike and said, "We're not really going to do that are we?"

"Of course not. He'll never know and wouldn't care if we did. This whole thing is just a show for the folks back home."

Jay Asher, our attorney, describes a time he had to testify about a memorandum he had written on color additives. Congressman Ted Weiss apparently kept quoting it and Jay was trying to explain that, although his own testimony was confusing, he believed he had made a point.

"So, as a result of all this, I was really depressed, because I figured I'm so inarticulate I can't get my point across. But after the hearing, [Commissioner] Frank Young came up to me and started shaking my hand and said, 'Great job. Great job.' He added, 'You've completely confused them. It was wonderful. Wonderful work!' [Laughter] And I just said, 'Oh. Oh, thank you, I guess.'"

One of the FDA's main interactions with Congress is through its annual budget request. FDA relies on Congress having a complete *tabula rasa* for memory.

Here's a section from the 2019 request:

> *FDA is implementing the FDA Food Safety Modernization Act to empower farmers and producers to help keep the American public safe from food-related illness through preventative steps aimed at controlling risk. We've taken new steps to promote healthier diets and beneficial innovation in new food products.*[41, 13]

---

13 It also reports the following:

They went on to say, "Outbreaks of foodborne illness and contamination have a substantial impact on public health" with an estimated 48 million foodborne illnesses occurring in the US every year.[14] It then went on to talk about the rules it promulgated, just like it has every year.

While relatively easy to mislead, the FDA relies on Congress to keep the money flowing and keep their distance. In his book about bureaucracy, James Q. Wilson cites Morton Halperin, who explained that bureaucracies "are often prepared to accept less money with greater control than more money with less control."[42] Wilson says, "If autonomy can reasonably be assured, then the agency of course will seek more resources or enlarged jurisdiction." The FDA has managed to do both with Congress: retain autonomy and continue to increase resources and jurisdiction.

The FDA keeps industry at bay through fear and favors. Fear comes in the form of premarket approval. You can't sell a medical device, drug, or food or color additive unless the FDA approves it first.

Daniel Carpenter describes this power concisely. He says, "Over the late twentieth century, few regulatory agencies of any sort, in any nation, possessed or exercised the power held by the Food and Drug Administration."[43]

Favors for large firms come in the form of approvals or, in the case of post-market regulation, putting their smaller competitors at a disadvantage. The seafood Hazard Analysis Critical Control Point (HACCP, pronounced *hassup*) rule was an interesting case of how small businesses are treated.

A lot of the requirements in the seafood regulation would cost the same amount of money whether you were large or small. For smaller firms though, the costs mattered more because of the size of the operation. It's like saying that we're going to tax everyone $5,000 a year. Five thousand dollars makes a big difference if you make $1,000,000, versus $20,000 a year.

Most of the commenters didn't want the FDA to exempt anyone, no matter how small or from any part, and the FDA agreed.[44] After all, large firms hire lawyers specifically to make these types of comments. The FDA concluded in the final rule by saying that we were "not persuaded...that

---

14 An estimated 128,000 hospitalizations and 3,000 deaths result.
Foodborne illnesses cost an average of $3,630 per case.
More than $36 billion per year in medical costs, lost productivity, and other burdens to society.

compliance for small firms, for monitoring, recordkeeping, equipment cleaning, pest elimination, administration, plan development, and mandatory training would cause 'undue harm.'"[45]

In fact, because of the large, fixed costs, some small firms found it nearly impossible to comply and stay in business. That was precisely what the large seafood firms wanted.

Beyond Congress and large firms, it's also important to keep the president's staff from intensive oversight. OMB's OIRA is the arm of the president that oversees all executive-branch regulations (the FDA is part of the executive branch). They can return rules that don't comply with the economic executive order or anything that the president (or his representatives, like the vice president or chief of staff) like. The FDA handles them masterfully.

They game their oversight. One trick is to propose an overreaching regulation with requirements the FDA doesn't care about and let OIRA save face by getting rid of the "bad requirements." Another, used extensively by the FDA, is to regulate by guidance, which is mostly exempt from OMB oversight. The FDA has actively used guidance in administrations where OMB oversight is enhanced.

I had a lot of fun writing about guidance in *Regulation* magazine. Here's a small quote from it:[46]

> *If you are not required to follow guidance, then for God's sake please never, ever, ever follow draft guidance, as that is only our current thinking. In fact, it expires the very second we write it because we are constantly in a regulatory fever and we have already thought of making you do something else. In fact, what kind of an idiot would act on draft guidance when it is perfectly obvious that we are (or rather the person appointed to think for us) is already thinking something different? We have already appointed someone else to do our current thinking for us. What's wrong with you?*

But the most common way to control OIRA is to lie to them.

At the end of the seafood final rule, the FDA told OIRA that we would look at the rule after a year to see if it was accomplishing its objectives.

When the time came, the Office of Seafood told OIRA that, upon reflection, Seafood HACCP is just part of a larger set of regulations, and it is impossible to "break out" the impact.

Next, the FDA must keep the (federal) courts happy. That's made easier because the law requires that courts give the FDA broad discretion. This is true for all agencies; the courts have given agencies massive discretion with their regulations when the law is vague, and even discretion to reinterpret their own regulations.[15]

Finally, there are the activists.

Right before he retired, I had dinner with a guy I admire and consider a friend. At the time, Michael Jacobson was the head of the Center for Science in the Public Interest (CSPI), the top food activist in the country. Mike and I'd had several public debates, including one on soda taxes. We didn't agree on much except that, for us, food safety and nutrition problems were worth spending a lifetime on.

I turned to Mike and said, "You know, after all the things we've done, many of which were at the behest of CSPI, we've accomplished almost nothing. Don't you ever get tired of this? Don't you think that maybe government isn't the answer to solving these problems?"

Mike said, "Richard, I see where you're going but I just can't get there."

I guess Leo was right after all: it's just a show.

---

15 See Chevron and Auer court decisions.

Chapter 8:
IT'S ALL TOO NEAT

THERE IS A COMPETITION in Washington that hardly anyone ever talks about for regulatory authority and the funding that accompanies it.

In 1992, I found out about the USDA's assault on seafood. I was on my way from our offices in Washington, DC, to Parklawn, our headquarters, in Rockville, Maryland, riding with our regulatory clerk. As he drove, he asked me if I knew about the seafood rule. I told him I hadn't heard about us doing anything with seafood.

"We're not doing it," he said. "This is being done by the commissioner's staff."

David Kessler, President Bush's pick, was a firebrand for an FDA commissioner (he changed political parties in the middle of his tenure).

My car colleague went on, "There's this attorney, Joe Becker, on the commissioner's staff who's writing it, but as a far as I know, he's never written a regulation before. You should find him and introduce yourself."

It turns out he wasn't hard to find. He was just down the hall from the commissioner.

Sitting there facing the open door was a pleasant-looking guy, about forty years old, alone in a small, windowless office, intent on the paper in front of him. He had curly dark hair, an intense gaze, and there was an intellectual look about him.

He looked up at me as I knocked. "What can I do for you?"

I introduced myself. "I understand you're writing a seafood safety rule instead of us doing it in CFSAN. What about the economic analysis?"

"What economic analysis?" He seemed genuinely confused.

I smiled at his question. Ignorance of presidential executive orders was almost a requirement for working in government. Even for lawyers like Joe.

"If this will cover all seafood producers," I said, "it's going to be a major rule, and it will need a regulatory impact analysis."

"I have *no idea* what you're talking about," he snorted, as though I was bringing up some bothersome detail that he would have known had it been important.

I launched into an explanation of how President Bush—George H.W. Bush—just like past presidents, required us to conduct an analysis of the costs and benefits of major regulations, and that regulating the entire seafood industry would qualify.

"OK," he said, "who does that?"

"Well," I responded, "since it's food, I assume I'm going to have to do it."

At that, Joe leaned back in his chair and relaxed. I could see him thinking, *I'm off the hook; I may as well cooperate."*

"What do you need from me to get started?"

"OK," I began, "how many illnesses will it prevent?"

"It won't prevent any. It's not intended to do that."

Joe stressed that if the FDA implemented this program now, it would keep regulation of seafood in the FDA and out of the clutches of USDA. He also told me that the Europeans wanted more federal oversight over seafood, or they would start blocking our exports.

I had a sinking sensation in my gut that I'd been here before. If this regulation wouldn't prevent any illness, it would never see the *Federal Register.*[16]

---

16 The *Federal Register* is the federal government's official sleep aid—coming to you each year in excess of 70,000 words in tiny type. It contains everything to do with federal regulations, including proposals, final rules, guidance, and even July 4th firework displays in Boston Harbor. It was suggested to President Roosevelt by a committee called the National Emergency Council and was quickly passed by Congress before anyone died from lack of the federal tome. No one actually *reads* the *Federal Register,* except lawyers who have committed a crime and are chained to desks with their eyelids stapled open and are forced to comment on it.

I took a breath and explained to him that his regulation would need to be cleared by the OMB. If there weren't any benefits—like preventing people from becoming ill from seafood—his proposal would be kicked back to the agency for reconsideration.

With requisite gravity he responded, "All I know is that this is David Kessler's highest priority. It has to get out."

He continued. "I don't know. Maybe it will prevent illnesses, maybe it won't. I have to get back to work on this, so just let me know if you need anything."

Here we go again. I know how this will go; what seems nice and friendly now will deteriorate when he realizes that he can't succeed without an analysis that supports his rule. Would he use that same logic if he were defending a client? "Maybe he did it, maybe he didn't, I just know he's too nice to go to jail." Well, the best I can hope for is that he's wrong; maybe it will reduce illnesses.

As I left to figure out my next move, I knew this: Joe did have to get back to work. Seafood safety had become a huge national issue. Caroline Smith DeWaal from the CSPI said, "People are turning to fish more and more as a low-fat protein source. The cruel irony is that a food that can be so good for you is much less regulated than other protein food, such as meat and poultry."[47] This would be, no doubt, the biggest thing Joe had done in his FDA career, and it would be a monumental boost to that career if he accomplished it.

The most pressing problem in seafood consumption doesn't come from the fact that tuna is stinky; it comes from raw shellfish, mainly oysters. Raw oysters are responsible for a mild disease, norovirus; a serious one, Hepatitis A; and a nasty number called *Vibrio vulnificus*. That last one can kill you if you are among the at-risk population, like people with liver disease or heavy drinkers.

If you live on Mexico's Gulf Coast, you get used to reading newspaper headlines that say, "Man contracts flesh-eating bacteria, has leg amputated, dies afterward." The flesh-eating bacterium is *Vibrio vulnificus* and it can infect you through either eating raw oysters or a cut on your leg when swimming in the ocean. The odds of surviving aren't good. One out of every two people infected will die, although, fortunately, it rarely infects people.

Joe was right, though; what really set off the seafood issue wasn't the illnesses. They played a role, but the actual battle was the food fight in Congress. The congressional issue was whether the USDA should regulate seafood instead of the FDA. The theory was, since the FDA hadn't passed new seafood regulations recently, it should be given to USDA.

Later on, the fight was over catfish. Vietnam and other Asian countries were selling all sorts of fish and intentionally mislabeling them as "catfish." The US catfish industry wanted USDA to do continuous inspections to get rid of foreign competition. In short, it was a typical DC turf battle. Ultimately, only catfish went over to the USDA, and the cost of continuous inspections drove many US fishermen out of business.[48]

But for the big seafood rule, was this really about helping consumers or was it just another political fight? If the latter, why would anyone care about the economic analysis?

The FDA and its congressional allies (committee chairs) planned to fight it. No one—not Congress, not federal bureaucracies—likes to relinquish control—of anything—ever.

By the time this contest surfaced in 1992, I'd been with the FDA for twelve years. I was chief of the economics branch of CFSAN. As I had explained to Joe, our economists were charged by the president's executive order to ensure that our regulations worked before they were issued. One reason, in my opinion, that the economic executive order is well founded is because regulations are often issued at the behest of the largest firms in an industry. Sometimes they result from activists who may have other reasons besides reducing risks for wanting regulations. Either way, health and safety rules that don't reduce risk hurt consumers, as they pull resources from productive uses to comply with useless regulations.

President Carter issued the first comprehensive economic executive order that required federal economists to examine benefits and costs of regulations. These analyses are called regulatory impact analysis. I am a fan of them, even more so than I am of the Washington Nationals. Both Presidents Reagan and Clinton followed up with similar orders, and Clinton's is still in effect today. His executive order charged economists to be regulation watchdogs, providing a check on the politics that so often drive misguided, unworkable regulations.

Economic analyses offer three checks on regulations. First, there must be a compelling need, that is, a problem that needs the federal government's attention. Second, there must be at least one solution to that problem. Finally, the solution's benefits must exceed the costs of implementing it.[17] In the dull halls of bureaucratic Washington, DC, there are both tiny and titanic fights over these analyses.

I started working on the seafood rule and, despite what Joe had told me about not accomplishing anything health-wise, I believed that the regulatory theory he was using was sound and *would* help make seafood safer. It looked like it should pass the three economic tests. If it did, that would mean I would not be in Commissioner Kessler's crosshairs, as OMB was unlikely to reject it.

In Joe's regulation, we were going to mandate HACCP, the first time the government had mandated these process controls. It was going to force manufacturers to keep a lot of records on how they processed seafood and, at least when I first learned about the theory, it seemed like it should work.

I should have known it was all too neat.

---

17 Clinton's executive order required that the costs needed to be "justified" by the benefits, but the reviewers in the president's OMB generally believed that meant that the benefits should exceed the costs. *Justified* meant that you could consider touchy/feely benefits like making animals feel better about themselves (just kidding, but really, it could mean virtually anything). In the Biden administration, benefits like "equity and environmental justice" have been emphasized.

"Good morning America, there's glass in your baby food." Pillsbury was forced to admit that in the spring of 1971. To fix the problem, Pillsbury went back to the Gemini space missions where food scientists had determined that astronauts like Neil Armstrong and Gordon Cooper were under so much stress that they couldn't handle any level of food poisoning. By the time the Apollo mission landed on the moon, Pillsbury was documenting places in systems of food processing where a chemical, physical or microbiological contaminant could either get in food, or it could be eliminated. These "critical control points" were written down and monitored and became part of the Hazard Analysis Critical Control Point (HACCP) system. It wasn't entirely new. W. Edwards Deming had written about statistical process control in 1939.

The Pillsbury scientist who had helped develop this for NASA, Howard Bauman, introduced the HACCP concept to the rest of the food industry a few days before it recalled the baby food with the glass fragments. Fifty years later, it is now required for the entire food industry.

Chapter 9:
LIE OR BE FIRED, AGAIN

WITH JOE'S REGULATION, the FDA would mandate HACCP for seafood processors whether they had already voluntarily adopted it or not.

The rest of the food industry heard about the FDA's seafood plan and was nervous. I recall attending one food industry meeting where a prominent industry scientist presented a paper claiming that HACCP was invented by the industry, currently used by the industry, and the government should have no role in overseeing how they used it. After all, he insisted, government bureaucrats had no expertise in using this tool. With so many kinds of food processing and foods, what could the FDA add?

I remember listening to him and thinking, *That sounds right. What do we offer other than making companies use it who don't want to?*

Despite my misgivings based on that speech, I still thought the theory was right, so I called in one of our new economists and assigned him to the cost side of the analysis. I decided to do the benefits myself, figuring that would be where any controversies were likely to be. I was wrong; there were controversies on both sides.

First, the program was costly. There were significant man-hours required to map out the processes and the critical points where things could go wrong, keep records, and making adjustments to the process when there were problems. But the costs wouldn't matter if the benefits were large enough.

As I said, the biggest problem was raw oysters, particularly from the Gulf of Mexico (bordered by Florida, Alabama, Louisiana, and Mississippi).

Our research found, not surprisingly, that oyster harvesters are not rich people. They're watermen who almost never go beyond tenth grade and who have grown up in the bayous and backwaters, engaged in the same occupation as their fathers and grandfathers, and often still using the same boats. They didn't use high-tech harvesting, but rather giant tongs to scrape their catch from the sandy bottom. Particularly in the South near the water, there is a bond between oystermen and oyster eaters—a culture that's existed for several hundred years. I hadn't met any oystermen, but the more I learned about them, the more I admired them. They are wary of government regulators and anyone who might affect their hardscrabble livelihoods. Here's a quote from, and about, a seventy-three-year-old oysterman: *"Unk Quick can read the floor of the Apalachicola Bay like a blind man reads braille."* [49]

The US had been having problems with its oysters for years and it wasn't like those problems weren't known to regulators. In fact, the National Shellfish Sanitation Program (NSSP) was created in 1925 by the US Public Health Service, and its members—federal and state governments and members of the industry—had been actively working on issues with oysters, clams, and mussels ever since.

The challenge with raw oysters is that they are harvested straight from the warm, contaminated waters of the Gulf and transported directly to restaurants. If you cook oysters sufficiently, both the viruses and the *vibrio* are killed. The effectiveness of HACCP relied on being able to prevent the pathogens from contaminating the oysters—not realistic—or cooking them, not possible, since customers were eating *raw* oysters.

Bottom line, the second economic condition for a successful regulation wasn't present. We couldn't solve the problem. And if you can't solve the problem, there are no benefits.

Now *I* had a problem. This was a regulation that the commissioner wanted, and I knew the economic analysis wouldn't support it. I had taught my staff to care more about getting the analysis right than about supporting a regulatory decision, but it would be tough to hold on to that theory for a commissioner's high-priority regulation. It took me right back to what had happened with lead acetate in 1981.

Meanwhile, Commissioner Kessler moved the entire issue out of his office to CFSAN, and he instructed us to create a new office of seafood. He hired a seafood expert to run it and transferred Joe to work as his deputy.

During this time, I stayed away from Fred Shank at work, although I continued to carpool with him. He was now the center director instead of just being the food standards director, where he had engaged in the whole head-banging routine over my contract. As center director, he was responsible for all rules including seafood rules. That meant I had to convince him to reduce the scope of the rule so the benefits would exceed the costs. I knew people in the seafood office wouldn't agree to that strategy.

I somehow hoped Fred wasn't going to be as grumpy—and for that matter, mean—at work as he was in the car. In fact, Fred was a hothead. When he was driving it was always entertaining. If we got behind someone who handed the attendant at the Dulles toll booth a large bill, Fred would scream, "Going to the God damn bank!" and pound on the steering wheel.

Maybe that was just Fred's way of dealing with the pressures of work. I also have to say that when my spouse needed emergency surgery, Fred called down to Duke University and got her admitted into one of the top programs in the United States. He'd never even met her.

Most people stayed away from Fred, so you could just go up and ask his secretary if he was free, and he usually was. There were a few people intensely loyal to Fred, and he treated them well. But then there was everyone else. Because I'd been carpooling with him, I assumed he had forgotten the fracas over food standards. I thought if I came to him and told him about the problem, I might not be in that "everyone else" category.

I knocked on his door.

"What?"

Fred's office was enormous, with an enviable stretch of windows looking out at the Capitol and a massive table that accommodated a dozen chairs. His desk faced the door and the table. He glared at me as I walked in.

"Do you have a minute?"

"What do you want, Williams?"

"I have some preliminary numbers on the seafood HACCP rule. It has almost no benefits and over one hundred-million dollars in costs. I think we need to rethink this rule."

I could see his face turning red and his cheeks blowing up like a pufferfish.

Oh my God, what was I thinking? I wanted a do-over button—one that stopped me at his secretary's desk, forced me to think it through and tell her, "Never mind."

"Get out of here, Williams! And fix that fucking analysis or I'll go down to USDA and find some goddamn economists who will do the analysis right! Now, get…outta…here!"

A few days later, just before I was ready to go home, I received an email telling me to go back to Fred's office for a meeting. No need to tell me what this was about. He was still fuming, and I assumed he would finish reaming me.

I walked into his office, but he wasn't alone. The first guy was an epidemiologist named Harry from the Centers for Disease Control and Prevention (CDC). I'd known him for years, a genuinely pleasant guy who worked on food-safety issues. But I also knew he was about to retire, so what was he doing here? He turned around and looked at me but gave nothing away. He just said, "Hi Rich," and turned back to Fred.

The other guy, George, was a microbiologist sitting on the other side of Fred. George was about fifty, with short gray hair and a secret smoking habit. Although he was Fred's deputy, everyone in the center knew there was no love lost between him and Fred. I also knew that he'd taken an academic job and was leaving in a week. George turned to me with a "hey" and also turned back to Fred.

I walked over and stood in front of the three of them and waited for Fred to speak. He wasted no time on preliminaries.

"*They're* going to tell you what the benefits are for the goddamn seafood rule."

What could they possibly tell me that I didn't know? I'd been studying this industry and the regulation for well over a year. There was nothing in it—nothing at all—that helped to reduce raw-oyster illnesses, and it didn't do much for fish either. But particularly without fixing oysters, the rule looked terrible from an economic perspective.

George looked slightly embarrassed and said, "Rich, it will prevent about fifty percent of the cases from occurring."

"Fifty percent of what?" I asked.

George looked at Fred as though needing his approval and said, "Everything."

"How?"

Fred turned to Harry who looked down and added, "Fifty percent is right."

He offered no explanation. I glanced at each of them, but they were staring at the floor, seemingly so uncomfortable they looked sick, like they'd eaten bad oysters. I knew right then that Fred had something on them.

At this point, Fred looked at me and said, "You got your answer, Williams."

"Would you guys mind writing that down in a memo—with your names on it?" I asked.

"No problem," Harry said, as though he were doing me the last favor I would ever ask of him. George just seemed relieved that this nightmare was almost over.

"Okay, thanks," I said and walked out.

I was dizzy. I wasn't quite sure where I was or what had just happened. I felt like I'd been dropped into the Twilight Zone and I wanted out. Fast.

I didn't go back to my office. I went straight to my car and drove home.

The situation only got worse from there. The next morning, I talked to the economist who'd worked on the costs of the rule. He told me he'd informed Joe that there were over $100 million in costs and almost no benefits. As a result, Joe sent over a woman from the seafood office to give us a copy of a book called *Quality Is Free*.[18] She said it should help us because it explained that there weren't really *any* costs associated with the rule. The theme of the book was, if you are improving quality, costs don't matter. She implied that, since their rule was improving seafood quality, there were no costs at all.

Did they really think this idiotic argument would somehow reverse economic logic? This was the FDA, not a fifth-grade debate. And even if it *were* fifth-grade debate, the "quality is free" argument would garner an F. The economist telling me this tale was laughing, but to me it wasn't a laughing matter.

---

18 This is an actual book by a guy named Philip B. Crosby.

Then he asked me about the meeting with Fred. As I was telling him what happened, he kept saying things like, "Weird, can they get away with that?" referring to George and Harry.

"They're leaving," I said. "And Fred doesn't care about anything but getting the commissioner's precious rule out."

Three days later, we met with Joe and his staff. As patiently as we could, we explained how and why requiring any change in what people do, whether they are fishermen or restaurant owners, incurs a cost. We dismissed the quality book's thesis, noting that improving the quality of products is something that people who make products routinely do, and that there was no evidence that HACCP would do that.[19] We didn't point out that the regulators in the seafood office probably weren't experts at improving seafood quality (they hadn't worked in the seafood industry). They continued to question us as to why there were costs. It was the Twilight Zone again, and I just wanted to return to my regularly scheduled programming.

Joe's unwavering position was that since regulation would help them run their companies more efficiently, and thus improve their quality, that was a benefit, not a cost. Our response: if they could find evidence of that, we would document it as a benefit. However, any mandated change in behavior is, by definition, a cost.

They never found any evidence. In fact, we found out they had conducted a survey of the costs to the seafood industry based on their likely requirements and discovered that the costs were massive. We were never shown those results and, strangely, the survey was accidentally thrown out over a weekend and was never seen again. At least, so they claimed.

That evening, after the meeting with the seafood guys, we were summoned to see Mary, the deputy director. When the two of us arrived at her office, she was sitting at her small conference table with a phone in front of her. She informed us that we were going to meet with the Office of Seafood by phone to discuss the economic analysis. They knew Fred had already taken care of the benefits, so now they wanted to reduce the cost estimates.

The first person to talk over the speakerphone was the woman who had delivered *Quality Is Free*.

---

19 In food world, "quality" and "safety" are different. Quality is about things like freshness and taste. Safety is about something that will not make us sick.

"Their costs are out of line with what this proposal requires. All anyone has to do is buy some yellow pads and pencils. That's it."

I asked her, "So, you helped write this rule, I assume you are doing it without pay and that the only cost was your computer?"

The deputy gave me a look as if to say, "Watch it."

The staff economist looked apoplectic. His fists were in a ball, and I could see that he was slightly shaking. His voice cracked when he spoke, and I knew it was taking every ounce of control *not* to throw something or just stalk out of the room.

He blurted out, "No."

"It requires people who take the time to do all the monitoring and write records. And that is only part of the costs," he continued. "It requires mapping out the entire process and putting in controls to clean the plant and keeping out insects and rodents. None of that, not one bit, is free."

Joe, from the seafood office, chimed in.

"They already do all of that."

"No, they don't. That's not true. We checked."

In fact, a few of the larger seafood firms were using HACCP and doing those things, but most were not. I could have added that if they were already doing these things, then there was no point to the rule.

The rest of the evening? Arguments flew. Tempers flared. We couldn't agree on anything and I felt like my blood pressure was ready to blow a hole in my chest.

Mary finally broke in and said, "Here's what we are going to do. The Office of Seafood will tell you what the costs are, and you will write them down. They're a little low on pest control, so the economists can use my estimate. The meeting's over."

I didn't acknowledge what she had said.

I'd had enough.

I walked out without looking back.

Two days later, I was sitting in my office on a Friday evening, grateful that one of the worst weeks of my career was over and contemplating the weekend. Maybe I would take a lengthy bike ride on a local trail. And that's when my boss, Ken Falci, who knew about the two meetings but hadn't taken part, knocked on my door and poked his head in.

"Got a minute?"

I nodded as he came in and sat down. I guessed what he was going to say.

"Rich, there's no other way to say this. You have to change the costs and benefits of the seafood rule."

There it was. Again. I'd heard it first from Dick Ronk on the lead-acetate rule years earlier.

"I've been talking to the deputy," Ken continued, "and she says if you aren't willing to change the analysis then you shouldn't come back to work on Monday. I'm sorry."

I'd never had an issue with Ken, and I could see the regret written all over his face. He was about my age and was a Vietnam vet like me. He was also a solid guy and a terrific manager. If anything, Ken had always been a staunch supporter. Although he was a fighter, he knew when to pick his battles. Ken promoted me to division director—and I was sitting in a big office with eight floor-to-ceiling windows overlooking DC with a view of the Capitol. The fact was, I loved my office, and I loved my job even more. But I was up against the commissioner, the center director, the deputy, the entire Office of Seafood, and who knows who else in the administration. He knew it and I knew it. This was a losing hand.

I needed to think. Giving in to this kind of intimidation to falsify an analysis represented everything I was against. I looked at Ken and said, "It's not your fault."

"Look," he said, "don't decide anything now. Go home. Think about it over the weekend."

Suddenly, I felt like I couldn't breathe. I might never be allowed back here after I left in the next few minutes. Could I just cave on what I felt was morally reprehensible? How would my staff feel about me if I did? But I had a mortgage and a wife and a small son. What would I do if I were fired?

I barely remember driving home, all the way down I-66 and out the Dulles Toll Road to Herndon. I pulled into my driveway and just sat there looking at my house. My mind was racing.

I know what I'll do, I'll call a press conference and tell the world what's going on. That's the way things work in Washington, DC, isn't it?

I went inside, and my three-year-old son ran up to greet me. I almost cried looking at his little innocent face as he babbled on about something important to a toddler. But I could scarcely listen.

My wife knew immediately that something was wrong. She asked what it was, and I gave her the abbreviated version. She didn't hesitate. "Well, you have to change it. What else can you do? You're in charge and it doesn't matter what your staff thinks."

I looked at her and said, "I'm going out."

I drove down Centerville Road about two miles to a country bar in a nondescript strip mall. I sat on a barstool apart from everyone else and downed a beer. Then another. And another. I couldn't hold a press conference. They would never believe me. They'd just say I was a disgruntled employee who couldn't follow directions. Besides, no one knew what a regulatory impact analysis was, and no one cared. I'd be painted as the FDA bureaucrat who didn't care about people getting sick from seafood. No one would ever hire me again. I would lose my job. I would lose my house. And I didn't even want to think beyond that.

I thought about everything I had been through, all the failures along the way, only to land here. Furious. Depressed. Powerless. I cared about this job, I cared about being a good boss, and I cared about doing regulations right, and this was wrong.

I sat through two more beers and knew I had to change the analysis, but I remembered one thing the guy who hired me used to say, "Revenge is a dish best served cold." Here, that dish was raw oysters—a food I've never been able to stomach since. That moment was cathartic for me. I would go in Monday and change the analysis, but find a way to never let this happen again.

Never.

I would never again allow people to trash me or my staff without serious repercussions. I figured out that I had been outmaneuvered at every turn by the Office of Seafood. I would have to become the best damn bureaucrat—the *smartest* damn bureaucrat—if I was going to beat these guys at their own game. If I didn't, we would keep putting out regulations that only served the interest of the FDA and the big firms, and small businesses and consumers would be the losers.

Someday, I told myself. *Someday I will tell my story.*

But for now, I would have to wait.

Chapter 10:
SMOKING SALMON

FORMER DEMOCRATIC PARTY PRESIDENTIAL CANDIDATE George McGovern, who lost to Richard Nixon in 1972, could testify to the small-business problems with regulations.

Using money made by giving lectures, McGovern bought Connecticut's Stratford Inn in 1988. After facing a barrage of regulations at every level, he asked why legislators so frequently fail to consider whether consumers will actually pay the higher prices caused by so many regulations.[50]

McGovern also speculated that too many well-meaning legislators lacked—as he previously did— "firsthand experience about the difficulties businesspeople face every day." After spending $1 million to buy the Connecticut Inn, Senator McGovern spent nearly $700,000 renovating 150 rooms. He might have survived that, but after all the regulations, taxes, mandates, and lawsuits, he was bankrupt four years later.

It prompted him to write the "Businessman's Nightmare" letter.

> *In short, "one-size-fits-all" rules for business ignore the reality of the marketplace. And setting thresholds for regulatory guidelines at artificial levels -- e.g., 50 employees or more, $500,000 in sales -- takes no account of other re-*

alities, such as profit margins, labor intensive vs. capital intensive businesses, and local market economics.[51]

He concluded, "I also wish that during the years I was in public office, I had had this firsthand experience about the difficulties businesspeople face every day."

Leslie Harlow, owner of a small salmon-smoking business in Maine, wished that the FDA inspectors knew something about the reality of trying to run a small food business.

Harlow's business was in Hancock, Maine—population 2,394. Its Atlantic salmon fillets come from the Bay of Fundy, just up the coast. You can watch them cure the fish with sea salt and brown sugar for seven hours through a window, after which the fish are smoked. In nearly thirty years of operation, they have never made a single person sick from a product that, as she puts it, "has been a part of our dietary heritage for centuries."[52]

Harlow's problems started back in 1995, when the FDA published its final rule—a complex program to make seafood safe (the HACCP rule).[53] Not surprisingly, large firms suggested that small firms should have to do everything they did. The FDA agreed, saying the costs of the regulation were "incidental" and "reasonable."[54]

In 2005, the firm built a new facility to comply with the new FDA seafood regulations. Two years later, she left the business to her original partner, who ran it until a 2015 FDA consent decree shut it down.

The decree was a nightmare. It had twenty-two pages of requirements to create plans for production, testing, hiring, cleaning, monitoring, and training—all costing tens of thousands of dollars. Everything needed to be overseen by hired experts and to the "FDA's satisfaction." The firm had to pay for FDA expenses whenever the agency felt the need to send multiple inspectors who would drive 274 miles from Boston to Hancock ($15,000).

The FDA requirements might help keep a food process safe that is operated by a 500-employee firm, but it would only distract a four-person process like Harlow's from focusing on time-tested and effective procedures.

In 2016, Harlow bought her former partner's interest and had her staff trained in the FDA rules. Despite spending tens of thousands of dollars, she remained shut down. After three years of back-and-forth with the agency, the FDA finally approved her safety program in 2019. Harlow couldn't reopen, though, because she needed another FDA inspection and, by then, there was a three-month government shutdown—in effect, another holiday season of sales lost.

The FDA recommended a lab to test her salmon, and after finding all of it in compliance, she was allowed to reopen in March of 2020. But a month later, the lab informed her that half of the batches were, in fact, out of compliance. The FDA shut her down again, and Harlow had to recall her products. She sent the same samples to a more reputable lab that told her that her products were—as they'd always been—in compliance.

At first, the FDA wouldn't accept the new lab results, but then relented and told her she could sell her products. Two days later, officials said they'd made a mistake, and she shouldn't have sold anything. She was again shut down. When asked when she could reopen, they replied that they were "really busy and will get to the matter when they can."

Another FDA request for more "supporting paperwork" and payment was the straw that broke the camel's back. Leslie Harlow had had enough and decided to move on from the business. Given the agency's performance, if there were a safety plan for FDA inspections, the agency would probably find itself with a consent decree of its own.

This could have been avoided if a more reasonable standard for small plants had been issued back in 1995. Maybe if the FDA had sought out or listened to people who had run a small food company, it would have, like Senator McGovern, concluded that one size does *not* fit all.

vLeslie Harlow was the victim of a game played in most governments. Economists call this game "rent seeking." To play, a firm spends money lobbying the government to put their competitor at a disadvantage. In return, when they do so, they get "rents," otherwise known as profits. The profits are expected to be larger than what they spend lobbying. It's another way to make money that doesn't involve making a better product or having a lower price. In regulations, it's usually small businesses that are the victims.

The most effective rent seeking game is "Bootleggers and Baptists." This is where Bootleggers (firms) have the same goal as Baptists (activists). Bruce Yandle from Clemson University described this situation where bootleggers wanted to get rid of legal booze, as did anti-alcohol "Baptists." When they tacitly team up, they become formidable, in that case, resulting in prohibition. In the seafood case, big firms didn't want any exemptions for small businesses, and they were supported by food activists.

Chapter 11:
WARNING BY AWARDING

THE DEFEAT OF THE ECONOMICS team (changing the seafood analysis)—and me personally—spread through the center like teenage gossip. I didn't care; I was determined that this would not happen again. I would fight for us to do honest analysis.

So, I was surprised to get a meeting notice from Ken, inviting me and the program office directors. I assumed Ken would bring them together to talk about how badly it reflected on the center to put out such a biased analysis and how we all needed to work together to make sure that we never had this kind of problem again. He might start with the economic executive orders, explaining that each president issued those because he wanted agency decision makers to consider the economic consequences of their regulatory decisions, and producing a biased analysis directly contradicted the president's wishes. Or something like that. There was no reason for me to talk to Ken prior to the meeting; he would know what to say.

The meeting was held in the commissioner's conference room. I was already there when the directors filed in. They were smiling and talking among themselves. I sat at the table looking at the notes I'd prepared to fill in whatever points Ken missed. I was armed and prepared to fire.

Ken walked in and sat at the head of the table; he waited until everyone was seated. Besides Ken and I, there were eight other people.

"Thank you all for coming here," Ken started. "This is probably a meeting I should have had a while ago but after the problems we had with the seafood economic analysis, I thought we should get together and see how we can work together more effectively."

Well, that's one way to put it.

I looked around the room, expecting to see people getting upset, but they all seemed to be blissfully unaware.

Ken continued.

"The first thing I want you to know is that, from now on, the economics branch will make sure that their analyses support your decision."

W*hat?* I was frozen. *What was he doing? Was he angry about the sea-food mess? Was he trying to save his job? Why would he do this to me?*

He asked if I had anything to add.

I looked down at my notes. There was nothing I could say after that.

"No," I said, and just sat there.

The office directors were all smiling and talking among themselves while Ken elaborated.

Finally, Ken said that the meeting was over, and he thanked everybody for coming. Ken and I had to walk back across the street to our offices. As soon as we were out of the conference room, I asked him what that was all about. He told me to wait until we were outside.

Many years ago, the Office of Personnel Management set guidelines for policy analysts. An excerpt from 1981 concludes:

> The policy analyst, as defined in this guide, is set apart from other participants in the decision-making process by his or her professional objectivity, nonpartisanship, balance, and ability to provide comprehensive advice and analysis. The policy analyst serves the political decision-making process by providing comprehensive, balanced information and analysis to all sides of policy issues rather than by advancing the ideas of a single decision maker, philosophy, or point of view.

This requirement was changed from earlier views that subject matter experts be used to "defend" policymaker's decisions (U.S. OMB, 1981).

"I know you're upset but let me tell you what's going on. Fred is still hot about seafood, so this was to put an end to Fred's interest. Some of the directors have been playing it up to Fred that your group aren't team players. We need to lay low for a while, but this doesn't mean that you will actually fake the analyses. Just let them think that."

A week later, the director for the Office of Nutrition sent me a note explaining that her staff was doing a small regulation and she had decided on her course of action. The note ended with, "Please make sure the cost-benefit analysis supports this decision."

I put it up our bulletin board and highlighted the last line. I called the team together and we all had a wonderful laugh over that. I told them we were never going to be in that business. I wasn't then, nor was I ever, planning on being a "good team player."

We weren't finished with seafood yet, as we had only gotten the proposed regulation out. After the proposal, you get comments for several months and then start the final regulation. The final regulation is supposed to respond to comments and make any changes in the actual rules that go into the *Federal Code of Regulations*.

It was around then I received an email telling me I would be the recipient of the Award of Merit. This is the FDA's highest award. For me it recognized "outstanding leadership in developing or implementing FDA regulations."

The awards ceremony was to take place two days from when I got the note. It was to be held in a hotel in Rockville, Maryland, near where the FDA headquarters was at the time. Ken was traveling, so I couldn't ask him how it happened.

When I went into the hotel that morning, there were signs directing me to the main ballroom. Several hundred people were already sitting in foldout chairs lined up in two large sections. I was directed to a specific seat by a guide. As we walked to the seats, she explained to me how this was going to happen.

Each row would be called individually, and we were to file up to the right side of the stage. When our name was called, we'd go on the stage, where our individual center directors would present us with a plaque, get our picture taken, and then we were supposed to return down the opposite side of the stage back to our seats, where we would remain until everyone had their award. I was in the tenth row on the right, meaning that I would get an award early and then sit through hundreds more.

Fred was going to give me an award himself. Maybe this was more about the sum of the work I had been doing for the last sixteen years.

I watched Fred give other members of CFSAN their awards. Then my row was called, and I stood in line waiting. When the announcer said, "Dr. Richard Williams, Award of Merit," I walked up on the stage watching Fred waiting on me. When I got close, he grabbed my hand to shake it.

He squeezed it hard and pulled me close to him and said, in a low, guttural voice, "This isn't for anything you've done, Williams; this is for what you *will do*!"

He handed me the plaque, turned toward the photographer, and smiled. I never saw that picture, but I can guess what my expression was.

Someone motioned me toward the other side of the stage, and I walked down the stairs and down the middle row. I saw one of the attendants motioning me to turn into my row toward my empty seat. I pushed right past him and continued walking past the people on either side of me and out the door into the lobby. I kept walking to my car, threw the award in the back seat, and drove home.

When I saw Fred on that stage, I should have known. For a moment, I dreamed of just quitting, but I knew I couldn't for the same reasons I couldn't call a press conference. On the way home, I reminded myself that this was just another battle, but I was determined to win the long-run war.

The seafood final rule came out with the bulls**t costs and benefits in it. The FDA tried to promote it by sending thousands of cups to a Florida State football game with a warning about *Vibrio* in oysters, which, apparently, did not find favor in the Sunshine State.

Fourteen years later, after I left the agency for a job at George Mason University, I looked again at the seafood issue while doing research for an op-ed. The annual number of cases of oyster poisoning from *Vibrio vulnificus* had doubled.[20]

---

20 In 1995, the FDA estimated that the number of cases of *Vibrio vulnificus*-related illnesses would be reduced from sixty cases to between thirty and forty-eight per year (60 Fed. Reg. p. 65096). In 2011, the Centers for Disease Control and Prevention reported 113 cases of illness caused by *Vibrio vulnificus* (9 National Center for Emerging and Zoonotic Infectious Diseases, "National Enteric Disease Surveillance: COVIS Annual Summary, 2011," Division of Foodborne, Waterborne, and Environmental Diseases, Centers for Disease Control and Prevention, August 2013,

Chapter 12:
KILLER LEMONADE

AS ED STEVENS DROVE around the corner in his Burke, Virginia, neighborhood, his regulatory antenna vibrated. An offender to the natural order had just come into view. It was a typical Washington suburb, four-bedroom colonials with small lots and a dog or cat in every other house. He didn't stop, didn't yell, but he slowed to make a careful observation of the little girl selling lemonade. He didn't know her name. She was the one who rode her bike with the pink tassels coming out of the handlebars. She lived in the house with a well-manicured lawn three doors down from him.

He didn't have to describe it for us; we'd all seen it before. One or more children, usually about eight or nine years old, with a card table and some foldout chairs. The cardboard sign would read "Lemonade, 25 cents," and they wouldn't let a car or a pedestrian go by without their sales pitch, "Want to buy some lemonade? We made it ourselves." Little did they know they had been observed by the chief regulator in one of the world's most powerful regulatory agencies, and he did not like what he saw.

Not one of the twenty-odd regulators in the commissioner's conference room, with that image in mind, blinked or even breathed as Ed pitched his story.

---

http://www.cdc.gov/ncezid/dfwed/PDFs/covis-annual-report-2011-508c.pdf.)

After admitting the crime took place right down the street from him, his voice went a little lower and was infused with serious intent, "I don't know…if that pitcher…or the glasses…were washed."

Not a stir in the room with everyone looking at their notebooks or shoes.

"In fact,"—here came his triumphant discovery—"I saw her stir it *with her hand.*"

I'd guessed where he might be going, but the way he said it sounded like he knew who the actual killer was on the grassy knoll.

"I think we should cover her."

He was oblivious to their reactions—a few sharp exhales and heads hung even lower. All I could think of was, maybe he was concerned she had booger fingers.

This meeting had resulted from a death. In 1996, baby Anna Gimmestad of Greeley, Colorado, died from drinking contaminated apple juice. Her death woke the whole regulatory apparatus. Anna was sixteen months old; she liked to parrot the whir of a helicopter and pause on each stair to kiss her parents through the banister. The press reported her death widely and noted that the cause was a product that was supposed to be regulated by the FDA.

We began with internal meetings, followed by a two-day public meeting in Pentagon City (near the Pentagon but not a military base) in Arlington, VA on December 16, 1996. The first FDA speaker set the stage by saying that it wasn't just one outbreak, that many juice products were contaminated. The next speaker, a former FDAer, thanked the moderator for giving him an excuse to avoid his Christmas shopping. He went on to say that absolute safety is, unfortunately, a myth. As events unfolded, this reality was lost within the FDA. He said that pasteurization has saved countless lives over the decades and we shouldn't just jump from apple juice to other juices, particularly those that are pasteurized, that may have no problems.

Not all bacterial cells are dangerous like the ones that killed the aliens in H.G. Wells' *The War of the Worlds*. Although some of the 39 trillion microbes living on or in us are dangerous, most are helpful, like gut bacteria that help you digest food, produce vitamins, or help to fight off infectious diseases. Some are just innocuous stowaways, but together they outnumber our 30 trillion human cells. In fact, modern biology and toxicology is now beginning to view regular exposure to microbes not as germs that will kill us, but rather as "partners" along with our own cells to help us live a healthy life. We have always known that people growing up on farms are less likely to get foodborne diseases because of regular exposure to pathogens (like us versus the aliens). Now, we understand that a diverse set of microbes in our gut and elsewhere is necessary for our immune, gastrointestinal, neurological, and respiratory health. We are beginning to use fecal transplants of healthy bacteria to help people following antibiotic treatments or with diabetes, depression, or obesity.

Sara Latta, *Body 2.0: The Engineering Revolution in Medicine* (Minneapolis: Twenty First Century Books, 2020), p. 65.

It wasn't just Anna who was affected by unpasteurized apple juice. Fourteen children were hospitalized with hemolytic uremic syndrome (destruction of red blood cells leading to anemia and kidney failure) caused by drinking raw juice. The FDA had inspected the plant that produced Anna's apple juice just three months earlier and found no issues. After Anna's widely reported death, something had to be done. Everyone turned to the white-coated scientists at the FDA. For me, it meant another food safety rule and an economic analysis.

It struck me that we were still dealing with the problem that Upton Sinclair had talked about in *The Jungle,* ninety years earlier—food contaminated with feces. But it wasn't obvious from rats running over meat, we had missed it in a previous inspection. We also knew more than Sinclair; we knew pasteurization would have destroyed the pathogens in the apple juice and Anna would still be playing helicopter.

The problem is mostly deer. They poop on the ground and the apples fall in the poop. Washing them doesn't get all of the poop off. When you press apples to make raw apple juice, the deer poop contaminates the juice.

That's the problem with raw apple juice; but FDA, perhaps like many agencies, never wants to let an opportunity pass to cover as many products as possible.

Covering products and firms in regulations that go far beyond the actual health or safety issues is not something that gets any coverage in the press. This theory of law, punishing all for the acts of one, goes back centuries. In the Qin Dynasty in the second century BC, entire families were executed for one individual's crimes. Perhaps it is a lesser outrage when a regulation goes well beyond the specific company or industry having a problem, but the theory is the same.

It was excess coverage that had us all sitting in silence after Ed, the senior regulator in the room, suggested we cover little girls' lemonade stands. After a few painful minutes of silence, the rule-writer running the meeting spoke.

"Thanks, Ed, let's move on now." *I held my breath; was Ed going to erupt over this challenge to his authority?*

Thankfully, he didn't say a word.

The meeting leader continued, "I think we have two decisions to make. Do we want to just cover raw juices, or do we want to cover pasteurized juices as well?"

Wait—had we already decided that all *raw juices were a problem?*

Jack Wilson, a senior microbiologist immediately piped in. "Orange juice can be contaminated too; it happened in Disney World."

This was news to me, although some people around the table nodded approvingly.

"They had vats of pasteurized orange juice down in Florida," Jack continued, "and frogs got into the vats and contaminated the juice with Salmonella. Eleven kids got sick."

Frogs, lizards, turtles, and snakes frequently carry Salmonella. That's one reason that, in 1975, the FDA banned those cute little pet turtles people used to give their kids.

Someone asked Jack, "Has anything like that ever happened before?"

Jack admitted that it hadn't, casting doubt on how far we could go with that line of thinking.

Governments shouldn't intervene unless the problem is persistent. One reason is that it takes an average of four and a half years to produce a regulation. If the government responds to every one-off issue, like a one-time contamination with frogs, it would issue hundreds of thousands of regulations that have already fixed themselves by the time the regulation is finalized.

Regulating one-off problems still happens, though. Unfortunately, as former administrator of the OIRA, Wendy Gramm, once noted, "One anecdote and you get a regulation, two and you get a law."

No one broached the subject of covering pasteurized juices for the rest of the meeting.

Jack Wilson, our microbiologist who taught us how to think big about budgets, ended the meeting by telling everyone he was certain that oranges could be contaminated on the trees and he intended to design a study to prove it. I walked out thinking two things, *Oranges contaminated on trees—that will be interesting.* And, *I can't wait to tell the econ staff the booger finger story.*

Chapter 13:
DUNKING ORANGES

WE STILL HADN'T DECIDED what juices should be covered after Ed's lemonade debacle and Jack's one-off Disney frog story, so our lawyers and regulatory scientists knew they had to get creative. The legal staff took the lead.

One problem was that we weren't supposed to be regulating all apple juices. The FDA, as a *federal* agency, is only supposed to regulate food in interstate commerce, that is, food that moves from state to state.[21] A lot of apple juice is produced and sold within the state, sometimes right on the road in front of the orchard.

If nothing else, the DHHS lawyers are creative, and we had one of the best in Jay Asher. Jay was a middle-aged guy, slender with blondish hair and an exercise and regulatory fanatic. He would get on his stationary bike at 3:00 a.m. every day and read federal regulations. I knew he'd know how to get around that pesky Constitution.

For those interstate rules that the FDA is allowed to regulate, federal preemption says that they override state rules. For example, Wyoming passed a bill in 2016 called the Food Freedom Act that exempts locally produced foods and direct farm-to-consumer food sales from federal oversight.

---

21 Article 1, Section 8, Clause 3—known as the Commerce Clause of the US Constitution.

One Cheyenne resident said, "I would much rather have food the way God made it than to have FDA-approved food that is not even real." Utah and Montana considered similar "cottage industry" bills, particularly to allow sales of raw milk. These laws shouldn't be necessary because federal preemption shouldn't apply.

But the FDA intended to use federal preemption under any circumstance. For the juice rule, Jay used the Public Health Act that said that if people get sick from a pathogen in a food, and somehow transmit that illness to people in another state, then the food is in interstate commerce. E. coli, Salmonella, or norovirus can be transmitted to another person, including by shaking hands with someone who is infected and didn't wash after using the bathroom.

Jay had other theories though that we could use to regulate intrastate commerce, as he explained in one of our juice meetings.

"If someone is selling fresh juice in a package, like in a jar made in another state, it is in interstate commerce. Even if someone is driving through a state from another state, and buys juice from a roadside stand, that is interstate commerce."

No one said a word; they didn't have to. Jay was good, and he told everyone what they needed to hear—I got your legal back. You guys want to cover a small roadside stand that sells juice right out of their own orchard to their neighbors? No problem. I don't know for sure, but I don't think we ever lost a court case with Jay at the helm.

A few months after our first meeting, Jack had finished his experiment to prove that oranges could be contaminated with pathogens like Salmonella or E. coli while still on the trees. He'd conducted his experiment as secretly as the Germans had created V-2 rockets. He would announce his findings to us and the entire world at the same time.

Word circulated in the building that Jack would hold a public meeting in our first-floor meeting room within a week. Because his study design was novel, he invited fellow microbiologists from around the country.

The room he selected held about fifty people, including ten from CF-SAN, one of my economists, Eric, and me. The other people were from the orange-producing states like Florida and California. I got there early and watched the guys—they were all men—come in and start shaking hands with people who had been friends for years. Jack was up front smiling and shaking hands with many of them as well. It was friends getting together with friends, and an all-around genial feeling was evident. It didn't last.

As I stood in the back waiting for the show to start, I started thinking about what Jack was trying to do. Think about an orange. It has a natural barrier, a thick peel compared to an apple skin, and oranges are usually picked off the tree. How could they ever be contaminated, at least inside the orange, while they are on the tree? Could something bore into them? If so, it would be obvious, so you wouldn't use them. I didn't know if Jack had travelled to Florida to investigate the problems with oranges on the trees, but I didn't think so.

He started with a smile and a welcoming note.

"Thanks to all of you guys for coming here. I know you're busy and I hope you find this worth your while."

Like good bureaucrats everywhere, Jack gave a PowerPoint presentation.

One thing about Jack I respected: he was creative, and this must have felt like his *pièce de résistance*. The first slide was a beautiful picture of an orange on a tree in an orange grove happily growing in the warm Florida sunset. You wanted to pluck it and eat it or just contemplate what a wonderful thing nature had provided for us.

That sentiment ended quickly. The next slide was several brown vats filled with purple water and heavy blocks of wood floating on the surface holding the oranges underwater.

Where on earth is this going? Had Jack created a "Bobbing for Oranges" game?

The rumblings began in the audience. Everyone in the room knew we were contemplating regulating different kinds of juices, including raw orange juice, and the pictures were making them uneasy.

Jack, still smiling, cleared it up. He told everyone that they infused the water with purple dye, and his next slides showed the drowned oranges that had subsequently been cut in half. There were tiny purple trails that went about three-fourths of an inch below the peel into the orange. He'd forced whole oranges under dyed water for hours with blocks of wood and, eventually, the water found a way in.

Now the murmurs became shouts. I heard one guy say, "What the f**k?" Jack must have heard it too, but he still had the same grin on his face. I turned to Eric, and we both smiled. We were witnessing a complete meltdown.

Jack spoke, "You can see by the micro-cracks that the dyed water has found its way into the oranges. We have proven that rainwater can find its way into the oranges and rainwater can contain pathogens."

Now they were furious. This was bulls**t regulatory science at its worst. I looked at Jack. He was serene, above the fury. He'd just justified federal regulation of unpasteurized orange juice.

In the cacophony, you couldn't hear one voice over the other.

"This is total bulls**t!"

"You're going to make us go through a bunch of regulatory crap because of that?"

One guy near the front was our former deputy director, a microbiologist who'd gone down to teach at the University of Florida. Years later, while doing research for this book, I asked him about that moment.

"That idiot," he said. "But I knew it wasn't going to make any difference, they were going to regulate raw orange juice no matter what."

In the end, the FDA included raw orange juice because we opined that the commenters to the rule didn't supply enough data to show that raw orange juice was *not* a problem. Plus, it's hard to compete with orange dunking.

Beyond unpasteurized apple and orange juice, we needed to decide what else it would cover. This regulation was to apply the HACCP principles, like we did with seafood, to juice products. Again, this meant lots of paperwork and lots of cost. We wanted the products to achieve a certain level of safety with HACCP, and we even specified what that level would have to be.

The next internal meeting was chaired by our center director, Joe Levitt. Joe was an amiable guy, completely unlike Fred Shank before him. He was short, balding, and somewhat round. He loved Dr. Seuss books, and I really liked that about him. He was smart and always smiling, and he worked hard to get the nasty CFSANers to not be so mean to each other.

"OK," Joe said. "Everyone seems to be here, so let's get started. Who would like to go first?"

Neither Ed nor Jack mentioned anything about lemonade stands or waterboarding oranges.

One microbiologist started, "Look, most of our evidence is on raw apples, but the fact is that pathogens are everywhere and, if a product hasn't been pasteurized to kill them, they can contaminate it. Maybe the reason we don't know about other raw juice products is because smaller outbreaks haven't been reported."

Joe nodded his head in agreement with that, and two other people talked about grape juice and cranberry juice. Then someone brought up frogs in Disney World and Jack had his opening: "I don't think we should miss the opportunity to regulate pasteurized juices. After all, they could be contaminated post-pasteurization."

Joe was firmer than I'd ever seen him.

"No," he said. "Let me absolutely clear. We are not, I repeat, not going to cover any pasteurized juices. That would just create a lot of senseless, high-cost paperwork."

A week later, I got a note from Jack asking me to meet with him. I took one of my new economists, Eric, with me so he could get an idea of how things worked in the FDA.

We walked into Jack's office at a small table surrounded by four bookcases crammed with microbiology books. His desk was piled so high with papers you could barely see him. He walked around and sat at a small table in front of his desk.

Eric and I sat at the table, and Jack began.

"Rich, I want to challenge Joe's decision. I don't think we should let the pasteurized guys off the hook for HACCP now that we're doing this regulation. The point of this meeting is that I don't want you to oppose me with Joe."

Well, it was instantly clear to me. Joe knew that if we covered pasteurized juices, there would be huge costs and zero benefits for that sector. Zero benefits because pasteurization kills pretty much every pathogen (they are very heat sensitive). He also knew it would be a lot harder to get the regulation through the department (DHHS) and particularly through OMB. When costs exceed benefits by a lot, that puts up a huge red flag.

Jack continued, "The thing is, we don't want to let these guys off of the hook just because they're pasteurizing. We've got to cover them."

Eric started to speak, but I put my hand on his arm signaling him not to talk. He looked at me like *I have to tell this guy how crazy this is.* I just nodded at him and turned back to Jack.

"Jack, I'm not going to stand in your way but, since this is your argument, I don't see that I could be of much value when you go to talk to Joe."

Jack said, "Fine, Rich, I got this."

We got up and walked out of the room. Eric's body language was so tight he could have made a diamond out of coal, had he been sitting on a lump. I motioned to him to stay silent until we were well down the semi-dark hallway of the building. He was seething.

Finally, he said, "How could you do that? You're supporting that bulls**t?"

"Nope," I said. "I didn't say I was supporting them; I said I wouldn't oppose them."

"But that's your job, it's our job, to advise people about benefits and costs and that will make the economic analysis look terrible."

"Eric, when someone is saying something you don't like, but they are digging themselves into an enormous hole, all you have to do is let them keep digging."[22]

His eyes widened. "Oh, you mean…."

"Yep, when they go to see Joe, he's going to tear them a new you-know-what."

Eric was smiling. Then he was laughing. "That was great."

We heard about it through the office grapevine. Joe had screamed at Jack and thrown him out of his office. That should have been the end of the story, but it wasn't. By the time we finished the final rule, it covered every juice product, including the pasteurized ones.[23]

---

22 I didn't realize at the time that this was from Sun Tzu in *The Art of War*: "Never interfere with your enemy when he's in the process of destroying himself."

23 Interestingly, in the final rule, the FDA presented arguments for including orange juice. There were two incidents where sick workers contaminated the juice. This is a problem that every food manufacturer and restaurant has—workers who do not look sick but come to work. If they are hourly workers and will not get paid for staying home, they will often come to work. HACCP can't help with this problem; if you don't know they are sick, it may be a

Shortly after that, Joe told me that as long he was center director, he would never agree to another HACCP regulation. Actually, as HACCP played out in its voluntary use by the food industry, it has been helpful, but, at least so far, the number of cases of food poisoning doesn't reflect the forced usage via regulation.

With the passage of the Food Safety Modernization Act of 2010, all food firms must do HACCP. I ran into Joe months later when he was a private attorney counseling firms on how to be in compliance with that law. His website says, "On behalf of the food industry, Joe was on the ground floor when Congress developed the landmark FDA Food Safety Modernization Act (FSMA). He was also a leading voice for the food industry when the FDA developed regulations that all food companies must now follow."[55]

"critical point," but you can't control it.

Chapter 14:
A COOL VICTORY

"FROM NOW ON, the economics branch will make sure that their analyses support your decision."

"I'll go down to USDA and find some goddamn economists who will do the analysis right!"

"Keep your nose clean and to the grindstone."

"This is for what you will do!"

"Now, get...outta...here!"

By 2000, I'd been at the FDA for twenty years, and it seemed like the entire time was just one debacle after the next.[56] Was I doing everything wrong? Or did they just hate economic analysis? By then, I knew that economic executive orders were not just for economists, but also for telling decision makers they were supposed to pay attention to the results of the analysis. No one at the FDA seemed to care about that. Commissioner Kessler said it most succinctly: "I don't need you."

Cass Sunstein, President Obama's OIRA director, was a powerful defender of cost-benefit analysis. He said, "It turns fights over policy into fights over concrete facts...and...the issues that most divide us are fundamentally about facts rather than values."*

He didn't stop there; he also said that benefit-cost analysis "serves as a corrective to...cognitive problems." One of the original proponents of behavioral economics, Sunstein is aware that decision makers, including those who decide federal regulations, suffer from some of the same behavioral decision-making biases as other people. For example, they may "anchor," where an individual relies too heavily on initially received information that causes them to make ill-informed decisions.**

*Dylan Matthews, "Can Technocracy Be Saved? An Interview with Cass Sunstein," Vox, October 22, 2018, https://www.vox.com/future-perfect/2018/10/22/18001014/cass-sunstein-cost-benefit-analysis-technocracy-liberalism.

** Cass R. Sunstein, "Cognition and Cost-Benefit Analysis," University of Chicago Law School working paper no. *85,* October 14, 1999.

With all the stuff going wrong, one thing I'd done right was to hire talented people. Eric was a relatively recent hire and, besides having a PhD in economics, the University of North Carolina had trained him in risk assessment. He not only understood risk assessments performed by FDA's science staff, but he could also do them.

Having Eric on staff helped when the FDA decided to confront the problem with eggs. I felt sorry for eggs. Eggs, or egg producers, had suffered a lot at the hands of the public-health community. In 1968, the American Heart Association warned that, because of dietary cholesterol, no one should eat more than three eggs a week. By 1984, *Time* magazine's cover pictured two sunny side up eggs and a bacon frown.[57] It turned out later that dietary cholesterol (in the yolk) is not a problem, and now eggs are considered a superfood.[58]

But egg safety is a problem. Eggs can become contaminated in chicken houses with rodent droppings and flies containing salmonella. Hens also infect their own eggs with salmonella. Research showed that an average of one out of every 20,000 eggs contain some level of salmonella. Given that Americans were eating, on average, 300 eggs every year, you would have about a 70 percent chance of getting ill from eggs during your lifetime.[59] Cooking thoroughly kills the salmonella, but over-easy, soft, scrambled, or sunny-side-up eggs can be a problem.

We had done an egg risk-assessment, but one of the egg associations came in and said that it had uncovered zero new information. Eric took the risk assessment and examined each possible new requirement that might reduce risks, how much risk would be reduced (marginal benefits), and how much each requirement would cost. Requirements included refrigerating eggs soon after being laid and making chicken coops more secure to keep flies and rodents out.

Because we were proposing to regulate farms, typically the purview of USDA, the DHHS wanted to be briefed on our proposal. Eric did a practice briefing for me, and by the time he finished, I felt comfortable letting him do the briefing.

His economic analysis, like the risk assessment he incorporated, examined every assumption and number where, if an assumption or number turned out to be wrong, he could explain how the overall results would change. This is called uncertainty analysis. It's vitally important because sometimes, if the estimate is off, like the one-in-20,000 estimate, it can change everything. That number is based on sampling, but the sample could have been biased. If it were, say, one in 50,000, the risks would be considerably lower and would change the entire analysis.

Similarly, cleaning up chicken houses, particularly chicken poop, or keeping out flies and rodents would have an effect, but how much? Was it worth it? It was uncertain then and still is. Eric had covered all of that.

The day before the briefing, I wished him luck; the next day I played a decent round of golf. The following morning, I got a call from my boss, Ken, who asked me to come in so he could discuss yesterday's department briefing.

"Rich, what were you thinking sending Eric all by himself? He hasn't even been here a year yet."

I protested, "Eric did his own risk assessment. He's been trained in it, and the economic analysis was perfect."

Ken came back, "That's not the problem. The problem is he had no idea what to do when the political appointees [George H.W. Bush's people], revealed how little they know about economics and risk analysis." I knew it could be political appointees from any administration, of course, but I hadn't really taken that into account beforehand.

"Why, what happened?"

"Apparently, when Eric started telling them about the areas where the data is uncertain, they asked him why he was so uncertain."

"I don't get it."

Ken continued, "They wanted to know why, before coming to brief them, he hadn't done his job so he could be certain."

"But correctly identifying where the data is uncertain is exactly what risk, and for that matter, economic analysis, is supposed to do. That's the sign of an excellent analysis."

"I know that, everyone in *this* building [DHHS was across the street] knows that, but these people had never heard of uncertainty analysis. They told him to get out and come back when he'd done his job and could be certain."

Another failure on my part. I should have been there.

"Sorry, it was a mistake, and it won't happen again."

I left Ken's office and went to find Eric. He related the entire story to me and was completely bewildered. He wanted to know if he'd done something wrong.

"No," I said, "I did something wrong. I should have been there, and I could have cut them off and explained how every analysis uses data that is inherently uncertain. You did an expert job."

We laughed a little, but then I related a story to him about why we probably shouldn't laugh at people's ignorance about what we do.

I told Eric about a recent occasion when I was with our consumer-studies team doing food-safety focus groups. The way it works is, we hire a professional moderator and give them a script to use with the focus group. The moderators present scripted questions to eight to ten people in a small room seated around a table. We, the FDA people, sit behind a one-way mirror watching and listening to them.

This one was about how people felt about irradiation. When asked, people started talking about how they didn't want to glow in the dark from eating "radiated foods." We were all chuckling about their ignorance, but then something hit me.

I turned to my staff and said, "You know, if we were on that side of the wall and the subject was quantum physics, there would be physicists in here laughing at us. There's no reason consumers not in our field should understand our stuff." Everyone stopped laughing.

After Eric's fiasco with the department briefing, I got together with my entire staff and we discussed how to do better briefings. We talked about careful preparation, practicing, and importantly, making sure we didn't talk over our audience's heads.

That wasn't the end of our problems with the department, however.

I went to the next egg briefing along with the center director, and this one got even weirder. One of the deputy secretaries was a muscular black man. My part of the briefing was to discuss how we would handle small egg farms. We had to analyze effects on small firms by law.

In 1980, Congress passed the Regulatory Flexibility Act that requires agencies to examine the effects of their regulations on small businesses. Sixteen years later, they amended it and gave small businesses the right to sue agencies if they haven't done the analysis correctly. The Small Business Administration, one of the president's many agencies, oversees these analyses.

I gave the standard Reg Flex briefing on the number of small businesses affected, what they would have to do, and how much it would cost them.

When I finished, I got a question from the assistant secretary I'd never heard before. He asked, "How will this affect black egg farmers?"

I went blank. Was I supposed to know the answer to that? Had I screwed this up as badly or worse than Eric?

Joe Levitt, the center director, saved me. He jumped in quickly and said, "We don't have an answer for that right now, but we will go back and immediately start to work on it."

On the way back across the street I turned to Joe and said, "What if I knew the answer to the question, which, in fact, I don't?"

He said, "There is no way we are ever going to answer a question like that, because no matter what you say, it's going to cause trouble."

We continued to work on the economic analysis while the program office—the Office of Land Food—continued to work on the rule. As usual, it was like two separate functions. They made all the decisions and paid no attention to what we were doing.

One humorous event happened during all of this. To see what the problem was with poop in chicken houses, we sent one of our best microbiologists to tour them. He walked onto a six-foot pile of chicken poop that had been there so long it was hardened on the top. Being only 5'4", he nearly drowned when his foot went through the crust and the entire thing collapsed. He was completely engulfed. I guess lack of oxygen would have gotten him before the salmonella, so it wouldn't have been recorded as a food-safety problem.

In the US, the vast majority of food manufacturers and retailers are small businesses. A lot of people, including farmers, have small flocks of chickens for eggs. Given that eggs have outgrown their bad publicity from years ago, egg consumption has grown from 250 per year to almost 300 since 1999.[1] The smaller egg producers are represented, as are all small businesses, by a dedicated group in the Small Business Administration (SBA), the Office of Advocacy. Formed in 1976, they represent small businesses to the regulatory agencies, do research, and talk to small businesses. They are needed because, like the comedian Rodney Dangerfield might have said, "Small businesses don't get no respect." They don't contribute to campaigns and they typically don't have a regulatory lawyer on board.

Early on in their existence, the SBA Office of Advocacy also didn't get a lot of respect, and they had to get creative to get noticed. One attorney was trying to get USDA's attention to her small-business issue. She examined the data they sent her and promptly sent a reply back saying: "You must have gotten your data from the Psychic Friends Hotline!"

That got her an audience with the Secretary of USDA (who complained). Despite his complaint, she was later promoted.

1. Source: United Egg Producers

Refrigeration surfaced as one of the most important issues. The Office of Land Food had written a proposal requiring shell eggs to be refrigerated at thirty-seven degrees right after hatching. The economists on my staff discovered that if egg manufacturers needed to buy new refrigerators, there was a cut-off point. Most farmers already owned refrigerators that chilled to forty-five degrees, but to go colder would require new ones. I'd asked Eric to calculate how many fewer illnesses there were likely to be by chilling the eggs an additional eight degrees. Like everything else he did, Eric was thorough.

We were scheduled to brief the deputy commissioner on this right after Eric finished. He and I went to the commissioner's conference room along with the head of Land Food and six people he had working on the rule. After the department uncertainty problem, I had no intention of missing any of these briefings.

William Schultz, the deputy commissioner in charge of the meeting, already knew a lot about the rule; it wasn't very long before he got to the question about temperature.

The office director jumped right in. "Obviously, we don't want to freeze the eggs, but we're pretty certain that thirty-seven degrees is the right temperature to set." His staff all nodded their heads approvingly.

Bill turned to me and asked, "What does economics have to say?"

No one had ever asked me a question directly about policy before. I didn't look at the program office director because I knew he would expect a perfunctory support answer.

"It will cost about twenty-million dollars more to go from forty-five degrees down to thirty-seven degrees because a lot of them will have to buy new, expensive refrigerators."

We'd briefed the office director on that fact prior to the meeting and he was ready with an answer.

He said, "It will be worth it, it will prevent more illnesses."

"How many more?" Bill asked.

The director turned to his staff, who immediately started checking their feet for answers.

This was the moment. They didn't know, and I did. I took a breath and said:

"We looked at the data and estimated that number. It's zero."

The office director turned back to his staff frantically looking for someone to contradict me. They had no idea.

"OK," Bill said, "Forty-five degrees it is."

The director continued to look at me as though I were a different person. In fact, I was. My staff and I had done our homework and spoken up on a policy matter, not just economics, and changed a program policy. It wasn't the first, but it was the first one where we directly contradicted an office director and won an argument.

Chapter 15:
GENERAL PATTON COMMANDS DIETARY SUPPLEMENTS

ONE OF MY FAVORITE PEOPLE at the FDA was Melody Fischer. She was one of the nicest, most reasonable people I knew, but she shocked me one day.

After the Republicans took control of the House and Senate in the 1994 midterm elections, the so-called Gingrich Revolution, they passed the Dietary Supplement Health and Education Act (DSHEA) in October. The FDA had tried for years to rein in the dietary-supplement industry, first going after vitamins and minerals in the 1970s, and then trying to stop their health claims in the '80s and '90s.

In truth, dietary supplements look like drugs, and the FDA wanted to regulate them as drugs. But drugs are heavily regulated and, according to one study, getting a single drug approved through the FDA takes $2.6 billion.[60] Also, from the time it's invented, it takes about twelve years to get a drug approved.[61] Not surprisingly, the dietary-supplement industry did not want that kind of a regulatory regime.

One reason the DSHEA bill wasn't more stringent was because there had been 2.5 million letters supporting "health freedom" sent to Congress.[62] People from all walks of life and all political sensibilities take dietary supplements and don't want them heavily regulated.

As a result, DSHEA said that dietary supplements were not food additives, nor were they drugs, both of which would require premarket approval. It also allowed supplement makers to make claims related to nutrient deficiencies, but they had to state, which they were apparently proud to do, that their claims were not evaluated or substantiated by the FDA.

For the FDA, the law was clear: it said that we could regulate dietary supplements *only* if we found a problem.

It didn't matter what caveat Congress expressed; we finally had the authority, and we would use it. The responses given to the proposed rule tell the story. Some commenters who apparently had read the law asked, "What do you need them [dietary supplement regulations] for?"

Here are some responses from the FDA written in the final rule.

> *Some comments state that dietary supplement CGMP (current good manufacturing practices) that regulate how to safely manufacture drugs and foods) requirements are not needed because the dietary supplements have a track record of safety. Other comments say there were more adverse events reported from drug use than from dietary supplement use and that a large number of Americans take dietary supplements, and on that basis suggested that dietary supplements are safer than foods or drugs.[63]*

Three out of four Americans take some kind of dietary supplements. People take them for energy, health, to fill nutrient gaps, and for healthy aging. Most take multivitamins, and most of those take vitamin D. Herbals and botanicals are growing, with people taking things like green tea and turmeric.

Supplement users tend to exercise more than non-supplement users (71 percent to 53 percent). They are more likely to eat better and see doctors regularly.[1] Interestingly, whether someone has or doesn't have a college degree does not affect whether they take dietary supplements. Users trust supplements, even if they are "hope in a bottle."

In February 2020, Commissioner Scott Gottlieb said the FDA needed to do more oversight because of "new potential dangers."[2]

1. 2019 CRN Consumer Survey on Dietary Supplements.

2. Markham Heid, "The Problem with Supplements," Medium, May 6, 2019.

The FDA's response:

> *We disagree with the comments asserting dietary supplements have a track record of safety such that dietary supplement CGMP requirements are unnecessary. Section 402(g) of the act does not require us to establish a "bad" track record of safety in the manufacture of dietary supplements before we may issue a dietary supplement CGMP rule.*[64]

In fact, that is exactly what Congress required, but, worse, the FDA also claimed that unless someone proved to them that the regulations we were establishing were *not necessary*, we would go forward.

Here's another response, essentially saying, "We don't have to prove that regulations are necessary; you, the public, have to prove that they are unnecessary."

> *We also disagree with those comments stating that the requirements in Part 110 [CGMPs] are adequate and that no additional requirements are necessary. The comments do not explain why the specific requirements set forth in the proposed rule that are not also in part 110 are unnecessary.*[65]

Unfortunately for the economists, we had to go out and find actual problems the regulations might solve to get the rule through the OMB.

Around the time we'd started on the rule, the center director, Joe Levitt, brought in one of his friends from the dietary supplement industry to manage the regulation. He had zero experience in government, but Joe told me, "Rich, you're really going to like this guy; he's just like you. He says what he thinks."

In retrospect, I found that to be a tremendous insult.

For our first meeting with Hank, I took the branch chief for economics and two additional economists who would be working on the rule. I couldn't stay, but I thought I should at least introduce myself to the new manager.

It started well. We all shook hands with Hank, and I introduced him to the other economists. He was about 5'6" with a bald head and compact build. Joe had also put him in charge of some of the food-terrorism rules. Hank explained to us he was working on "top secret" rules.

He said, "If I told you what I was working on, I would have to kill you." No one managed even a smile at that tired old joke. I left after that.

After that meeting, the branch chief came to see me.

He looked morose.

He said, "It never ends. He's at least as bad as the program office directors. After we explained about how economics works in the government, how he is supposed to use the results to help shape the regulatory decisions, he dismissed us. He said, 'I don't need you guys to help me make decisions; I'm a decision maker. I don't see any need for us to meet anymore.'"

I told the branch chief not to worry; just do the job and we would figure out how to handle General Patton later. We called him that because we figured he would have been happy to sport pearl-handled pistols while he did his super-secret work.

After months of looking for problems with how dietary supplements are manufactured, we were nearly empty-handed. I went to see one of the few people I knew to be reasonable in the Office of Nutrition, Melody Fischer. It was still their regulation, even though Hank had been given oversight.

"Hank's driving us crazy," I told her. "He won't listen to a word we say. In fact, he doesn't even want to meet with us. We've looked and looked for months, and we haven't found any serious problems with how they make these things. We don't have to do this rule. Why don't we just announce that there isn't enough of a problem to do it?"

Melody said, "But Richard, *we have to get these guys somewhere.*"

I couldn't believe what I was hearing.

We have to get them? That's our regulatory philosophy?

In fact, it was our philosophy for just about everything, but I'd never heard it spoken out loud before.

Eventually, Hank settled on a whole series of requirements for dietary supplements. The two that made the least sense were that he wanted to require companies to test every single incoming ingredient for safety, and then, when the product was completed, test the whole thing again. I asked him about it.

He responded, "Look, they have to test the incoming ingredients. Suppose they don't, and then they just go ahead and make the supplement. When they test the final product, they're going to find out that they got a bad product. They'll have wasted all of that time and money on producing the stuff because then they have to throw it out. You see?"

I finally had an opening to help make this regulation a little less crazy.

"OMB is going to hate this, but here's an idea. Why should we take the hit for more extensive regulations and save those guys money? If they're stupid enough not to test their incoming ingredients, then—you're right— they're going to lose money. Screw 'em!"

Hank smiled. "You're right. Let's just make 'em test the final product. If they don't figure it out, the hell with 'em."

Using Hank's mindset, I'd figured out a way to reduce the costs; at least we would get costs a little closer to the ridiculously small benefits. This was my last big win in the agency before I retired. After I left, the FDA sent me another award for the dietary-supplement rule.

It was only after I left the government that I started to think about my big "wins." With the egg rule, I'd actually gotten economic and risk analysis into a decision. The same thing happened with the dietary-supplement rule. But these regulations didn't really help consumers much. In some cases, economics and risk didn't play any role at all; in others, the analysis had to be either manipulated at the start or had to be changed to fit the decision. What exactly was I winning?

Chapter 16:
WILL I DIE WAITING FOR FOOD LABELING?

COMMISSIONER DAVID KESSLER didn't even smile when he said, "Well, you could eat more fruits and vegetables." He was responding to a question a young woman reporter asked in the Great Hall of the Department of Health and Human Services in Washington, DC.

"While we wait for two years for these regulations to take effect, what are we supposed to do?" she had asked.

I was in the back watching it even though the staff weren't supposed to be there; there was fear that reporters would find us and start asking questions that we weren't cleared to answer. I was also grimacing so I wouldn't be caught laughing at the question. All I could think of was that he could have said, "I'm sorry, ma'am, there's nothing I can do for you so you should probably just update your will."

He could end by making the sign of the cross; that would have shown that she was in God's hands now.

Commissioner Kessler's press conference in 1993 was to announce the publication of the twenty-six nutrition labeling rules and regulatory impact analysis. It was the end of our two-year struggle, but the government's focus on nutrition started long before then.

One starting point might be in 1933, when Hazel Stiebeling, employed by the USDA's Bureau of Home Economics, published *Food Budgets for*

Nutrition and Production Programs. In it, she suggested that there should be "dietary allowances" for some vitamins and minerals.[66]

In 1939, following Stiebeling and at the suggestion of the League of Nations, Canadians proposed daily values for calories, fat, protein, and calcium. If you don't know what daily values are, don't worry; by the end of this book, you won't care either.

All of this was fine and would have done no harm if this information had been kept in dusty nutrition journals and books. Alas, it wasn't to be, at least at first. At the time, we were mostly concerned with whether people had enough to eat.

That was still true in 1967 when Robert Kennedy, the son of multimillionaire Joe Kennedy, went to the Mississippi Delta and found that people not growing up in tony Brookline, Massachusetts, were *poor* and hungry most of the time. On the other hand, many were also obese (from overeating awful food when it was available).[67]

Kennedy revealed his findings:

> *Although the children of West Africa melt away from starvation, America stands in ironic contrast as a land of overindulged and excessively fed. In many ways, the well-being of the overfed is as threatening as the undernourished.*[68]

The media got into it as well when, in 1968, CBS aired *Hunger in America*, showing American children starving to death.[69]

Nine years later, Senator George McGovern started a Senate investigation of starvation in America but ended up focusing on diseases related to diets. His hearings and committee produced the *Dietary Goals for the United States* in 1977. The report indicted red meat as a major source of disease, causing the meat industry to fight back like hungry carnivores.

There were also weird reactions to the report, including inmates in the Montgomery County Detention Center who began throwing frozen TV dinners against the wall in anger because they felt they'd been "dehumanized."[70] I'm not sure why they hated frozen dinners but, apparently, a switch to eating fresh foods re-humanized them. Bruno Bettelheim, who may have overstated the case for the inmates' concern, said:

Eating and being fed are intimately connected with our deepest feelings. They are the basic interactions between human beings on which rest all later evaluations of oneself, of the world, and of our relationship to it.[71]

Eating and being fed? I thought it was love.

The FDA paid attention to the McGovern hearings, and in 1973, when firms made claims about how their foods prevented diseases, we got into the food-labeling business. We decided that if a manufacturer wanted to say something nice about their food (i.e., make a health claim), they also had to tell you about the nutrients in their food. The rationale back then was:

Without full nutrition labeling, such claims or information would be confusing and misleading for lack of completeness and could deceive consumers about the true nutritional value of the food, its overall nutritional contribution to the daily diet, and its nutritional weaknesses as well as strengths.[72]

FDA Commissioner Charles C. Edwards wasn't so sure that the required labeling was a good idea. In 1973, he stated in the classics' journal (otherwise known as the *Federal Register*), "Experience under this new regulation (labeling amounts of different nutrients) is required before expansion to all foods on a mandatory basis can be considered."[xi]

Not everyone was alarmed by our poor diets, though. In same year as the McGovern committee was holding hearings, Larry Groce came out with a hit rock and roll song called "Junk Food Junkie," singing about the glories of Ding Dongs and Pringles.[73]

Meanwhile, professional wrestler André the Giant, who typically consumed 7,000 calories worth of booze per day, set the world record for the number of beers consumed in a single sitting by drinking 119 twelve-ounce beers (18,000 calories) in six hours.[74] Perhaps Americans were more attuned to André and Groce than McGovern, because Americans haven't seemed to learn much. We now eat more oils, meats, and dairy foods than they did back then.[75]

In 1990, Secretary of Health and Human Services Louis Sullivan said, "The grocery store has become a Tower of Babel, and consumers need to be linguists, scientists, and mind readers to understand the many labels they seeVital information is missing, and frankly some unfounded health claims are being made." [76,24]

By the time of the Babel speech, we'd had the McGovern Committee, multiple reports from nutrition societies, the 1973 labeling rules, lots of science linking food components (nutrients, macronutrients) to chronic diseases (cancer and heart disease), and the beginnings of a food activism explosion. The Nutrition Labeling and Education Act (NLEA) was the natural result of where everyone involved wanted to go: giving consumers information on specific nutrients (vitamins, minerals), macronutrients (fats, carbohydrates, and protein), ingredients, and calories.

In the NLEA, Congress instructed the agency to put nutrition labels on all foods such that:

> *The required information is to be conveyed to the public in a manner which enables the public to readily observe and* comprehend *such information and to* understand *[my underlining] its relative significance in the context of a total daily diet.* [77]

At the time, only about 30 percent of foods were mandatorily labeled under the 1973 law. CFSAN had floated a *Federal Register* document and held public meetings asking the public what else people wanted from food labels. Following that, we started writing proposed rules, but Congress didn't want to let the opportunity pass to take credit for any new food labeling. In 1990, they passed a law mandating what pretty much what we already had written in our draft proposals.

---

24 This quote, particularly the reference to the Tower of Babel, has been repeated everywhere for years. That included even people who don't read the Bible. I confess I didn't know what the Tower of Babel was, so I looked it up. I found out that Nimrod (a great-grandson of Noah) made a tower in Babel (possibly in northeastern Syria today). With the tower, the people they decided they didn't need God anymore. God was so annoyed he made them start speaking different languages so they couldn't understand each other. Carrying on the tradition, the FDA created the nutrition-facts panel to ensure that people couldn't understand what they were eating either.

Assuming we'd already done most of the work, Congress gave us one year to get the proposals out.

In the regulation office, we began with a meeting. Ed Stevens, our office director, had never had a single meeting with his managers before, so it was a big surprise when he summoned us to his office one morning in 1990. His small regulatory staff included attorneys, economists, and the people charged with writing regulations.

He started off with a big smile.

"Good morning. I've just come from a meeting with Fred, and we are starting the largest regulatory project in my time here so far and, I believe, the largest one we will ever undertake."

He seemed genuinely excited, and we had no idea what it was all about.

"We are going to revise the food labels and make nutrition labeling mandatory for all packaged foods."

Then he said, "Each of you needs to look at your vacation plans from now until next year and cancel them. We have to get this done."

A week later, Ed left for a month's vacation.

The consumer studies branch was charged with studying different labels to see which would be the most useful to consumers. They did focus groups, consumer surveys, and experimental studies in malls to try to understand what consumers knew, what their attitudes about food and nutrition were, and what they believed. Even prior to the law, they'd already been testing label formats, but Congress was specific about what information had to be listed. Had Congress been more flexible, we might have ended up with something better.

The economists NLEA role was to look at the benefits and costs of different labeling options. For me particularly, I had to learn nutrition, just as earlier I had learned toxicology and risk analysis for food-safety rules.

Right before he left for his vacation, Ed came into my office one afternoon to issue a warning.

"Rich, this will be a big political issue, and OMB and the department are going to have their own ideas about what we should do. You need to stay away from those guys, particularly Walt Francis at the department and John Morrall at OMB."

"Uh, OK, I've heard of those guys, but I don't really know them," I said.

"That's good, that's good, I just wanted to warn you in case."

About a month later, at an economics conference in DC, I was on a panel of economists talking about regulations. The guy sitting next to me on the stage turned out to be John Morrall.

I smiled at him and said, "So you're the guy I'm supposed to stay away from?"

John, a blond-haired man in his middle forties with a tan and a slender build from running, replied, "What?" with a quizzical smile.

"Yeah, I was just warned by my office director about staying away from you because you're one of the guys who will review our nutrition labeling rules and try to interfere with what we want to do."

"Does this guy know we both work in the executive branch for the same president?" John responded.

I laughed. "Well, come to think about it, he may know that, but he, and I guess just about everybody I work with, thinks you guys are the enemy."

John just shook his head as if to say, *Will this bulls**t ever stop?*

"Richard, why don't you come over in the next few weeks and meet the staff?"

I agreed to do so, despite Ed's warning. I mean, weren't we all on the same team under President Bush?

I spent all day with the regulatory arm of OMB, OIRA. They worked in the New Executive Office Building near the White House, and I came to realize that, unlike us, they were the president's regulatory staff. Their desks had giant stacks of papers, regulations they had to review, that poured in every single day. They were mostly young, in their twenties and thirties, but all of them were smart. They were also bound together by the fact that they knew how much they were hated by the regulatory agencies. I attended one meeting with them while I was there and the condescension from the agency managers toward these young upstarts was palpable.

Much later, my experiences with OIRA prompted me to give testimony in the Senate entitled "David Versus Godzilla," because the fifty or so people at OMB were outnumbered by nearly 200,000 regulators.[78]

After meeting with the OIRA staff, I realized that I would have to deal with them later when the labeling analysis got to them, but right now I needed to think about how the new nutrition labels would work. Somehow, consumers had to get new information, make better choices, and their health had to improve.

If consumers saw the nutrition panels and understood what they were seeing and how each nutrient and macronutrient fit into their daily diet, then nutrition labels could be beneficial—but I had less than a year to prove it.

I knew Ed was right. This was huge, it needed to be done fast, and a lot of people would be watching.

One of the nutrition office directors once said to me: "There are 10,000 things that could go on a food label. The problem is deciding which are the most important."

People are becoming more and more concerned about what was previously thought to be irrelevant information about food. We could, for example, list the country that grew, made, or packaged the food. We could talk about the practices of the farmer or rancher, such as the types of pesticides and herbicides used, the quality of the water and soil, and how the animals were treated. We could also talk about how the workers on the farms or in manufacturing plants were treated and what they were paid.

Rather than just calories, nutrients, and ingredients, we could talk about the chemical makeup of the foods. We could also list where and for how long the food has been in storage and transported, and whether those facilities were sanitized.

We could also talk about the food's contribution to greenhouse gases, how much water is needed to grow it, whether it contributes to agricultural runoff affecting streams, lakes, and oceans. Is it genetically modified or engineered? Is the packaging from sustainable sources? Is the manufacturer or farmer small or is it owned by a minority? Has it been sued lately or had any recalls?

There's no end to possible food facts.

Now think about the size of the average can of food which has the name of the food and the manufacturer and the nutrition-facts panel. There's not a lot of room left for anything else.

Chapter 17:
THE SMALLER YOU ARE, THE HARDER YOU'LL FALL

"I MAKE CANDIES in my small shop and *everybody* knows they're wicked. You don't need a label to tell you that!"

As I looked at relabeling packaged foods, it was difficult to believe how expensive it was. The costs of mandatory label changes included first trying to understand the regulations; having the micro (vitamins and minerals) and macronutrients (e.g., saturated fat, protein, carbohydrates), sodium, calories, and fiber analyzed; printing new labels; throwing out old labels; and, if necessary, reformulating the product. Not counting reformulation, the average cost was about $7,000 per product.

From the comments to our proposed regulations, we realized small firms would be crushed by these rules. In the 1973 rule, the FDA had concluded that if labeling information is necessary for informed decisions about food, it should be provided regardless of the manufacturer's size. Moreover, enforcing a regulation based on the size of the regulated firm would be expensive for USDA and the FDA.[79]

When Congress wrote the NLEA, they pulled language from a previous law (as the lawyers informed us they do from time to time)—in this case, an exemption for small businesses. It exempted far too few firms.

It wasn't just the fact that they were small businesses, it was actually more the case that they produced fewer products each year. The problem is that if you produce a product that only sells a few thousand items a year, it can't compete with a product that sells ten million products.[25]

Even before having to relabel, I discovered a lot of small food businesses were barely making rent, payroll, and other operating costs every month. Because of that, most didn't have enough retained earnings to pay for new labels.

They also couldn't go to the bank and ask for a loan. The first thing the bank would ask them is whether relabeling would increase their business. They wouldn't increase sales because everyone would be doing the same thing.

For food labeling, the FDA tasked me with going around the country to get firsthand experience by holding hearings with small business owners. I had to find out exactly what Senator McGovern wished he'd known when he tried to run his Connecticut Inn. The FDA would not have done this except for one small businesswoman who looked at the cost of changing her labels and wrote a friend of hers, a senator, and said it would put her out of business and she would have to let her thirty employees go.

I was excited to go out and meet people who knew their odds of survival weren't good—20 percent of businesses fail in the first year and, by five years, only half survive. They scheduled me to go with three people from USDA who were working on their version of the food-labeling rules to three cities across the country: Atlanta, Kansas City, and San Francisco.[80]

Our first, and most memorable meeting, took place in a downtown Atlanta hotel in 1991. The FDA had booked a large auditorium for me and the three people from USDA. When I walked in, there were already about 300 men and women sitting and talking among themselves in the room. On the

---

25 Here's an example. Suppose you have two candy bars that compete with one another and each one costs one dollar before labeling. Let's call one Tiny Bars. Tiny Bars sells 2,000 candy bars every year. The other candy bar, call it Big Bars, sells 2 million bars each year. Each one must be relabeled, and the cost for each product line is $7,000. I'll do the math for you. If you passed on all the costs of relabeling to consumers, Tiny Bars would now cost $1.28. Big Bars would cost $1.01, as the cost per bar is not even a penny per bar. Many consumers would not be willing to pay twenty-seven cents more for Tiny Bars so would switch to Big Bars. As a result, Tiny Bars would go out of business.

stage, there was a podium with a microphone and chairs for the three people waiting to speak. Because most of the people attending were expected to be under FDA rules (as the FDA regulates all foods except meat and poultry), I was chosen to go first.

I'd been to a lot of meetings with food-industry executives, but they were all from big companies. This would be my first time meeting small-business owners. They weren't like the high-paid DC lawyers or the regulatory compliance chiefs in big food firms. These were owners/operators of their own businesses. I knew there were many thousands of them across the country but, I confess, I didn't really understand them. While I was there to brief them on what we were proposing, I was about to go to school on running a small business.

I walked up to the podium with my notes and the room quieted down. The three USDA people sat in the chairs next to me. I began.

"First, let me welcome you and thank you for attending this meeting that will be about one of the biggest changes in food regulations the FDA has ever undertaken. The FDA is implementing the recent law, the Nutrition Labeling and Education Act of 1990 that mandated that all labels—not just those making claims—will have to have nutrition information on their packages. There are many other parts of the legislation, such as what it will require you to do if you want to make a health claim, but the part I want to talk to you about today is what the required changes will cost you. The people you see to my right will follow me and talk about USDA's efforts. We want this talk to be interactive. We also hope you will interrupt us whenever you have a question or a comment. We are recording it so we will be able to take your questions and comments back with us so they can be considered in our final rule.

"First, let me ask if there are any questions at this point about why we are here or anything else?"

The room went from quiet to a black hole that sucked in all sound.

"OK," I responded with as much cheer as I could manage, "let me talk a little bit about the small business analytical requirements Congress has imposed on us and then go into our preliminary estimates of what this will cost you.

"By now, most of you may have heard about the Regulatory Flexibility Act. This is a law passed by Congress in 1980 that mandates that we consider having different requirements for small firms. It means we are required to study the impact on small firms and then, as a result of that research, we must give consideration to different options for you, such as fewer requirements or more time to comply with the regulations. This law is to protect you, and it also gives you a voice, through ombudsmen from the US Small Business Administration, who comment on your behalf."

Again, I paused, waiting for questions. I went on to describe our estimates of the different required labeling activities and the average cost of $7,000. That figure drew the first reaction from the crowd. I heard multiple sharp intakes of breath.

I asked again, "Any questions or comments on this?" Once again, silence, although there was a little uncomfortable squirming.

"There are two ways to comment: here in this hall, or you can write letters to us during the comment period. If you have issues, though, you must raise them with us either verbally on tape today or by written comment."

Nothing. Nada. No one spoke.

I then turned it over to the USDA folks and, after their brief speech, they got the same reaction.

The USDA speaker called me back up, and we both thanked everyone for coming and called the meeting to a close.

That's when the real meeting began.

Immediately, a crowd formed around me down in front of the stage. I looked over and the same thing was happening with a smaller group in front of the three USDA folks.

One man started off with nods from those around him.

"I didn't want to say anything in front of everyone and, in particular, you know, on tape. I don't want anyone to know who I am so I'm not going to tell you my name. I just want to know if you guys really get it. You talk about seven thousand dollars as though it's nothing. I recently bought a fax machine, and I agonized over that purchase for three years before spending three-hundred-fifty dollars."

I said, "Thanks, that's what I'm here for, to learn more about how this will affect you."

He didn't reply.

The next person to speak was a lady about sixty years old, with jet-black hair and dressed as though she were going to church.

She said in a strong Georgia accent, "Well, *Ah* don't know why your regulation would have anything to do with me. I make candies in my small shop and *everbody* knows they're wicked. You don't need a label to tell you that."

I laughed and said I would see if there was any thought to exempting candy, although I doubted it.

I talked to a dozen more people and, finally, one woman who'd deliberately stayed in the back came forward when everyone else left. She had soft graying hair and tired eyes with a hesitant smile on her face.

"Dr. Williams," she began gently, "I hope you can help me."

"I certainly hope so too."

"I have a small jam company; it's my own recipes that I worked on over many years," she said with just a lilt of a Southern accent.

"I think I'm successful. I actually have a few people that work for me, and I have a small building where we cook the jams and put them in glass jars. But this thing that the FDA is doing is going to ruin me. I can't afford seven thousand dollars."

At this point, I could see a tear just beginning to form in one eye.

As she continued, her voice became a bit more Atlanta Southern. "My husband is a successful businessman, and he has always told me I had no head for business. Even now, he keeps telling me my business is going to fail, and I need to get back in the kitchen. But my kids are all grown up now and gone from home and I don't want to go back in the kitchen all day."

By now she was quietly crying. It was obvious why she waited to the end.

"Is there anything you can do, anything that can help me?"

I said, "Well, there are two possibilities. First, I could follow you back home and explain to your pig-headed husband that, if your business fails, it's not your fault. But I don't think that's what you have in mind. The second option, the one I will do, is to go back to Washington and persuade them we have to change the small-business exemption. I swear to you I'm going to get that done."

She took my hand with two of hers, looked into my eyes, and said, "Thank you, *thank you*."

I went back to Washington and we "helped" members of Congress craft what was called a technical amendment to the NLEA law that would exempt small businesses with small product lines. I liked to think that lady went on to grow her successful jam business, eternally pissing off her husband.

Chapter 18:
GOOD ENOUGH FOR MCDONALD'S

IN MOST CASES, heads of agencies don't like to be told anything by OIRA. They feel like anything from the OMB "bean-counters" is an assault on their expertise. Having done a short detail at OIRA, I knew the impossible job the OIRA analysts were asked to do, particularly with all the politics involved. The food-labeling rules were the quintessential example of our interactions with OIRA.

After the Meeting from Hell with Ken and the office directors putting me in a "support role," I decided I would take a different approach to the benefits of food labeling. The hardest issue we had to deal with was how, if people changed their diets, would it affect their health? Rather than go it alone as we normally did, I decided to involve Susan Tindall, the nutrition-office director, in the benefits analysis. Susan almost never smiled and had a voice that would be well suited to lecturing inmates at a high-security prison. I didn't know the nutrition literature, but it was Susan's entire life.

Susan's office on the first floor was tidy, with her diplomas and FDA awards neatly posted on the wall. I sat in front of her and told her about the model I created to estimate the benefits of health changes from the new labels. We needed to get to actual changes in health, reductions in chronic diseases from changes in diets.

Surprisingly, she was ready to help.

"Let's call my friend at the National Heart, Lung, and Blood Institute (NHLBI). He'll know what's out there that can help."

She began flipping through the cards on her Rolodex until she hit on one. "Here he is. I'll get him on speaker phone."

He answered on the first ring and Susan quickly explained that we needed his help. She told him I was in charge of studying the benefits and costs of all of our nutrition labeling rules and then said, "I'll let Rich explain what he needs."

I jumped right in after saying hello.

"Here's the problem. We need to quantify some diet-disease relationships. So, for example, if we have information that says a million people reduced their consumption of saturated fat by five percent because of labeling, how many cases of heart disease would that eliminate?"

He said, "You can't do that, that can't be done."

"Oh, let me explain," I said. "We have an economic executive order from the president that says we have to estimate the benefits of what we're doing; in this case, we have to estimate the reduced number of cases of heart disease and cancer."

He said, "That doesn't change the fact that you can't do that. There is no information that will allow you to do that."

Idiotically, I persisted, "But we have to—it's a presidential directive."

"Sorry, I can't help you. Nice to hear from you, Susan." He hung up.

Susan turned to me and said, "How important is this?"

I explained that the costs of the new labeling regulations had to be justified by improving health outcomes, like reduced cases of cancer and heart disease.

I knew Susan didn't really understand about OIRA in OMB. I explained to her why OIRA was a big issue for us.

President Carter created OIRA as part of implementing the Paperwork Reduction Act of 1980. In 1981, when President Reagan took office, he gave OIRA, part of the executive branch, the additional authority to review cost-benefit analyses he required of the regulatory agencies. Since then, all presidents, Democratic and Republican, have used the small staff at OIRA for both functions.

About 90 percent of everything OIRA does is related to oversight of regulatory impact analyses, while 10 percent (according to some critics) is to undermine the independence of executive agencies by enforcing the will of the president, vice president, or chief of staff.[81] For example, the president can tell the OIRA staff to ignore the economic analysis of a regulation and instead tell the agency exactly what he wants done on a particular issue.

In fact, that had happened with the seafood HACCP analysis. One analyst in OIRA who had objected to my bogus analysis had written a single-spaced, twenty-five-page objection.[82] He challenged the cost estimates of the "FDA experts." They ordered him to "look away," and because he didn't, they sidelined him from that and other rules.

I'd witnessed the politics when I worked at OIRA on a detail. They assigned me to review a large Department of Labor Occupational Safety and Health Administration (OSHA) regulation to prevent chemical explosions in the workplace. When I read it, I wondered if the OSHA economists figured that no one would ever carefully read their analysis.

Their economists had estimated that, if the rule were in place, it would prevent 80 percent of all workplace explosions. For proof, they offered a footnote that was a reference in a past *Federal Register*. I looked it up. It was a relatively recent regulation (that had no relationship to explosions) where the OSHA economists had estimated that the rule would solve 80 percent of the problem. Curiously, that analysis also had a footnote for proof that referred to an even older regulation whose benefits were estimated to prevent 80 percent of that problem. That was their number, and they were sticking with it.

I turned in my review of the OSHA regulation and it went to the acting director, James Macrae. He sent the word down that based on my analysis, he would return the rule to OSHA the following day. The next day, the morning news described an enormous chemical explosion in Texas. Macrae sent me the signed return letter for my files and said he was sorry, but politics prevented returning the rule. I understood the position he was in but wondered just how many times rules were not returned because of politics and the workload.

But the NLEA economic analysis was bound to get a lot of public scrutiny, so whether or not OIRA had political clout in this instance, the analysis would have to be a good one. I expected OIRA to take a hard look at the regulatory impact analysis for labeling because it was a gigantic set of twenty-six rules.

I knew it would make a bit of difference that the OIRA analysts liked information regulations as opposed to more severe and expensive regulations, but the combined impact of these regulations was huge and they did end up fighting us over them.[83] In his memoirs, Mike Taylor noted that in the fight with USDA over the label format, OIRA was "one of the big problems."[84]

For me, I had to do what the NHLBI guy told me "couldn't be done." We first needed to know how consumers would react when they saw the new labels. Fortunately, we had a study done in conjunction with the Giant grocery stores: they'd put little shelf flags reading things like, "low saturated fat," on particular foods. They tracked changes in sales of the flagged foods relative to the similar foods that did not have the flags. Obviously, the flags were different than reading a nutrition-facts panel, but it was all we had to go on.

Along with the shelf-flag study, we needed answers on diet/disease relationships, the ones that the NHLBI guy refused to answer. If consumers made changes to their diet, how would it affect their health? Fortunately, I found a study done for the department that did just what I needed. A computer model developed by a physician, Warren Browner in San Francisco, estimated how many additional cases of cancer and coronary heart disease would be reduced if there were reductions in fat, saturated fat, and dietary cholesterol.[85]

Browner used research from a nutrition researcher at Harvard named Mark Hegsted. Years later, in an article published in 2016, a University of California researcher found out that the Sugar Research Foundation had paid Hegsted and another Harvard nutritionist to downplay the role of sugar in heart disease.[86] The authors concluded that Hegsted and two other authors had purposely and erroneously blamed atherosclerotic vascular disease on dietary fats and carbohydrates.[87]

Hegsted had also helped draft Senator McGovern's 1977 Senate committee report, *Dietary Goals for the United States*, which launched the Dietary Guidelines Committee. That first committee report launched the low-fat/low-cholesterol diet advice. Today, and who knows if it will last, dietary cholesterol and total fat (not trans or saturated fat) seem to be off the hook.[88] Sugar, at least for the moment, is indicted as a big offender.

Nevertheless, I now had a diet/disease model and the consumer-change model. Before putting all of that together, I wondered how it would all work. Would we be able to show that the benefits exceeded the costs, keeping Fred and everyone else off our case? I wasn't going to fudge the numbers, but before I started, I called the economist on my staff into my office who was responsible for the costs. I wanted to run the benefits problem by her. It was Pat, who later became a powerphile.

I started, "Here's the problem: the math may not work out."

I handed her a sheet of paper that repeated the steps and put some sample percentages attached to each step.

1. First, some consumers must see the labels. 50 percent

2. Second, some of those consumers must read the labels. 50 percent

3. Third, some of those consumers must understand the labels. 25 percent

4. Fourth, some of those consumers must make healthier food choices based on what they read. 25 percent

These numbers were a check on what we were seeing with the Giant shelf-flag studies. I continued, "I just made those numbers up, but they seem like reasonable upper bounds to me. Each of those events must be multiplied by the others to get the percentage of consumers who'll make healthier choices."

Pat had scribbled the numbers down, multiplied them, and said, "I see what you mean; that's about one and a half percent."[26]

---

26 Here's how this works. Suppose there are 100 million shoppers and only half actually notice that there is a label on the back. Of the 50 million who see the label, suppose only half of them, or 25 million, read it. We're going to assume only one out of four, or 25 percent, understand it, so now we are down to 6.25 million people. Again, we are going to assume that, of those who understand it, only one out of four will change their eating habits based on what they read. That leaves just over 1.5 million people out of the original 100 million (1.5 percent) who made a change.

"Exactly, that might be the upper bound of the percentage of people who will be making healthier choices."

"True," Pat said, "but whatever the effect is, you get to multiply it by two-hundred-fifty million Americans."

"That may be what saves us."

"Great," she said, "here we go again. We already know this will be expensive, but we might end up not being able to support these rules."

"I know, and I'm worried."

One thing saved the analysis. The fact that the labels only had to be changed one time, except when products were new or reformulated, meant we had big upfront costs, but the changed behavior would continue, and once the reduced illnesses kicked in, there would be benefits every year (we calculated out to twenty years).

When I looked at the research our consumer studies had done, however, it occurred to me that they hadn't tested the types of information (e.g., calories, fats), just distinct ways to display what Congress had required. Some of the ways we could have done it are in the chart below:

Labeling Options	
(USDA) Saturated Fat	8 grams
(FDA) Saturated Fat	12%
(Current) Saturated Fat 8g	12%
(Faces) Saturated Fat	☹
(Stoplight) Saturated Fat	🚦

USDA wanted to have numbers, like the number of grams per serving. The FDA wanted to list percentages (of a 2,000-calorie daily diet) for each nutrient. Our consumer studies staff tested other things like happy faces and stoplights, but our research showed that people wanted numbers.[89] If we went with percentages, would people really get it, particularly the same way they got the little shelf-flags that said "low saturated fat"?

It got worse. An FDA survey based on 1976 sales showed about 24 percent of all foods in supermarkets carried nutrition labeling.

This is a summary of what they found:

> *Consumers have had 17 years of experience with the current nutrition label format (by 1991), but public comments received by FDA, recent consumer research about revised food labels[90] and the preference results from this study found that consumers want a short, easy-to-read, easily interpreted food label.[91]*

When lead researcher Jacob Shapiro had completed most of this work, I went to his office to ask him about it. Jacob was a contrarian and overconfident of his abilities to an astounding degree. He once told me the FDA could not do without him and that, if I wanted to discuss any faults he might have, he would resign immediately. I called out to my secretary to start drawing up papers for Jacob's resignation and he immediately backed down. Nevertheless, I learned more from disagreeing with Jacob than I did from most people at the FDA. He was often right.

I came into his window office with books and stacks of papers on the floors, desk, and on the windowsill. "I hear you have some interesting results in your shopping-mall study."

This is a study where the consumer researchers go to shopping malls and "intercept" people and get them to answer questions. In this case, they went to eight shopping malls around the country and asked people questions about different label formats, including the one you see today.

Jacob said, "Yeah, it wasn't unexpected; the findings are supported by my theories. When you ask consumers, they always say they want more information."

"And?"

"There was a clear pattern that the labels consumers liked, the ones with numbers, were not the ones they were good at using."

"What do you mean?"

"It means we asked them which labels they liked and then we gave them some tests to see if they could tell how much of a nutrient they were consuming. The ones they liked were the ones we will probably end up with, but they couldn't do the math."

This went right to the heart of any possible benefits consumers might get from food labeling. How on earth did we get here?

I pushed him. "But we're using the shelf-flag study, which is a heck of lot easier for them to use. That means we're way overestimating how many people will respond to this stuff. What can we do?"

"That," said Jacob, "is an excellent question."

I decided to only project the number cases of cancer and heart disease that would be reduced for the next twenty years. I ended up estimating that we would prevent 35,179 cases of cancer, 4,028 cases of heart disease, and within those cases, 12,900 deaths. All of that would happen because people would eat less total fat, saturated fat, and cholesterol.[92] Some commenters to the proposal said there would be much bigger impacts.

We estimated the costs of our rule at between $1.4 and $2.3 billion, with benefits ranging from $4.4 to $26.5 billion because of reducing the numbers of cases of cancer and coronary heart disease.[93] USDA came forward with similar numbers for meat and poultry. The Browner/Hegsted studies saved us, as well as the exceptionally soft Giant shelf-flag study. I knew it probably overestimated the benefits, but it was literally all the information we had.[27]

While we were working on our proposals and the regulatory impact analysis, USDA was on its own track. They had their own nutrition label and thought that percent daily values were inappropriate because people couldn't understand them. CFSAN people thought that USDA felt that way because our label would make meat look bad and they were trying to protect their constituents. There were lots of White House meetings; neither USDA Secretary Edward Madigan nor DHHS Secretary Louis Sullivan would back down. It got tense.

---

27 Warren Browner didn't comment on the proposed rule to us, but he came out and said that even if you ate less saturated fat and cholesterol, it would only increase a woman's life span for three months and man's for four months. Fortunately, I never saw that article at the time.

The NLEA law would take effect even if our rules didn't get published but USDA was not operating under a specific law. President George H.W. Bush said there would only be one label, and it had to apply to both FDA and USDA products.

The two agencies sent representatives to meet in the Oval Office. The arguments went on for a while but, finally, when told that McDonald's was already using the FDA nutrition-facts panel in their tray liners, President Bush yielded to DHHS. Secretary Sullivan told him that mandating the FDA label was the right thing to do from a "public health perspective." Perhaps the broccoli-hating president preferred McDonald's fare.

Once decided, Commissioner Kessler held his news conference with the reporters' lamentation that people would be lost until the label appeared. Secretary Sullivan declared, "The Tower of Babel has come down."[94]

For the CFSAN employees who'd worked on it, we shed our concerns about choosing healthy foods and diet/disease relationships and went to a nearby military base and celebrated our accomplishments with pizza and beer.

Chapter 19:
FOOD LABEL SAVANTS

HER FACE DARKENED with pure hatred that sucked in the surrounding light. I suppose I deserved it. After all, I had just reduced her entire life's work, her passion, to a tiny symbol. My reaction to her hate rays? I was inspired.

That reaction was to a speech I gave ten years after the nutrition labeling regulations passed.

By that time, at least for some of us, the problems with the food label were insurmountable. One thing was obvious; my estimates of preventing 12,000 deaths over twenty years were unlikely.

By 2004, we had a new nutrition office director, Maria Wagner, the one whose hateful glare lit up my life. Later, when she was talking to me again, she told me, "If I could just sit down with every American family in their living room for fifteen minutes, I'm sure I could make them understand how to use the food label."

For a highly educated nutritionist like Maria, these are wonderful labels. She looks at them and sees everything she studied over decades of nutrition research illuminating the path for consumers to healthier eating. No doubt lots of nutritionists feel the same way. Fifteen minutes is quick, however, when you consider what author Bonnie Taub-Dix needs.

Taub-Dix, author of *Read It Before You Eat It,* calls the food label a "powerful weapon that can…cut through the confusion," and by reading her book, she can help you become a "label reading expert."[95]

Really? If you just master her 283 pages of label interpretation, perhaps you *could* access this "powerful weapon." Maria claimed she could do in fifteen minutes what Taub-Dix said would take five to six hours of reading her book.

But even in the FDA, some wouldn't even try. In the early 2000s, I had quietly asked some members in the Office of Nutrition—that is, professional nutritionists and dieticians—if they used percent daily values when food shopping.[28] The answer was no. I never told Susan Tindall about this, particularly after she'd started a meeting off with, "We've created such a wonderful label, I just don't know why people aren't using it." Apparently, she'd never quizzed her own staff.

After he'd left the commissioner job, Kessler called the nutrition-facts panel "iconic," and the FDA historian who interviewed him said it was "the most recognized graphic in the world."[96]

And yet, it's still a problem. Is the problem that people haven't had Maria come to their living room or read books on how to read the food label?

Perhaps not. Start with the fact that nutrition information on packaged foods is primarily pointed at highly educated and highly motivated individuals. Omri Ben-Shahar notes in *More Than You Wanted to Know*:

> *Over forty million adults are functionally illiterate; another fifty million are only marginally literate. In one study, 40 percent of the patients could not read instructions for taking pills on an empty stomach. Innumeracy is worse. In a test of basic innumeracy, only 16 percent could answer three (really) simple questions (like, how much is 1 percent of 1,000?).*[97]

---

28 The percent Daily Value (%DV) shows how much of a nutrient in one serving of food (as defined by FDA) will contribute to an average daily diet (2,000 calories). Nutrients to limit should have low percentages; nutrients to increase should have high ones.

It's not just illiteracy. Showing a nutrition-facts panel to consumers with a college degree, a CDC study found that just under 50 percent could correctly answer questions like, "How many calories are in the whole container?"[98] Here's an example of math that a lot of people get wrong. A bat and a ball cost one dollar and ten cents in total. The bat costs a dollar more than the ball. How much does the ball cost?

If you said ten cents, you're wrong; it's five cents.

We're expanding this complex labeling to multi-chain restaurants where 44 percent of restaurant calories are consumed. One consumer group noted, "We don't need government to tell us the difference between a salad and a twelve-piece bucket of chicken."[99]

In an understatement, nutrition researcher Eric Matheson said, "I think people really have a hard time interpreting what food labels mean."[100] A survey by the American Heart Association found that "95 percent of shoppers at least sometimes look for healthy options, but only a little over a quarter say it's 'easy' to actually find healthy foods."[101]

In another survey by the International Food Information Council, one consumer said, "Figuring out what to eat is harder than doing your own taxes."[102] And sure enough, a 2007 USDA study found that while nutrition labels improved intake of fiber and iron, it had no effect on total fat, saturated fat, or cholesterol (the FDA targets of the food label).[103]

The result? When the NLEA was passed in 1990, 6.2 million Americans, or 2.52 percent of the population, had diabetes. Fifteen years later, that figure jumped to over 23 million (7.4 percent).[104] Childhood diabetes has tripled.[105] Worse, heart disease—the primary target of food labeling—is now on the increase again.[106]

By 2003, when Mark McClellan became our new commissioner, I knew the food labels weren't working. McClellan was the first economist to become commissioner of the FDA, but he also has a medical degree. He brought a Swedish health economist who was an expert on FDA's issues on to his staff.

Tomas Philipson is a large, muscular, good-looking man with black curly hair and an easy smile. He studied pharmaceutical regulation at the University of Chicago and agreed to come to the FDA for a year to advise Commissioner McClellan. I got a call from him one morning and he suggested we go to lunch. Tomas told me how he'd been on the Swedish national volleyball team but he'd changed direction and got a PhD in economics after breaking his leg.[29]

We talked about food safety and nutrition, my specialty; then he told me about the FDA science forum. I told him I'd never been invited.

He asked, "What would you talk about if you were invited?"

I responded, "The food label. It doesn't work."

"What do you mean?"

I told him that after ten years, people just didn't know how to use it.

I also told him I had just discovered something that might work: the *Keyhole*.

"Apparently, it's on some foods in Europe and it just combines all of the nutritional information into one symbol. If it's on a food, it means it's a good nutritional choice compared to all of the others...."

He didn't let me finish the sentence. "Richard, that symbol comes from Sweden. You need to come and talk about it at the science forum."

I got excited for a moment, but then I said, "You don't understand, they won't ever invite an economist to that meeting."

Tomas broke into a broad grin and said, "It won't be a problem; I'll just tell Mark you need to be there."

With the commissioner's backing, I knew I had just gotten a coveted invitation. I also knew I wouldn't have to clear the speech with any of CFSAN's nutritionists, so I could say what I wanted.

The FDA science forum was held in the Walter E. Washington Convention Center, a 2.3 million square-foot building in the center of DC. There were about 250 people in the room and, other than the ones from FDA, they were food executives and company scientists.

I had worked hard to get this talk just right. I went back and read all of our consumer-studies papers on the food label and spent hours getting the slides perfected. I knew the CFSAN nutritionists would be watching it, as well as the key players in the food industry. I couldn't afford to make a single mistake. After all, no one had ever made the argument I was getting ready to make.

---

29 In 2020, he was the acting chairman of the Council of Economic Advisors under President Trump.

I told the audience to look at two nutrition-facts panels on two fictional soup labels. I called them Nature's Soup and Mother's Soup. The first claimed it was organic and the second claimed it was just plain good for you. I used the claims because when some people see a claim, they assume it's a healthy food. Of course, poor old Campbell's tried to advertise, "Soup is good food," but got slapped in 1989 by the Federal Trade Commission (FTC) for misleading advertising.

With the two slides up, recalling the questions Commissioner Edwards wanted people to answer way back in 1973, I asked the audience, "What is:

1. The true nutritional value of the soup;
2. Its overall contribution to your daily diet;
3. Its nutritional weaknesses and strengths?"

Take a look at the two labels below and see how well you do.

Nature's Soup

Nutrition Facts

Serving Size 1 1/3 cups
Servings Per Recipe 6

Amount Per Serving

Calories 160

	% Daily Value*
Total Fat 5.5g	8%
Saturated Fat 2g	10%
Trans Fat 0g	
Cholesterol 80mg	27%
Sodium 200mg	15%
Total Carbohydrate 20g	7%
Dietary Fiber 10g	20%
Sugars 3g	
Protein 27g	
Vitamin A	140%
Vitamin C	6%
Calcium	6%
Iron	15%

* Percent Daily Values are based on a 2,000 calorie diet. Your Daily Values may be higher or lower depending on your calorie needs.

Mother's Soup

Nutrition Facts

Serving Size 1 1/3 cups
Servings Per Recipe 6

Amount Per Serving

Calories 150

	% Daily Value*
Total Fat 4.5g	6%
Saturated Fat 4g	20%
Trans Fat .5g	
Cholesterol 60mg	20%
Sodium 475mg	20%
Total Carbohydrate 80g	27%
Dietary Fiber 20g	80%
Sugars 8g	
Protein 35g	
Vitamin A	100%
Vitamin C	16%
Calcium	20%
Iron	5%

* Percent Daily Values are based on a 2,000 calorie diet. Your Daily Values may be higher or lower depending on your calorie needs.

To answer those questions and make a healthy choice for your lunch, you must be able to compare everything from each label. You want to know which food is better in calories, micronutrients (vitamins and minerals), macronutrients (fats, proteins, and carbs), and ingredients (e.g., sugar and salt). You also need to know how to weight the calories, micronutrients, macronutrients, and ingredients relative to their importance.

Then I showed them some answers.

	Nature's Soup	Mother's Soup
Calories		✓
Total Fat		✓
Saturated Fat	✓	
Trans Fat	✓	
Cholesterol		✓
Sodium	✓	
Fiber		✓
Sugars	✓	
Protein		✓

The checks in each category indicate that one soup is better than the other in a particular category. These are just some of the things you would need to compare but, based only on what you see, can you now say which soup is better for you? If you don't know, that's all right—no one else knows either. For example, the check marks don't say anything about quantities.

But, of course, even if you could put all of those checkmarks in the right places, that's still not enough information to know which is the healthier soup. You would also have to know:

1.   Which of the above categories are most important? How should they be ranked and how much higher or lower do they have to be to make them more important?

2. What about the stuff at the bottom of the label: the vitamins, iron, and calcium? Are they important?

3. How much does it matter what was eaten before or what will be eaten after the soup?

4. How do health issues, levels of exercise, levels of stress, intake of dietary supplements and medicines, microbiomes, or genetics matter as to which one would be healthier for an individual?

5. Does it matter how the food is cooked, what was added such as salt, pepper, or other spices? For example, if the foods were proteins, does it matter whether they were fried, steamed, or broiled?

After getting the audience's attention with the two labels and questions like the above, I presented an alternative—the Swedish Green Keyhole.

"Why not just give people something simple so that they don't have to try and figure out the complicated nutrition-facts panel, or how to think about food health claims, or, for that matter, food claims in conjunction with the facts panel? The Keyhole is only allowed on healthy foods in Sweden."

At this point, I looked down the center aisle and there was Maria, on the edge of the aisle, ready to explode with her nuclear hate bomb. I thought I knew what she was thinking. *Reduce all that wonderful, complex nutrition information to a stupid symbol? Never!*

She didn't approach me afterward; in fact, she didn't speak to me for a few months after. I'm pretty sure she told her whole office what happened because they were all mad at me. Even though I'd worked hard to make friends in this group, I also knew the chance Tomas had given me was a one-time affair. I forgot about getting along, promotions, and the things that successful people do. Instead, I gave the best talk I could.

I can't be sure it was my talk that changed everything, but it sure seemed like it.

First came the food companies with things like "Sensible Solutions" from Kraft.[30] Then trade groups got into it with the "Whole Grain Council Stamp" and the "National Dairy Council Stamp." The American Heart Association started making money by selling their "Heart Check" stamps. Supermarkets started with symbols like the "Hannaford Guiding Stars," and Olive Garden restaurants had their low-fat "Olives." Applebee's started putting Weight Watchers symbols on their menus. Other countries had their own national symbols like Canada's "Health Check" and Australia's "Pick the Tick" (which sounded to me too much like pulling a blood-sucking insect off your leg).

The US food industry decided they needed to do something more comprehensive, so the manufacturers contacted the Keystone Group, a non-profit with a reputation for bringing disparate groups together. They formed a group consisting of academics, consumer advocates, and federal advisors to create an icon for all foods. After leaving the government, I was asked to join the group.

It was difficult; there was a lot of jockeying by food groups, and it took two years, but the "Smart Choices" symbol finally emerged. At the very end, there was a push to put added sugars into the program but most of the group agreed there was no difference between natural sugars and added sugars. That came back to hurt the whole program in a big way.

Mike Jacobson of the CSPI pulled out at the very end because of the missing added sugars. At the last meeting of the group, I begged the food companies not to put the symbol on something obviously not good for you, even if it fit into the Smart Choices category.

It didn't work. One of the food companies put the symbol on a high-sugar kid's cereal, and that allowed the FDA nutritionists to come out against it. One detractor wrote, "Maybe they could just slap a big checkmark on the front of the package that screams, 'Don't think; just eat this.'"[107] Actually, that was the idea—eliminate the requirement to get a master's degree in food labeling.

---

30 It is a front-package labeling system that provides consumers with "practical information to help them easily choose from hundreds of healthful options for breakfast, lunch, dinner, and snack time. It will be used on more than 500 products," Progressive Grocer, April 20, 2007.

Eventually, Maria came up with her own symbol: FDA's "Label Man," with its own video, "The Food Label and You."[108] All you have to know, according to the twenty-eight-minute video, is "calories, serving size, and Percent Daily Value." It's longer than her fifteen minutes in your living room, and it tries to be cute with things like "CSI, Calorie Scene Investigators."

First Lady Michelle Obama was into nutrition, so together with a White House chef, she asked the food industry to come up with a front-of-package symbol. Since they'd failed with Smart Choices, they came up with a "Facts up Front" label that had calories, saturated fat, sodium, and sugars in a little box on the front of packages.

But the FDA nutritionists were having none of that. They wanted to keep the food label the way they designed it, consumers be damned. Eventually, the CFSAN nutritionists decided to revise the food label with "calories" and "servings per container" larger and in bold, along with added sugars.

The former First Lady's goal was, "In the end, our guiding principle here is simple: that you as a parent and a consumer should be able to walk into a grocery store, pick an item off the shelf, and tell whether it's good for your family."[109] I credit her for trying.

Just adding sugars and putting calories in bold letters isn't going to do it.

There won't be a national icon anytime soon. Meanwhile, people are getting fatter and sicker and revising food labels is like pushing the elevator button more times to make it come quickly.

Chapter 20:
LEARNING TO LOSE TO WIN

I WAS WRONG about trans fatty acids. I was sure trans fat should be combined with saturated fat on the food label. Consumers already knew that eating too much saturated fat was bad for them. Since trans fat was at least as bad as saturated fat, combining them to let people know how much of both of the "bad" fats they were consuming would make it easier for them.

As I mentioned earlier, by the year 2000, only 13 percent of Americans knew that there was such a thing as trans fatty acids. Six percent thought they were bad for you and 7 percent thought they were good for you. Improving awareness of trans fatty acids in food had been our PART goal. If I'd won my argument with the nutritionists, I don't think we would have affected consumption of trans fatty acids anywhere near as much as what ultimately happened.

Think about the messaging we've heard from the public health community over the last few decades. Cut down on saturated fat and total fat; eat less sugar; cut down on red meat, eggs, sodas, nuts; avoid too much salt or MSG; avoid trans fatty acids; and avoid dietary cholesterol.

Some of these messages turned out to be misguided; some of them were good for some people but not for others; and some were just wrong. In truth, there is uncertainty in each recommendation. Whether focused on specific foods, ingredients, or macronutrients, policymakers who created these targeted messages usually ignored the fact that when consumers or manufacturers cut back on one thing, *they replaced it with something else.*

By way of example, USDA researchers found out that when advised to cut back on red meat in the 1990s to reduce fat consumption, women replaced the meat with salad dressings and ice cream. The amount of fat consumed stayed the same or even went up slightly.[110]

We didn't start eating trans fatty acids by accident. The food activists insisted that it was better to have hydrogenated vegetable oil than animal fats.

The first hydrogenated food product (i.e., trans fat) was Crisco from Procter & Gamble. It was introduced in 1911, and within a few years it became wildly popular with American housewives. Not only did it have the consistency of lard (pig fat), it was also cheap, tasty, made from plants (cottonseed oil), didn't smoke, and was even kosher.[31][111] Along with margarine, Crisco introduced trans fatty acids widely into the American diet.

Concerns started later. A USDA scientist, Luise Light,[32] began to study the relationship of trans fats to heart disease in the late '70s, but USDA quashed the study to protect margarine.[112]

In the 1980s, CSPI and other advocacy groups pushed restaurants to replace saturated animal fats with trans fats. Both CSPI and the National Heart Savers Association accused manufacturers of "poisoning America… by using saturated fats."[113] In 1986, CSPI called Burger King switching to vegetable shortening (trans fat) "a great boon to Americans' arteries."[114] Again in 1998, CSPI said, "All told, the charges against trans fat just don't stand up."[115] In 1990, in response to questions about trans fat (hydrogenated vegetable oils), Bonnie Liebman, CSPI's nutrition director, dismissed the

---

31 Lard is back but, like everything else, who knows for how long. See, Christoper Doering, "Lard makes a comeback as trends play to the maligned fat's strengths," *FOODDIVE*, May 13, 2021.

32 Luise Light was the USDA director of dietary guidance and nutrition education research, and in the 1980s, she provided the recommendations for the first food pyramid. After submitting it to the secretary of agriculture, the recommendations were substantially changed, increasing the amounts of carbs (breads and cereals) and decreasing the five to nine servings of fresh fruits and vegetables to two to three servings, http://www.whale.to/a/light.html.

concerns with, "That's not to say trans fatty acids are artery-cloggers." She concluded, "The bottom line [is] trans…schmans."[116]

Four years later, in 1994, CSPI petitioned the FDA to require trans fat on the nutrition-facts panel. By then, CSPI director Mike Jacobson was arguing that labeling trans fat might save between 2,100 and 5,600 consumers from heart disease.

I had a conversation several years later with Mike about trans fat and the whole approach we were taking.

"The problem with trans is that you guys didn't think about what would replace it if it was removed from the food supply," I told him.

Mike said, "Richard, we just didn't know about trans back then."

"Exactly my point."

It turns out that getting rid of saturated animal fat and replacing it with trans fat was just another example, similar to the baby-formula problem, of the Whac-A-Mole game. In the 1997 book they edited, *Risk vs. Risk*, John D. Graham and Jonathan Baert Wiener called these phenomena (pop-up risks) "countervailing risks," meaning that as one risk decreases, another one increases.[117] When DDT was eliminated, other toxic pesticides were used in its place.

That wasn't the reason that nutritionists were against adding trans fatty acids to the food label, though. Sofie, the nutritional epidemiologist in my division, came to my office one day to discuss it.

She said, "They don't want to do it. They think people consume so little trans compared to sat [saturated fats] that they think it will distract them. They're also petrified that people will go back to butter."

"Oh, I'm guessing you think they're wrong?"

"It's not just me; the economists don't like it either. We've been trying to get people to reduce saturated fat for decades and it hasn't worked. This stuff is intentionally added into foods, largely unlike sat, and manufacturers can just stop doing that. Once people know about this, manufacturers will have to stop using it."

"Wait, why would they do that?"

You would think we would do better at nutrition given how many agencies are involved in it, particularly at the federal level.

FDA has the Center for Food Safety and Applied Nutrition.

DHHS also has:

> The Agency for Healthcare Research
> The Assistant Secretary for Health including the Office of Disease Prevention and Health Promotion (ODPHP)
> The Office of the Surgeon General
> The Centers for Disease Control (CDC)
> Division of Nutrition, Physical Activity and Obesity

USDA has:

> The Food and Nutrition Service (FNS)
> The Economic Research Service (ERS)

The Department of Defense has:

> The Defense Education Activity (DoDEA) including:
> The Joint Culinary Center for Excellence
> The Army Public Health Center

NASA has its focus on space nutrition.

The National Science Foundation has Biological Sciences.

"It's true that people eat a lot less trans but it's worse than saturated fat. It affects both LDL [low density lipoprotein, the bad fats], and HDL [high density lipoprotein, the good fats]. It's most likely a lot worse for heart disease."

But the nutrition office was in charge; they would write a rule to allow firms to *voluntarily* label trans fatty acids. They would also allow manufacturers to make a claim of "no trans fatty acids" but they wouldn't allow a "not a significant source of trans fat" claim.[118] They hadn't counted on a new director at OIRA, John D. Graham, of *Risk vs. Risk* fame.

I knew John from his previous job as the director of the Center for Risk Analysis at the Harvard School of Public Health.[119] He had invited me to be on their advisory board, which I was happy to do because they were doing some groundbreaking work on risk/risk analysis.

John wanted OIRA to be proactive. He wanted to prompt agencies to send over rules that had benefits exceeding costs. To that end, his branch chief, John Morrall, called me to ask about trans fat.

"Hey, I'm calling you to ask you about a rule you guys are doing—on trans fatty acids."

I didn't know how he knew we were working on it at that exact moment, but I said, "Sure, what about it?"

"John [Graham] is looking for rules that have benefits exceeding costs so he can make OMB look more positive by asking agencies to send those rules over."

"I can't guarantee that this one will; right now, it's a voluntary rule and I don't know who would volunteer to add it to their label. Not that many people know anything about trans. If it's mandated, that's a whole different story given how bad trans is compared to sat."

Morrall said, "Great, that's just what we needed. Thanks, Rich."

That brief phone conversation led to a prompt letter from Graham to the commissioner, telling us to hurry up and send over a mandated rule. Unfortunately, the commissioner didn't know the rule was going to be voluntary. He told someone on his staff to call the center director and make it a mandatory rule, which is what he wanted all along.

The nutritionists were so upset that they didn't want to write the rule. Hannah came to my office to tell me about the change.

She said, "This is awful. We aren't sure whether we should even try to fight this. I don't know if we can defend a rule like this in the preamble."

"OK, Sofie knows this stuff backward and forward. Why don't you just let her write the first draft and then you guys can edit it?"

"Would she do that?"

"I'm sure she would."

Yes, I did feel a little weird about the whole thing. If OIRA had called anyone else, they might have been given a different story, but I just told them what I thought. From an economic perspective, benefits *were* much more likely to exceed the costs of adding trans fat to the label if it was mandatory. I probably should have told someone about the phone call, but I didn't. In my mind, we all worked in the same executive branch and we all had the same interest. I know others didn't feel that way—more like OIRA was the enemy. I just didn't think that way.

Sofie wrote a draft in a month. When she sent it to the Office of Nutrition, they were infuriated. She'd written how much worse trans fatty acids were than saturated fats on a gram for gram basis. I had also asked her to combine saturated fat with trans fatty acids on the label so consumers could more easily keep their total amount of "bad fats" down.

When the Office of Nutrition read her draft, they threw it in the trash. They decided they had to draft it themselves. But now they had a problem. Everyone involved with the rule knew trans and sat had been added in our draft to make it easier for consumers, but they wanted them separate to keep the attention on saturated fat. All they had to do was convince me.

I got a notice for an hour-long meeting in Melody's office at 10:00 a.m. one Monday—that probably meant they had been thinking about how to handle this all weekend. I decided not to bring anyone else with me. There was a lot of foul blood at this point between us and the nutrition office.

When I arrived, Susan Tindall, Hannah Becker, and Melody Fischer were seated around a small table with one empty chair. I could tell by the notes they'd scratched in front of them that they had been there for quite some time.

The meeting started amicably with Susan.

"Hi, Rich. Come on in, have a seat. We wanted to get together to talk about how trans goes on the label."

"I thought that might be what this was about."

Hannah jumped in, "We can't put trans fatty acids and saturated fat together."

"Why not?"

"They're two entirely unique chemical entities."

"Why would consumers care about that?" I asked.

"Well, we care about the integrity of the label, but that's not the only reason. Trans fatty acids are a minor part of the food supply; we don't even think they should be on the label," Hannah said.

Melody joined the mob.

"We want to keep the focus on saturated fat, so we want saturated fat on its own line."

In a burst of inspiration, I changed my mind, knowing I would have to explain it to Sofie and the economists.

"So, what you are proposing is that trans fatty acids have a separate line with the amount of trans in the product?"

Susan replied with an eager, "Yes," as she detected acceptance in my voice.

"OK, I agree, but not for either of the reasons you suggest. I think once people learn about trans' effect on LDL and HDL, then trans will become the new demon to avoid. People will mostly forget about saturated fat, at least for a while."

They didn't care about my reason because they'd won.

The final rule went into effect on January 1, 2006, with a separate line on the nutrition-facts panel for trans fatty acids. The FDA did not allow "trans-fat free," "reduced trans fat," or "reduced saturated fat and trans fat" claims.

The nutritionists thought they could control the messaging, but it went exactly as I'd predicted. The FDA finally decided that trans fat was pretty much like poison, so that as a food additive it could no longer be considered "generally recognized as safe."[120] Three years later, on June 18, 2018, the FDA banned trans fats in all foods sold in restaurants and grocery stores.[121]

I'd lost the argument but ended up with a public-health win. I felt great about this one. But in the end, the nutritionists also won, as once trans is gone, people will start worrying about saturated fat again. Well, maybe that's a win; we'll talk about that later.

Chapter 21:
OBCT

WHY DID SANTA have to be fat? Was it because we had "visions of sugar-plums dancing in our heads"? Really, the idea of sugarplums is gross. Then there's Valentine's Day. We get little candy hearts and give ladies big hunks of chocolate while that fat little cherub goes around shooting everyone in the butt to make them fall in love. Don't even get me started on Halloween and Easter candy.

We reward ourselves with food on holidays. We reward children for being good. In fact, every eating occasion is supposed to be fun, or like Santa, jolly.[33] Food as pure enjoyment for most people started around the time Santa was invented to visit Union soldiers in Civil War camps (1862).[122] Until then, people ate so they wouldn't starve.[123] But in the middle of the nineteenth century, we developed an interest in the culinary arts, that is, gourmet cooking and eating for pleasure. We even have a name for the extreme food lovers— "foodies."

With pleasure and plenty came portly. All of this came to a head, at least in the US, in 1980, when Ronald Reagan was elected, John Lennon was assassinated, the original Pac-Man came out, and we started getting

---

33 "Jolly fat people exist, but they may be a minority. Obesity dramatically raises the risk of depression, anxiety, and dementia," from Scott C. Anderson et al., *The Psychobiotic Revolution: Mood, Food, and the New Science of the Gut-Brain Connection*, p. 222.

fatter. It was also the year I started at the FDA, but I'm reasonably sure I wasn't responsible for initiating the obesity crisis.

By the early 1990s, the federal government became concerned about poundage; it fell to the FDA and USDA to *do something* about it. I remember that right after we launched the effort, I was visiting USDA talking to a Bush (the elder) appointee.

I'd been invited to talk with him about some of the things we were doing as a part of the obesity working-groups that we'd started with the DHHS. USDA had their own groups. We were sitting in his rather large office in the USDA building with windows that looked out on Independence Avenue and another big, gray USDA building. He was a middle-aged black guy who told me he came from a small Texas town. He'd gone home recently and driven by his old elementary school.

"It was morning, and I stopped outside the front door when I saw a school bus pull up. When the doors opened and those kids got off to walk the sixty feet to the front door, I saw that half of them were out of breath. I wanted to cry."

"That *is* bad," I said.

"Yeah, but what can we do about it?"

I had no idea, but I did know we had to find out what had changed.

The kids in that Texas town are like the kids in a lot of towns. Today, two in ten children aged two to nineteen are obese, and another one in ten is overweight.[124] That's about the average for Texas, but go next door to Mississippi and the figures jump to four in ten for children being overweight or obese.[125]

When they grow up, they keep getting fatter. About seven out of ten adults are overweight or obese, and of those, four out of ten are obese.[126] It's going to get worse. A study by Harvard's T.H. Chan School of Public Health predicts that about half of the U.S. population will be obese by 2030.[127] What really matters is when your body-mass index (BMI) gets to thirty-five and above; that's when actual health issues kick in.[128]

When we started in 1990, only one out of ten adults were obese.

My role was primarily as a part of our cleverly named obesity working-groups (OWG).[129] We got it kicked off as the secretary of DHHS, Tommy Thompson, made national remarks that he'd noticed that "far too many Americans are literally eating themselves to death."[130]

The first task for my group was for the consumer-studies staff to hold focus groups on obesity. The first set was parents of school-age children, and what I heard shocked me.

The moderator asked, "How many of you have children you consider overweight?"

Every one of the eight attendees raised their hand.

He continued, "OK, what are you doing about it?"

One woman spoke up, "I don't think it matters, they're just kids. They'll run it off over time." Everyone else nodded in agreement.

In our first OWG meeting, I asked the lead investigator to report on this fact. I assumed it would be critical for the group to know whether this was a universal sentiment. Our group consisted of economists, consumer-studies researchers, nutritionists, dieticians, and a few senior managers along with representatives from DHHS.

Our consumer-studies researcher gave her report, focusing on the issue of the parents dismissing concerns about children.

She next said, "I believe the data is pretty clear that if they are overweight or obese at a young age, they tend to keep that weight when they grow up."

She looked around and people nodded their heads, but no one said anything.

Finally, the OWG lead said, "OK, thanks, let's move on to the next item on the agenda."

I couldn't believe it. Admittedly, it was just a focus group, but this seemed like it should have been important enough to follow up.

For our next set of focus groups, we had a group of teenagers, boys in one group and girls in another, and we asked them how they controlled their weight. Girls said that if they ate a big breakfast, they would eat less for lunch. Boys said that if they ate a big meal, they would work it off later.

Finally, we had adults, and they were clear: they knew what the problem was but said they didn't have time to watch what they ate. They also did not want the federal government to "help." People know they are fat and feel like they know what to do about it. Concern about weight inspires a 70-billion-dollar industry, with books, diet programs, gyms, and trainers, but the results of all those expenditures are not encouraging.[131]

> Linda Bacon and Amee Severson in *Scientific American* claim that so-called "health experts" are sending incorrect and destructive messages about the relationship between weight and wellness. The real problem for the overweight is "fearmongering" that "puts them at risk for diabetes, heart disease, discrimination, bullying, eating disorders, sedentariness, lifelong discomfort in their bodies and even early death." They claim the idea that being overweight on its own is a health problem that has its roots in racism and slavery and other attempts to "rank bodies."[1]
>
> [1] Richard Williams, "Should We Fight Obesity or Accept It? Both," InsideSources, September 26, 2019.

There was no discussion about what the focus groups were revealing about how people thought. I thought that what they revealed about parents of overweight kids was particularly alarming, but there was no reaction.

Rather than think about those things, the nutritionists turned to the food label as the answer.

It took a while, but the FDA's solution finally showed up in 2016. We put calories on food labels in twenty-two-point BOLD letters.[132] Problem solved.

I started thinking about what changed in 1980 that began the upward weight trend. One major change is that women joined the labor force in droves (a wonderful thing). Women working outside the home jumped from 38 percent in 1960 to 57 percent in 1990—a 50 percent increase.[133] It jumped to about 60 percent in 2000. With two working parents, families tend to go out more and eat in restaurants. Sure enough, food consumed away from home jumped from about 18 percent in 1977 to 50 percent in 2010.[134] In addition, over one in three adults consume fast foods every single day.[135] Food in restaurants has bigger portions and more calories. So at least one issue contributing to the obesity epidemic is people eating a lot more large, high-calorie meals in restaurants.

In 2018, the FDA's rule for menu labeling in restaurants kicked in. Calories had to be posted and additional information had to be available on request.[136] A Harvard study found that, on average, the labeling was responsible for a sixty-calorie reduction per meal served in the first year but then it trailed off to twenty-three calories.[137] The FDA has done lots of education on restaurant labeling but the truth is it won't make a pound's worth of difference in the long run.

One bit of information contradicts that. Our consumer-studies team discovered that for restaurant foods, people wildly underestimate calories. I recall that for chicken sandwiches with mayonnaise, people's estimates were low by 300 calories. For the average person, who should consume 2,000 calories per day, that's a lot. There may be lower-calorie foods that would be a better substitute.

One recommendation that didn't make it out of the OWG came from the commissioner's deputy secretary for communications. He'd come from a Madison Avenue advertising firm, and in one of our first meetings announced that he would come up with a slogan, like a "tipping point," that would solve the obesity problem. He said he just needed a few months to come up with this fabulous slogan.

Several months later, we were all sitting at a table waiting for him to report the results of his research and the new slogan. There were about thirty people in the room, and we all waited for the commissioner, Lester Crawford. The guy was already positioned next to the commissioner's chair, but he was not giving a clue about what was to come. The commissioner came in and everyone was breathless.

Commissioner Crawford sat down and said, "What have you got?"

An enormous smile lit up the deputy's face. He said, "What you are is what you eat."

There was a long moment of silence. Finally, someone at the table said, "You mean, 'You are what you eat'?"

His slogan wasn't even grammatically correct. I don't think anyone had the heart to tell him that the phrase was over 150 years old.[138]

The commissioner just laughed a little. The poor guy was deflated. People know they overeat; they don't want or need a slogan. It's also not clear whether new information will help.

OBESITY—SOME THEORIES

There's one theory that we didn't examine when we looked at what was causing the obesity crisis—sedentary mothers passing on fat cells due to lack of exercise. We have known for years that fatter mothers are linked to fatter babies.

One intriguing theory is that lack of physical activity during pregnancy may have caused babies to have more fat cells and thus have a permanent, irreversible disposition to being fat.[1] In this story, more fat cells are the only thing that distinguish fat from thin people.

The theory is that, during the twentieth century, women became more sedentary, leading to weight gain.[2] This weight gain is passed on to babies in the form of more fat cells that "grab" energy (calories from food) away from other cells like muscle. When they do, they store the fat (in the fat cells) instead of burning it off (by muscle cells). It gets worse.

Because the children's muscle cells are starved for energy, they send signals to the brain requesting more food, particularly more calorie-dense food, and send it faster between meals, leading to more weight gain and, unfortunately, diabetes.[3]

When I asked Edward Archer, one of the leading proponents of this theory, he said, "I am not a voice in the wilderness when I say that diet (as opposed to exercise) is a trivial risk factor for chronic disease." In one of his papers, he called the diet/disease theories, "Diet-Centrism," the tendency to attribute everything to diet while neglecting the fact that different people handle (metabolize) foods in different ways.[4]

[1] Edward Archer, et al., "Maternal Inactivity: 45-Year Trends in Mothers' Use of Time," *Mayo Clinic Proceedings* 88, no. 12 (December 2013).

[2] Timothy S. Church, "Trends over 5 Decades in U.S. Occupation-Related Physical Activity and Their Associations with Obesity," *PLOS ONE* 6, no. 5 (2011).

[3] Edward Archer and Samantha McDonald, "The Maternal Resources Hypothesis and Childhood Obesity," in Mulch and S. Patel and Jens S. Nielsen (eds.), *PostNatal Programming and Its Influence on Adult Health* (Boca Raton: CRC Press, 2017).

[4] Ibid.

PART II:
THE SCIENCE

ONE REASON WE WEREN'T solving any problems was because a lot of the science behind what we were doing was poor.

1. In 2005, John P.A. Ioannidis said, "It can be proven that most claimed research findings are false." Although most research findings are about positive relationships, he said, "Simulations show that for most study designs and settings, it is more likely for a research claim to be false than true."[139]

2. The editor of the *New England Journal of Medicine* echoed that sentiment: "It is simply no longer possible to believe much of the clinical research that is published, or to rely on the judgment of trusted physicians or authoritative medical guidelines."[140]

3. Finally, Richard Horton, editor-in-chief of the prestigious *The Lancet* said, "Much of the scientific literature, perhaps half, may simply be untrue. Afflicted by studies with…an obsession for pursuing fashionable

trends of dubious importance, science has taken a turn towards darkness."[141]

It was only very late in my FDA career that I came to realize that FDA scientists were often the victims of poor science.

Where does science fit into regulations? There are three stages of health-and-safety regulations, and science is important for two of them.

- *What is the problem?* Science and risk-assessment answer what the problem is, how large the risk is, and how widespread it is.

- *What can we do about it?* Again, science, along with economics, may help suggest some possible solutions which must be evaluated as possibilities to the extent mandated or allowed by law.[34]

- *What should we do about it?* Economics can help here, as can law, but ultimately, it is about values, and that is primarily decided by politics.

Obviously, if the science isn't right at the beginning, the whole thing falls apart.

---

34 Law includes our "sacred documents," including the Constitution, the Declaration of Independence, and the Bill of Rights, as well as all subsequent laws and decisions.

Chapter 22:
NONSENSE

You can fool some of the people all of the time, and those are the
ones you want to concentrate on.
—Robert Strauss, Democrat, advice to George W. Bush[142]

AFTER A DECADE OF WORKING closely with nutritionists, I understood there is a big difference between nutrition science and nutrition policy. I angered a few nutritionists by telling them nutrition policy is way too important to be left solely in the hands of nutritionists. Diets and labeling are, or are supposed to be, the result of nutrition policy. There are disagreements in every science, even including quantum physics, but nothing beats nutrition for conflicts and confusion.

Commissioner Crawford was the first person to start me thinking about the science of nutrition. Having spent time on toxicology, microbiology, and some chemistry for food-safety issues, I'd blithely assumed nutrition was just another reliable science. In 2004, during one of the FDA's OWG meetings, Commissioner Crawford challenged that understanding. He was in his mid-sixties with a shock of white hair. He understood food more than most commissioners, as he'd presided over the Center for Veterinary Medicine in the FDA and the Food Safety Inspection Service in USDA. Everyone knew him and most people liked him, particularly his irreverent humor.

In an OWG meeting, for once, Commissioner Crawford was not the last person to arrive.

The last two to walk in were the CFSAN head nutritionists, Susan Tindall and Hannah Becker. They were known behind their backs as the Ice Queens for their ruthlessness. They took their job very seriously and together were formidable.

As they walked in, Commissioner Crawford said, "Here they come, nutritionists, who do what I like to call 'non-science.' Then I just shorten that to 'nonsense.'"

I had no idea at the time what he was talking about, but I realized fairly quickly that the nutrition we are expected to use in conjunction with food labels may be mostly nonsense. For example, there is the 5/20 rule. If you haven't heard about it, or don't really get percent daily values, don't worry about it, it's not that important. Nevertheless, here it is:

- 5 percent daily value or less is low—the FDA now lists saturated fat, sodium, and added sugars for things to get less of. There is no recommended amount for added sugars, so there is no DV for sugars.

- 20 percent daily value or more is high—dietary fiber, vitamin D, calcium, iron, and potassium fall into the "more of" category.[143]

The idea is that you go down the list of a nutrition facts panel and you select foods lower than 5 percent of the daily value for bad things and greater than 20 percent for good things.

As long as you don't count restaurant meals and meats, seafood, and produce that are unlabeled, or worry about how much of each type of food you eat, you'll be healthy as a house...wait...a horse, healthy as a horse, not a fat horse, but a regular horse that gets lots of exercise. Maybe. Well, it depends.

While the FDA's nutrition program is vested in the food label, Congress said that USDA is supposed to be the "cornerstone of Federal Nutrition Programs and a go-to resource for health professionals nationwide."[144]

To do this, USDA is primarily responsible for the dietary guidelines that come out every five years and their version of the 5/20 diet, MyPlate.[35]

Are these helping you? Let's start with the dietary guidelines. They have been coming out with a lot of fanfare every five years since 1980 and—get this—they "encourage individuals to eat a healthful diet."[145]

You have to keep up with the latest versions. In 1980, the dietary guidelines told us to avoid too much total fat and cholesterol.[146] In 1990, it recommended choosing a diet low in fat, saturated fat, and cholesterol.[147] By 2015, recommendations for reducing total fat and dietary cholesterol were gone. For most of us, it appears not to matter too much; only 3 to 4 percent of people follow them anyway.[148]

There is also the question of how much to believe them at any point in time. Denise Minger says, "What reaches our ears has been squeezed, tortured, reshaped, paid off, and defiled by a phenomenal number of sources."[149]

If the dietary guidelines aren't that helpful, what about just a simple picture, that is, USDA's MyPlate? MyPlate has a picture of fruits, grains, vegetables, and protein with dairy (like a glass of milk) on the side. All the portions look about the same, so it's not clear if that is exactly what you are supposed to eat. Think about trying to use it as you eat during the day. To get the proportions right, you must add up each portion of each type of food for every meal.

What do you do with a meat pizza? It has bread (grains), meat (protein), cheese (dairy), and tomatoes (vegetables). Do you have to know the proportion of each and square it up with the MyPlate portions?

---

35 This used to be the Food Guide Pyramid.

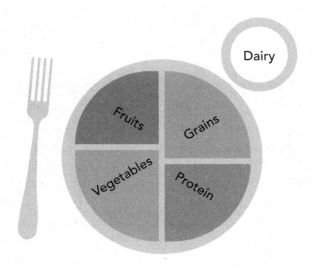

One nutritionist said about MyPlate, "An icon isn't going to help you eat smarter, lose weight, get in shape, or feel better about yourself."[150] A 2013 study found 57 percent of Americans were unlikely to visit ChooseMy-Plate.gov.[151] It's not like USDA is consistent, either. The CDC found that the foods USDA subsidizes makes people 37 percent more likely to be obese.[152]

Because much of government advice is either too complex (the food label) or too simple (MyPlate), there is a host of people outside the government all too eager to jump in with dietary advice. It's not clear who's winning, but consumers are losing. For example, only 13 percent[153] of the population meets the guidelines' recommendations for vegetables, while about 16 percent of the population goes on fad diets every year.[154]

It doesn't matter whether it works; they just keep doubling down on the same approach.

On the private side, we have doctors who get an average of twenty hours of nutrition education,[155] and actors like Professor Gwyneth Paltrow or activists like the Food Babe Vani Hari. You can find every kind of diet, including ones that recommend you eat charcoal, baby food, or raw foods, and eat with blue-tinted glasses, or eat what Jesus did.[156] That's just for advice. The weight loss products market now has reached $72 billion, even though the number of dieters has decreased.[157]

THEIR FOOD SLOGANS AND MINE

Theirs

"If you can't pronounce it, don't eat it." —Michael Pollan

"Count chemicals, not calories." —Arland Hill

"Don't eat anything your great-grandmother wouldn't recognize as food." —Michael Pollan

"Eat white man's food and end up in white man's hospital." —Somebody not white

"I'll eat eggs from chickens I know." —Ellen DeGeneres

Mine

"Don't eat anything bigger than a bowling ball in one bite."

"If you can't pronounce it, take a class or stop reading."

"Don't let people who lie for a living (actors) be your dietician."

"If you put a turnip in a toaster, you get what you asked for."

EAT RED MEAT

There are diets that tell you to eat more red meat and diets that tell you to never eat red meat.

The dietary guidelines says that "red meat" means beef, pork, lamb, veal, goat, and wild animals like bison and elk. They suggest that everyone eat no more than twenty-six ounces per week of these.[36] In 2020, the guidelines told mothers that children under two need to be fed red meat, suggesting, "If we can establish those healthier patterns right away, it will get them used to eating these types of foods."[158] At the same time as the 2020 guidelines were being developed, the NutriRECS group, led by researchers from Canada, Spain, and Poland, examined the data linking red and processed meat to heart disease and cancer and found it "weak."

---

36 You also apparently have to guess that "saturated fat" is a code word for red meat.

There are many people who also subscribed to the NutriRECS conclusions. One particularly colorful crusader is journalist Nina Teicholz who wrote *The Big Fat Surprise: Why Butter, Meat and Cheese Belong in a Healthy Diet.* She thinks meat is OK but went well beyond the advice to limit it; she took on all of the government's nutrition advice.[159]

She wrote:

> *The U.S. government's nutrition advice since 1980 has mainly been to increase consumption of carbohydrates and avoid fats. Despite following this advice for nearly four decades, Americans are sicker and fatter than ever. Such a record of failure should have discredited the nutrition establishment. Yet defenders of the nutrition status quo continue to mislead the public and put Americans' health at risk.[160]*

DON'T EAT RED MEAT

The anti-meat cult was scandalized by the NutriRECS findings. Harvard School of Public Health's Walter Willett found the study to be "the most egregious abuse of data I've ever seen."[161] David Katz called it "an assault on public health, and public understanding."[162] The *New York Times* called the advice not to eat meat "a bedrock of almost all dietary guidelines."[163]

How strongly do they feel that way?

David Katz summarized it on his blog:

> *Don't. Not if you would like to reduce your risk of dying prematurely from any cause. Not if you would like to avoid heart disease. Not if you would like to avoid cancer. Not if you would like to avoid diabetes. And not if you care at all about the fate of the planet and all life currently on it.[164]*

The health theory Katz espoused can be summed as two hypotheses:

1. Eating less saturated fat lowers blood cholesterol.

2. Lower blood cholesterol reduces the likelihood of getting heart disease.

Also, eating less fat means less cancer.

Some suggested that the "don't eat meat/saturated fat" theories may be true for some individuals, but only extend life by a few months.

WHO IS RIGHT?

Is saturated fat in meat so bad for you it shouldn't be in your diet at all? For me, the answer is, *I don't know*. I don't eat meat or poultry and haven't for almost fifty years. I made that decision because I was eating fast food hamburgers every day and I felt sick every day. But one thing I think is true—all these diets, from the FDA's 5/20 rule, to MyPlate and the dietary-guidelines reports, to the Mediterranean diet pushed by Dr. Katz, and to whatever on earth the Food Babe is pushing, are all telling us that there is one diet right for everybody.

For me, I think Mr. Rogers had it right.

Mr. Rogers, the television star of the children's show, *Mister Rogers' Neighborhood* was talking to children, but he could have been talking to all of us about our diets:

> *You are a very special person. There is only one like you*
> *in the whole world. There's never been anyone exactly like*
> *you before, and there will never be again. Only you.*

That's the message we're getting from the practitioners of precision nutrition and precision medicine these days, that you are unique in many ways. The ways that you are unique will determine what you should eat and, for that matter, how you should exercise and what medicines you should take.

We've known for a long time that people are different in their tastes and preferences, environment, incomes, age, race, sexual preferences, political views, and health. Beyond that is new information about genetic background and the mix of bacteria in your gut. Eventually, all of this will affect what you should eat.

For right now, there seems to be some consensus on what you shouldn't eat—a lot of sugary junk foods. And I would guess you should stay away from the truly weird diets. Remember, it's not just your weight issue you are trying to solve; it's your entire health profile.

Chapter 23:
EPIDEMIOLOGY PEOPLE IN/GARBAGE OUT

WHEN THE NIH SCIENTIST told me that no one can link dietary changes to heart disease quantitatively, I did it anyway. He was right; there wasn't enough sound science behind it. Nevertheless, everyone in the FDA seemed pleased by the large benefit-estimates, and not one person in the center questioned the science.

There are two primary types of scientific evidence the FDA uses for foods: animal studies (studying animals to understand human diseases) and epidemiology (the study of the distribution, patterns, and determinants of health and disease, including humans and animals). Both have issues. Animals, particularly rats and mice, are small and don't always respond to chemicals the same way we do. People, on the other hand, are extremely hard to study because they won't cooperate.

What that means is that they won't follow instructions and change every single facet of their life so we can get a clean study. We can't have Harvey Wiley's Poison Squads anymore, and prisoners have rights about subjecting them even to "minimal risk."[165] I used epidemiological (epi) evidence to get the NLEA answers. I know now the evidence I used was substandard.

Part of the problem is that it's very difficult to find epi studies that conclusively prove a particular food *causes* a health outcome—either positive or negative. What they mostly find is that people eat something prior to getting sick and it *may* be related—that is, eating and being sick are *correlated*. Eating doesn't necessarily *cause* the sickness.

Early on, I assumed that if I found a paper in a scientific journal, it was gold. Some of these papers are randomized controlled trials (RCTs), which are considered "the gold standard" because they randomly separate people into a test and a control group. If the test group gets the effect and the control group doesn't, it suggests a cause because the test food is the only difference.

The problem is, for most food issues, RCTs are nearly impossible because you would have to lock people up to make sure they eat and do only what you want. You also can't give them something likely to make them sick. Instead, you rely on just watching what they eat over time or ask them what they ate in the past.

Because of that, an epidemiological study showing causation is rare.

Some epi studies claim causation even when they don't have it. This is one reason we continually see reversals in dietary guidance—because lots of things can be correlated with a disease and not be causative, and the very next study can find no relationship.

Shortly after I took over the epidemiology branch as part of my division, I needed to hire an epidemiologist. I went to the national conference to learn more about them and hire someone at the same time. The keynote speaker announced at the start of the conference that he had exciting news: there was *almost* a new policy based on an epidemiology paper. It was then I realized that this is the Rodney Dangerfield of sciences: "It don't get no respect."

Within the last ten years, information has surfaced about why epi studies are essentially "weak." Some of these issues apply to other sciences as well. It starts with funding.

Scientists in universities must get funding to publish and they must publish to get tenure. Universities pay their salaries, but funding for studies must come from elsewhere. Many funders, whether public (like the FDA and NIH), private (like food companies), or non-profits (like the Pew Research Center), look to fund people who are likely to find their preferred results. Although most people think there is something uniquely biased about accepting industry funding, government agencies are also looking for specific answers. Usually, government agencies want to find out something is risky so they can regulate it; industries want the opposite.

Not only must scientists get funding and find answers their funders will like, but they must also get their results published. Often, that implies having results that appeal to journal editors. Some editors like papers that support their own theories or are consistent with their political/scientific views. Editors definitely prefer positive studies (e.g., eating red meat causes cancer, as opposed to eating red meat doesn't cause cancer) and ones that make headlines. When a study has positive effects and the effects are arresting, editors are much less likely to be picky about scientific integrity. Alternatively, they hate retractions because that means they have allowed a worthless paper on their watch.

For epidemiology, one huge issue leading to weak papers is the problem of confounders. A simple example comes from the fable "The Rooster Who Crowed Too Soon," about a rooster who believed that his crowing caused the sun to rise.[166]

There's a funny example from World War II that illustrates the problem. In 1974, physicist Richard Feynman described a model that was missing important information.[167] During WWII, South Sea islanders in New Hebrides watched Allied planes bringing food and supplies to the soldiers. After the Allies left, the islanders made runways and put fires alongside them at night. They also built bamboo antennas and huts near the runways and had men sit in the huts with pieces of bamboo over their ears that looked like headphones. Sadly, despite these heroic efforts, no more planes came.

The islanders had a model—planes will land with supplies (dependent variable) if we have runways and huts (independent variables). Their model was wrong because they were missing confounding independent variables; that is, they left out Allies with supplies and orders to deliver them.

Let's look at another example. Suppose you want to know the cause of higher death rates in Florida. You know there are more alligators in Florida than other states and decide that it is your independent variable. Are alligators the reason for higher death rates in Florida?

No, there are two confounding variables: "snowbirds," older people who go to Florida in the winter, and year-round, older retirees in Florida. If you are missing the real causes—the retirees and snowbird confounders—

all you have is correlation, not causation. More alligators will be correlated with more deaths, but they are not the cause.

In 2008, *The Lancet* published a study of only twelve people who got a measles, mumps, and rubella vaccine, considered a "landmark study that turned tens of thousands of parents around the world" against the vaccine.[168] The claim was that the vaccine caused intestinal problems and autism. There were six reviewers who missed the massive flaws in the study, and it took twelve years before it was withdrawn. There are still politicians (e.g., Robert F. Kennedy Jr.) and Hollywood stars (e.g., Jenny McCarthy) claiming it's true.[169]

Here are three models (compiled by the Genetic Literacy Project, with permission from the authors) that correlate different independent variables with autism.[170]

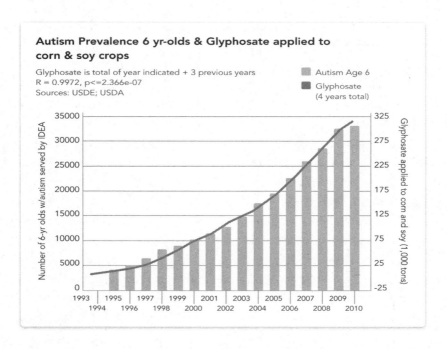

That seems to be obvious—glyphosate is related to autism; in fact, it seems to cause it. But wait a minute, what about this?

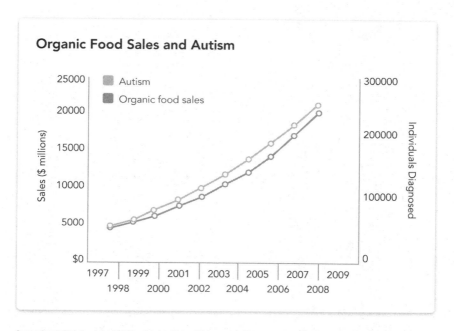

Organic Food Sales and Autism

Sources: Organic Trade Association, 2011 Organic Industry Survey; U.S. Department of Education, Office of Special Education Programs, Data Analysis System (DANS), OMB# 1820-0043. "Children with Disabilities Receiving Special with Disabilities Education Act.

Could organic food be causing autism? The correlation is practically perfect, and note the statistical p-value.[37] Most papers are accepted if the p-value is less than .05, and this one is fifty times less than the acceptable number. If you think there is some weird chance that organic foods cause autism as illustrated by the above chart, keep reading.

Here's another possibility. You may recall various celebrities warning you against vaccinating your kids. One was Jenny McCarthy, who said, "If you ask 99.9 percent of parents who have children with autism if we'd rather have the measles versus autism, we'd sign up for the measles."[171]

---

37 A p-value is a statistical measure of the likelihood of finding the result you did. In the example, a very low p-value indicates that the probability that there is no relationship between consumption of organic food and autism is very, very low. The problem is that it doesn't tell us that there actually is a relationship; there might be something else going on that is causing the curves to match up this way. I'm sure the organic industry has lots of alternative explanations.

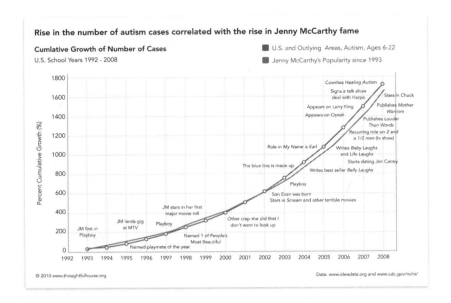

Rise in the number of autism cases correlated with the rise in Jenny McCarthy fame

The issue with this and many other published epi papers is that, if you have a huge data set to work with, you can get any answer you want. One way this is done is through something that statisticians call "p-hacking," which is just a fancy word for trying out different statistical analyses or different data sets until a correlation pops up as "significant" (i.e., a low p-value). Once you have that, it is likely to be publishable.

This is helpful for scientists that need to get funding and get positive results to get their paper published.

The most reported case of using large data sets to get correlations, or p-hacking, was in food psychology—the Brian Wansink case.[172] If his graduate students couldn't find a correlation, he told them to go back and "torture the data" into finding some combination that was significant. The last thing he wanted was to try to publish something that didn't show any correlation—a negative study. Negative results now account for only 14 percent of published papers, but some scientists feel that if all studies were published, most would be negative.[173] The problem for Wansink was that he got caught because he instructed his students via email (the Freedom of Information Act was his downfall).

A former editor of the *New England Journal of Medicine* said, "Authors and investigators are worried that there's a bias against negative studies. And so, they'll try very, very hard to convert what is essentially a negative study into a positive study by hanging on to very, very small risks or seizing on one positive aspect of a story which is by and large negative."[174]

In nutrition, this is worrisome. This may be one reason different researchers are coming up with different answers on red and processed meat. Another issue may be red meat is bad for some people but not for others.

The same issues and questions are relevant for salt. It's one of the big three targeted now (along with saturated fat and added sugars) by food agencies around the world. John Vanderveen, a senior nutritionist in CFSAN, once said there was "no conclusive evidence that salt consumption causes hypertension. It's only a hypothesis."[175] In fact, very low sodium diets have been linked to increases in triglycerides and blood cholesterol, which are linked to heart disease.[176] But one psychologist, Michael E. Oakes, said the salt debate is "a testimony to the lack of objectivity of science in practice," with those favoring salt restriction calling rivals "shameless carpetbaggers."[177]

Some scientists are just bad statisticians. As Gary Taubes put it, even if studies find a statistical effect, it's not clear that it's a meaningful clinical effect.[178] A paper may confuse a very weak connection with a meaningful one.

ABSOLUTE VS. RELATIVE RISK

A really good way to confuse people and get big headlines is to talk about relative risk instead of absolute risk. Here's the difference.

Suppose you have a test group in the exposed population where two out of 1,000 people get an illness and in the control population only one out of 1,000 gets the illness. That means that, from a relative risk point of view, the test group *is twice as likely* to get the illness; two is twice as big as one. That sounds scary. But the absolute risk, the actual odds of getting the disease increase is actually 0.1 percent. Increasing the risk by 100 percent, twice as likely, sounds a whole lot more dangerous than a 0.1 percent increase.

Another issue is that some researchers aren't very good statisticians. I know I had difficulty with what we called "sadistics" in graduate school. I felt a little better after I heard a story at a conference about a heart surgeon who was using statistics in his medical paper and ran into a statistician. The surgeon says, "Hey, I'm doing a statistical paper, and I was wondering if you could recommend a good book on statistics to help me to work on it next week?" The statistician says, "Sure, I'm doing some heart surgery next week, and I was wondering if you could recommend a book on that?"

The problem with statistics is, it's hard, but it's required in most science papers. The good thing is that more papers now have multiple authors with different disciplines, so there's an easy fix—include a statistician.

Another big issue in food epidemiology is bad data. To find out what people eat, the CDC conducts a survey called the "What We Eat in America Database."[179] Besides being asked about general dietary behavior, such as whether they have been told to change their diet, and questions about food frequency, participants are asked to answer questions about what and how much they have eaten in the last twenty-four hours.

There are two problems with this approach—participants either can't remember, or they don't tell the truth. No one will admit eating a quart of ice cream while watching reruns of *Friends*.

The result: across the thirty-nine-year history of the survey, 67.3 percent of women and 58.7 percent of men did not report eating enough food to stay alive. Remember, a bunch of these people are vastly overweight or obese.[180] These data are used in about four out of five epi studies to estimate diet-disease relationships.

Do you know what the researchers do to fill in the additional food people don't report? They eliminate people who report having low food intake or make up what they think they were eating.

We're never going to get anywhere using this data. It needs to be collected electronically with novel technologies that, hopefully, are nearly here.

Look at this chart from Jonathan Schoenfeld and John PA Ioannidis that shows the results of multiple food studies. Each dot is a study result.

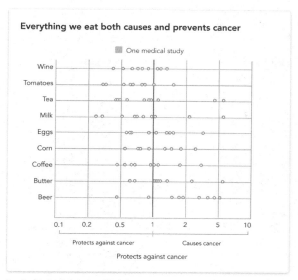

Everything we eat both causes and prevents cancer

One medical study

	Protects against cancer		Causes cancer
Wine			
Tomatoes			
Tea			
Milk			
Eggs			
Corn			
Coffee			
Butter			
Beer			

0.1   0.2   0.5   1   2   5   10

Protects against cancer   Causes cancer

Protects against cancer

Source: Schoenfeld and Ioannidis, American Journal of Clinical Nutrition

It's not surprising that we get reversals and fights over dietary recommendations. They start with bad data sets and use them in epi studies that only show correlations.

In one way, I'm almost glad I didn't know most of this when I was doing economic analyses in the center. I would have questioned the science underlying our decisions even more than I did and made people even madder at me for the questions I raised.

Chapter 24:
TURNING GOLD INTO STRAW

"Every day FDA scientists carry out scientific research actions that have a profound impact on the health and well-being of all Americans. They work hard to make sure that the foods Americans eat are safe and healthy."[181]
—FDA Website

THE FDA PRIDES ITSELF on being a science agency. It has a list of eleven principles on its website, beginning with, "Maintain a firm commitment to science-based, data-driven decision-making."[182] That's precisely the commitment you would want from a science agency, but that's not always practiced for regulatory decisions.

For me, there were many issues where the FDA's use of science in policy were problematic. By the mid-1980s, I was already sure that the science behind determining whether a food or color additive was a carcinogen made little sense. I was beginning to doubt that, given the way we did animal studies and the conclusions we drew from them, we were banning additives that never caused anyone to get cancer. Of course, being in the FDA did not allow me to say or write anything, which was frustrating.

What was worse though, was the double standard—evidence-based science for the industry and "good enough" science for the FDA's policies. This was made clear to me during our implementation of the NLEA.

Right from the start, CFSAN hated health claims, probably for a good reason. Besides food interactions, your health depends on your genetics, health status (current illnesses), environment, exercise regimen, gut microbes, chemistry, stress, and medications (legal and illegal). The idea that eating one particular food every day is going to reduce your resistance to disease is farfetched.

Nevertheless, making a health claim on the front of a food package is a big seller for the industry. In fact, most consumers don't realize there are three kinds of claims that manufacturers make:

1. About a particular nutrient and its effects (e.g., "A good source of calcium").

2. A claim about the overall effect of the food (e.g., "Calcium may reduce the risk of osteoporosis").

3. A claim about how a certain food affects the "structure or function" of the body (e.g., "Calcium builds strong bones").

It doesn't matter which of these claims a manufacturer makes, they all have the same marketing effect, as consumers don't know or care about the difference between them. In fact, we did multiple studies to show that consumers interpret all of them to mean that any of the claims above showed that the food, overall, must be healthy.[183]

In 1984, Kellogg's linked consumption of high-fiber cereal (All Bran) to a reduction in the likelihood of getting cancer on the front of the cereal box—that is, a health claim. It helped Kellogg's that the National Cancer Institute (NCI), another member of the DHHS, along with the FDA, endorsed the message. Kellogg's included the NCI's message on their cereal box.[184] My old boss, Fred Shank (the grumpy one), was head of the center back then, and he wrote that any such claims were either misbranded or an illegal drug (not like cocaine, but a medical drug not approved by the FDA).

But 1984 was three years after President Reagan admonished that the "government is not the solution to the problem; government *is* the problem," and by 1987, we were forced to publish a proposal to allow claims. One of the FDA criteria in a proposed health-claim regulation was that, "The information should be based on and consistent with valid, reliable, scientific evidence that is publicly available."

Meanwhile, both the surgeon general (of DHHS) and the National Research Council (of the National Academy of Sciences) published reports that said that poor diets were causing heart disease, cancer, strokes, and diabetes. They urged reduction of total fat, saturated fat, cholesterol, and sodium, and increased consumption of complex carbohydrates and fiber.

Americans immediately changed their diets to follow this advice and... wait, sorry, that was in a parallel dimension.

Following the election of George H.W. Bush in 1990, the NLEA legislatively allowed health and nutrient content claims, and following the FDA's earlier criteria, there had to be "significant scientific agreement" that the claim was true.

One of the first petitions under NLEA was for authorization of a health claim for dietary supplements containing vitamin E and reduced risk of heart disease. The studies were mixed.

After reviewing the evidence, the FDA concluded in 2001 that there wasn't enough science validating taking vitamin E to lower the risk of heart disease.[185] It prohibited the health claim.[186]

In other words, "No significant scientific agreement, no claim."

But the guy who filed the petition sued the FDA because he claimed the FDA didn't have the power to ban speech under the First Amendment.[187]

FDA lost the case.

We were still trying to prevent four health claims and the agency was in a panic as we continued to lose court cases. Jay Asher, our attorney, came into my office to tell me what was happening. He was distraught as he sat down at the table in front of my desk.

He said, "The court told us trying to ban claims, like the one on omega-three fatty acids reducing the risk of heart disease, was arbitrary and capricious."[188]

"But we've been preventing these claims for years. Why did we lose now?"

"I think it's because some of our sister agencies have turned against us. They think this is valuable information consumers should have."

He was talking about the relatively new Office of Dietary Supplements of the National Institutes of Health (NIH), which had been studying the beneficial effects of supplements. That would give food and dietary supplement manufacturers evidence to use in claims.

"Does it mean we're out of this business entirely, and they can do anything they want?"

Jay said, "I've been thinking about that. Before, we could put the burden of proof on them. If they could think of some way to phrase a claim where consumers wouldn't be confused about what the science was actually saying, we let them have the claim. That was hard for them because most consumers don't really get scientific disagreement. Now, it's on us."

"What does that mean, 'It's on us'?"

"It means we have to make sure there is nothing, no way on earth, to, you know, remedy consumer confusion before we can ban a health claim."

"Sorry, Jay, I still don't get it."

"It's on us," he repeated. "We have to do research that tests every possible way you could explain how much, or how little, scientific backing there is to a claim. That means if a claim is based on a few poorly done studies, before we could stop it, we have to test every conceivable way you might be able to make consumers understand that fact. But that's the only way we can ever again prevent a health claim."

"But that's bulls**t. There are an infinite number of ways you could craft a message like that. We could never test them all."

"Now you're getting it," he said.

"And that's it?"

"No."

"I wonder if most of the NLEA would even survive in this kind of environment."

He looked sad and slowly stood up. "See ya," he said, and walked out.

The point is that the FDA cannot ban a "qualified claim" unless they do massive amounts of research.

I didn't tell him, but I was thrilled by the result. I considered the First Amendment the most important law in the history of human civilization.

According to FDA rules, food manufacturers still have to assemble massive evidence to make a claim to prove that there is significant scientific evidence if they don't want a qualifier added to their statement.

But why do manufacturers have to assemble all of this evidence and the FDA doesn't?

Here are three instances of weak scientific evidence the FDA provided to support its rules.

WEAK EVIDENCE NUMBER 1

Under the Food Safety and Modernization Act of 2010, Congress required the FDA to perform a risk assessment to see which types of produce had food-safety problems so they could target their produce regulations. In 2014, the regulation for produce safety was called "Standards for Growing, Harvesting, Packing, and Holding of Produce for Human Consumption." The rules were supposed to cover any fruits and vegetables that had past outbreaks. The FDA did the risk assessment and determined that there were significant risks for foods that are typically consumed raw, but very low risks for those that were cooked and "rarely consumed raw."[189]

Coffee beans weren't covered in the regulation because you cook them, but celery and grapes were covered because they are consumed raw. The problem is that celery and grapes have never had a food-safety problem.[38]

In fact, FDA's own analysis shows there had never been a problem with *46 percent of all produce.*[190]

In June 2019, I sat down with members of the California Farm Bureau, a member of the Heritage Foundation, and the FDA in their headquarters in White Oak, Maryland, just off the capital beltway. The meeting room was just inside the front door, so I assumed they didn't want us walking through the halls.

---

38 In 1989, there was an apparent cyanide-poisoning attempt by injecting it into grapes in South America. A telephone call to the US Embassy in Chile alerted authorities to this. This was not something the produce rule would have addressed.

The three of us were on one side of the table with Frank Yiannas (deputy commissioner for food policy and response), the deputy CFSAN director, and four or five others on the other side.

We were there to question why they ignored their own risk assessment, ordered by Congress, that showed that nearly half of produce that had never had an outbreak was covered in their very expensive regulations.

I started, "Congress asked you to do a risk assessment. You did it, but then ignored it. Why?"

Yiannas responded.

"We look at a risk assessment as something that tells us about the past. But we want to be forward looking. We know sometimes there are fruits and vegetables that have never had an outbreak but then they may have one sometime in the future. That's what I mean by forward looking."

"You realize you have gone well beyond risk assessment with that statement," I said.

Yiannas just smiled while the other FDAers glared at me.

It appeared we were not going to get anywhere, so we thanked them for their time and left. We stepped outside the building and started walking toward the parking lot about fifty yards away.

As we walked, the California grower asked, "What the hell just happened in there? Why would they ignore their own risk assessment?"

I responded as though I was from the FDA. "Because you have to look forward. What if a Martian came down and peed Martian pee on some lettuce? Just because it has never happened doesn't mean you shouldn't include it."

He let out a weak laugh, but his face was gloomy.

WEAK EVIDENCE NUMBER 2

As part of the NLEA, we had the authority to regulate package slack fill.

Think about a box of cereal. When you open it, there is space between the top of the box and the cereal, the so-called "slack fill." After the box has been moved and set down a few times, it settles and leaves a little more space at the top. No one should care, because you can compare cereal prices based on the price per ounce of the food. Putting the same amount of food into a bigger box that has a little empty space doesn't really buy manufacturers anything. If anything, the bigger box with empty space costs them more in packaging.

If we found that slack fill misled consumers, we could regulate it. In a meeting in the commissioner's conference room with Mike Taylor, then deputy commissioner for policy in charge of NLEA, I explained why this wasn't a problem.

"Rich, what about this?" Mike asked.

"It's not a problem, Mike. Look, I just spent months trying to persuade the Canadians that we should have free trade and that they shouldn't have standardized can sizes. Canada standardizes in metric sizes so we can't send excess supply [of already packaged foods] across the border without repackaging them. Their logic was that US packages are misleading because they can't be compared to their metric packaging. But consumers can compare prices based on the actual amount of food compared to the price, like price per ounce. Package sizes don't matter."

I sat back. *That should do it. No one could regulate based on package size logic.*

Mike said, "What's that have to do with slack fill?"

"Because slack fill doesn't matter one bit. Who cares if it's an inch or five inches, if it's the same amount of cereal?"

Mike persisted. "Isn't it cheating consumers to sell it in a bigger box with the same amount of cereal?"

"If they are buying food based on the size of the package, and one package is bigger than the other but they both say twelve ounces, then the only people that will be confused are, well, idiots."[39]

Mike then turned to the consumer safety officer, the person charged with writing a regulation if we determined it would be needed, and asked her. Donna was in that period of life between late twenties and early forties and was otherwise indeterminate in age. When she spoke, it was soft and cautious, properly purposeful and scientific.

"Donna, what do you say?"

For once, I knew I'd won this one. There was nothing she could say to counter my logic.

---

39 Of course, the FDA has an internal motto that says, "We protect the food, not the damned food."

tion to each end of the cut and pull the wire off the earth the same amount all the way around. How far off the earth would it be?

1. Enough to slide a razor blade under it.
2. Enough for a man to crawl under it.
3. Enough for a man to walk underneath it.

I got the wrong answer using my common sense but so did every single scientist in the room. They forgot to model it. The answer lies in estimating the change in the circle's radius where the model is $\Delta D/\pi$ (the change in diameter divided by pi—i.e., 10 feet/3.14 = 3.18 feet). A man could crawl under it.

Everyone gave the razor blade answer. They objected to the answer, "Come on, you only added ten feet to eight thousand miles?"

The next day they all came back and said they "got it."

To emphasize the importance of what they were learning, I invited the deputy commissioner for policy on the commissioner's staff to come in on the last day of the class to talk about the importance of economic analysis. I hoped he would mention that he had recently read an eighty-page regulatory impact analysis that I had written with a new economist on staff.

That proposed regulation was to ban sulfites, a common preservative used on salad bars and in food. In fact, sulfites had been an issue back in Wiley's day.[40] Because this was such a huge rule, I knew the regulatory impact analysis had gone to the deputy's office.

Donald Blackwood was a wiry man with red hair that had been at the FDA for two decades. I didn't know him well, but I did know that he looked at regulatory impact analyses for major rules.

I called him from my office.

"Hi Don, I don't know if you have heard but I am putting together the first-ever classes on economics for CFSAN rule writers."

Don replied, "I hadn't heard that."

---

40 The rule we were promulgating was based on allergic reactions to sulfites, mostly as a result of indiscriminate spraying on salad bars. Wiley had fed his Poison Squad large amounts of sulfites and made them sick. He lost his battle with the secretary of USDA to ban them. See Deborah Blum, *The Poison Squad*, (London: Penguin Books, 2019), p. 174–175.

"Yes, well, the point of the classes is to help us get regulations out faster by getting me some help with the economic analyses. I'm hoping that they get just enough economics to help write a first draft with the information I need." There was no need to mention Larry; I think Don knew that.

Don said, "How can I help?"

I replied, "I'm glad you asked. I wonder if you would give a short talk at the end of the class. I want you to talk to them about the importance of doing the analyses and getting it right for review at OMB."

"Glad to."

I introduced Don and sat down. Nothing could have prepared me for what he said.

"OK, I know you have just been given three days of training in economic analysis, but I don't want you to take it too seriously. This is just a perfunctory compliance exercise we have to do because of this new economic executive order. You need to know it doesn't play any role in FDA decision-making."

I stared at him and couldn't hold myself back.

"What about the eighty-page economic analysis of sulfites where we concluded it would be a major rule? OMB is going to be reviewing that."

"Yeah, I read that and threw it in the trash. I substituted a half-page analysis that said it wasn't a major rule."[41]

The class just sat there watching us without saying a word.

"Well, that's Mister Blackwood's view, but I can tell you that no analysis is leaving this center without it being economically sound."

Blackwood and I glared at each other, newly discovered enemies. He left the room without saying another word. The class departed silently as well.

Lawyers never ask a question of a witness when they don't know what the answer will be. I should have applied that theory to Blackwood, who I really didn't know.

Several years later, I again put together courses in cost-benefit analysis and taught it across the center, but I no longer had guest speakers. There was still a lot of fighting going on when the economic analysis didn't fully support decisions. The classes helped, but we were still getting in disputes like the seafood HACCP regulation.

---

41 If it's not a major rule, no analysis is required.

I continued to believe that classes helped, however. In 1996, I met Nell Ahl, who oversaw the newly formed Office of Risk Assessment and Cost-Benefit Analysis in USDA. Nell was older than most of her colleagues, and she was short, round, brilliant, and determined. USDA was way behind the other agencies in both risk assessment and cost-benefit analysis. As to the latter, they thought they should write it to support decisions, not inform them.

Nell was on a mission. Right from the start, we realized that a big problem with both economics and risk assessment for both of us was that a lot of the staff for both agencies, particularly those dealing with foods, didn't accept either risk or economic analysis. Nell came up with the idea of us working together to create classes in both. Because I was the one who was bringing it to the FDA, I decided to go ahead and do it and, as they say, "apologize later." Nell got the USDA graduate school interested, and we created courses on risk analysis (which includes economics) for food. It surprised us when they filled up immediately. I guessed that, like me, many younger people saw risk analysis as the future and wanted to learn it.

My role at first was to give the last lecture in the risk classes, and I always ended with the same message: "Your job is to get the analysis right. It should not matter what decision makers do with your analysis, what decision they make, as long as you have given them the best possible analysis. For now, decisions are not in your pay grade and you should not try to shade your analysis either way."

I still tell people that, but I do periodically get objections from those who feel more of a religious-type affinity for regulations.

Today, as part of the Joint Institute for Food Safety and Applied Nutrition, the risk courses Nell and I developed have been taught to thousands of people around the world.[191]

PART III:
INVENTING OUR WAY AROUND FDA

ALTHOUGH I WAS SUCCEEDING in getting the FDA to use economics and risk in their decisions, I realized we weren't really making any progress in public health. The budget kept going up, but the regulations weren't accomplishing anything. This lack of progress led me to search for answers that went beyond just getting manufacturers to change their practices (regulation and inspection) and force-educating consumers to change their food choices related to nutrition.

New innovations are coming so fast that the FDA cannot keep up, particularly with precautionary approaches. They risk becoming irrelevant, or worse, an obstacle.

As Adam Thierer states:

> *The intensifying pace of technological change pushes out the frontiers of what is possible, forcing policymakers to either bring archaic regulations in line with new realities or risk being ignored by evasive entrepreneurs and an increasingly technologically-empowered public.*[192]

It's an exciting time for food innovation. The challenges we face today—from food safety and nutrition, to global warming, world population growth, land degradation, water shortages, treatment of animals, animal vectors for deadly viruses, lake and ocean eutrophication, food deserts, and declining fish stocks—are all an open invitation to inventors and entrepreneurs around the world.

Chapter 26:
UNNATURAL FOODS

"Just because something is natural it does not mean that it is good and just because something is unnatural it does not mean that it is bad. Arsenic, cobra poison, nuclear radiation, earthquakes, and the Ebola virus can all be found in nature, whereas vaccines, spectacles, and artificial hips are all man-made."
—Simon Singh and Edzard Ernst[193]

"People don't want to eat technology."
—Food Technologist at the Grocery
Manufacturers Association [42]

THE GROCERY MANUFACTURERS ASSOCIATION (GMA) represents many of the country's largest food producers. At their headquarters in Washington, DC, while talking about a food safety problem, I had mentioned that I thought technology would be the answer, not regulations. The food technologist I was speaking with wasn't so sure about technology. He said he'd formed his opinion from talking to client food companies.

Eating new foods produced by modern technologies is a frightening idea for many, and there are plenty of people pouring gas on that fear. For example, we have the Food Babe, the Environmental Working Group, and

---

42 Now called the Consumer Brands Association.

other self-styled experts telling us to "avoid chemicals" and "eat naturally." The idea of eating, and for that matter, living naturally goes back decades, reflected in Henry David Thoreau's rejection of modern business and moving to Walden Pond in the middle of the nineteenth century. Hippie youth communes followed one hundred years later. It can't help but be appealing, but is it the right course for us today?

One of the popular proponents of this view is the Food Babe, Vani Hari. She wrote:

> *If you can't pronounce it, that probably means the material has been part of the human diet for a minute period of time in terms of the human evolutionary or developmental process. Using many of these substances is a grand experiment that many people would prefer not subjecting themselves or their children to.*[194]

In short, if you can't pronounce it, don't eat it.

Not wanting to stop with just health, Mark Hyman sees all the world's evils caused by food technology:

> *When taken as separate issues, the problems of poverty, racism, chronic disease, corporate manipulation of the poor and minorities, health inequities, violence, crime, suicide, mental illness, declining academic achievement, national security, and farmworker and food worker abuses seem overwhelming. But when filtered through the lens of food injustice and social justice, they are all connected to our modern industrial ultraprocessed food and agricultural system.*[195]

People have always been frightened of technology. They were once afraid of coffee; it was "regarded as a devilish drink unfit for children, women and men concerned about their virility."[196] I suppose caffeine is still scary if we list its ingredients: caffeine (3,7-dihydro-1,3,7-trimethyl-1H-purine-

2,6-dione), tannin, thiamin, Xanthine, Spermidine, Guaiacol, Citric Acid, Chlorogenic acid, Acetaldehyde, Spermine, Putrescine and Scopoletin.[197]

In fact, there are 1,500 chemicals in coffee.[198]

But eating natural, when taken to extremes, can be dangerous. In 2014, twenty-three-year-old Jordan Younger, who blogged as the New York City Blonde Vegan with 70,000 followers (at the time), noticed that her hair was falling out in clumps. She was a "gluten-free, sugar-free, oil-free, grain-free, legume-free, plant-based raw vegan."[199]

She was suffering from orthorexia, an obsession with consuming foods that are perfect looking. Her periods had stopped, and her skin had an orange tint from the sweet potatoes and carrots she was consuming.

She quit all of that and confessed her change in diet to her followers, who accused her of being a "fat piece of lard."[200]

Some don't even buy into the whole-foods trend. Mark Hyman feels that, "When you grind it into flour, whole wheat or not, it is worse than sugar."[201] Of sugar, he says, "The history of sugar is closely linked to slavery… and today…sugar, especially in its new form, high-fructose corn syrup, is connected to a new type of oppression—food oppression, which makes people of color sick."[202]

Another modern fad, along with food labels themselves, is to only buy foods with "clean labels." These foods advertise the absence of artificial colors and preservatives and having only "natural" ingredients. Those searching for clean labels feel that the fewer the ingredients, the better.

The label may say broccoli, but it contains glucobrassicin, carotenoids including zeaxanthin, beta-carotene, Kaempferol (a flavonoid), glucosinolate and sulforaphane (natural pesticides), dithiolthiones, indoles, glucoraphanin, s-methyl cysteine sulfoxide, isothiocyanates, and indole-3-carbinols. It is also loaded with formaldehyde.[203]

Whether you are searching for clean labels, trying to avoid chemicals, or eating whole foods, one thing that most food activists agree on is that food should be "natural." In her newest book, food activist and nutritionist Marion Nestle states, "In their largely unprocessed forms, foods from the earth, trees, or animals are healthful by definition."[204]

Is it true? Like animals, plants are part of the millions of years of evolution, the Darwinian struggle to survive. Part of that survival is the struggle not to be eaten. Animals evolved by developing speed, teeth, claws, spines, size, poison, and intelligence to avoid being eaten. Similarly, plants developed poisons, bad taste, thorns, and foul smells to keep from being eaten. Ed Yong notes that plants "fill their tissue with substances that deter plant-eaters—poisons that harm, sterilize, cause weight loss, initiate tumors, trigger abortions, lead to neurological disorders and just plain kill."[205]

Clearly, some plants and plant components are healthy, but not all. For example, the death cap mushroom is just one of the mushrooms that kill. Apple seeds contain cyanide.

Part of the "eating natural" mantra is avoiding pesticides. Marion Nestle points to the Environmental Working Groups' "Dirty Dozen."[206] Strawberries top the list as the most pesticide-polluted produce. But they don't tell you how much pesticide residue is on strawberries, or whether the residue is toxic at the levels they contain. Scientists looking at the dirty dozen concluded that the EWG list "lacked scientific rigor or subsequent credibility" and found that "substituting organic for conventionally produced products would not appreciably reduce risks."

ARE PESTICIDES DANGEROUS?

A study by food scientists tried to answer this question. Most pesticides are designed by nature so that plants can defend themselves, but we have found a way to supplement natural pesticides. Functionally, pesticides kill or repel insects, prevent plant diseases, or kill weeds by poisoning them. Although a few epidemiological studies have found that pesticides affect childhood intelligence and have reproductive effects, those studies turned out to be flawed. Most research finds no connections.

Like any other poison, it is the dose that determines the harm. When you read a report that says something like, "A study has found that a vegetable *contains* a dangerous pesticide," you know that's a trigger alarm, not a scientific finding. A warning based on science would be about risk. Reporting about risk would tell you the level of exposure of a pesticide that could be dangerous, not the presence of a pesticide.

The standard for pesticides to be allowed on produce is that they must present a "reasonable certainty of no harm." To get a reasonable certainty, we have to know both how much people are exposed to (through eating or, for farm workers, inhalation) and compare that to how much of a pesticide is allowed on a plant—known as a "tolerance." At the Environmental Protection Agency, the tolerance for pesticide residues is called a Reference Dose (RfD).

To get a RfD, you feed rats or mice different doses of the pesticide until you find a dose low enough where there are no effects (called the No Adverse Effect Level or NOAEL). That dose, however, is not yet considered safe for humans. To get the RfD, you then take the level where is no effect in rodents, the NOAEL, and you divide it by between 100 and 10,000. In other words, from the rodent no-effect level, which is a dose low enough so that the rodents experience no harm, the RfD is set 100 to 10,000 times lower.

FDA laboratories enforce RfD pesticide tolerances set by the EPA. In 2016, the FDA found that less than one out of 100 domestic food samples were violative, that is, above the RfD but still far below the NOAEL.

A study done in 2015 looked at typical risks associated with violative samples. Over half of the violations were one million times lower than the dose at which there was no effect, the NOAEL. Less than 1 percent of the violations were within one tenth of the NOAEL.

In other words, all of the residues were so low as to not cause harm to consumers, that is, there is a reasonable certainty of no harm.

We add pesticides to complement plants' own pesticides, but 99.9 percent of all pesticides (by weight) are the plants' own.[207] Further, every year, the USDA does a survey that shows that the human-added pesticide residues are well below levels where they present any danger to you.[208]

No one pays any attention to it.

Just as plants and animals developed their defenses to being eaten, predators developed their own tools. We are also predators and use intelligence as our tool.

We began "domesticating" plants around 10,000 years ago. In modern times, right around the Civil War, Gregor Mendel started cross breeding pea plants. Today, 99 percent of corn, wheat, soybeans, peanuts, and many other plants are human-developed hybrids.[209]

Corn is a prime example of man's influence. Look at the picture below that shows "natural" corn, otherwise known as "teocinte." Teocinte was a wild grass with an ear about three inches long and an average of seven kernels in a hard shell. A typical corn plant has about 800 kernels.

Teosinte   Modern Corn

Nicolle Rager Fuller, NSF

But we have also bred animals by cross breeding them for several hundred years to get the protein and fat characteristics we want.

What all of this means is that there is absolutely nothing in nature that competes to be safe or healthy so you can eat it. Further, virtually everything we eat has had the technological hand of man involved in producing it—and there is nothing natural about that.

Tom Standage, in his excellent book *An Edible History of Humanity,* says, "The simple truth is that farming is profoundly unnatural...and all domesticated plants and animals are man-made technologies."[210] He adds, "Corn, cows, and chickens as we know them do not occur in nature, and they would not exist today without human intervention. Even carrots are man-made."[211] Chocolate does not exist in nature.[212]

And yet, the fear of chemicals and technology is rampant.

If you're concerned about processing, remember that even cooking causes "a huge alteration in the DNA molecules causing them to unravel and fragment."[213] In fact, processing can help or hurt foods. For example, cooking carrots makes beta-carotene (a carotenoid that is good for eye and health) more available to your body, but it can hurt when it destroys vitamins.[43]

I'm not saying that there's anything wrong with the fruits and vegetables in your grocery store. By all means, eat them; over the years, they have been accumulating useful properties with each new improvement. One good reason to eat fruits and vegetables, even though they're a product of technology, is that they can help us keep a healthy, diverse microbiome.[214]

But you need not choose the more expensive organic foods. Back when organic foods first began to be popular, I was invited to a meeting at USDA. I guess they chose me because many of the people in the meeting were USDA economists and I was the chief foods economist at the FDA. But the meeting turned out to differ greatly from what I'd expected.

I walked from the FDA to the old USDA building in southeast DC, the one that has dark hallways and musty-smelling meeting rooms.

The large meeting room held about twenty chairs around a table, and they were already filled when I walked in. Most of the people in the room were women in their twenties and early thirties. One of them, an energetic thirty-something at the front of the table, started the meeting.

"Thank you all for coming today. This is not an official meeting in the sense that it comes from upper management. This is more about bringing us together to talk about what we can do to promote eating organic produce and animals."

There were smiles and nods around the room.

She continued, "As you know, we are working on a policy to define what it means to be organic, but just having a policy to tell farmers what

---

43 Of course, processing does disguise what you are eating. In *Future Foods*, David McClements (p. 327) asks, "Which is not in strawberry yogurt: cow's hooves, seaweed, or strawberries?" In fact, it has gelatin from cow's hooves, carrageenan from seaweed, and the strawberry flavor is chemically synthesized.

they have to do to use the organic label will not be enough. We need to put together a program to warn people about the dangers of pesticides and other harmful chemicals that are being put on our crops and being fed to animals.

"I'm proposing today that this group put together a campaign and then present it to upper management at both agencies for approval."

There was a lot of excited discussion as people talked over one another about all the conceivable things we could do, as I just sat there, somewhat stunned.

Finally, I stood up. Everyone stopped and looked at me.

"I think being from an agency that is more focused on science than activism disqualifies me from being with this group. I know that there are not enough pesticide residues on produce to be a health concern. I don't think I can help you."

The smiles stopped, and the glares began. The young woman at the head of the table glared at me and said, "I'm sorry you feel that way, everyone else here feels that this is tremendously important."

I picked up my notebook and walked out. I never followed up on what they did, but they were more in the Marion Nestle camp than I am.

Sometimes it feels like the food world is divided between those who are trying to produce and sell you food, and those who are trying to scare you away from certain foods. There are hucksters on both sides of the equation. The problem for consumers is how to get away from promotion and agitation toward objective, competent science.

It's not too hard to find bunk promotions. Here's a health claim from 2010 from POM Wonderful juice and POMx supplements. This one was so bad that even the FTC, which is generally much more lenient than the FDA, went after them.

> *SUPER HEALTH POWERS!...100 percent PURE POME-GRANATE JUICE.... Backed by $25 million in medical research. Proven to fight for cardiovascular, prostate, and erectile health.*[215]

The studies showed nothing of the kind. For example, the studies showed that POM juice was no more effective than a placebo for erectile dysfunction.

Here's an example from the other side, the activists who are trying to scare you. A friend who retired from the food industry described a recent meeting he attended as illustrative of what's happening in the world of science and technology versus food activism.

> *The meeting was about the latest consumer food trends. One session provided an overview of approaches being taken by new businesses who cater to consumers who like natural organic foods that are produced by small manufacturers and sold by small retailers. The session opened with an overview provided by a noted food blogger and moved into a discussion that included the blogger, a natural foods retailer, and a new producer of organic meat and sauce products. A major part of the discussion focused on the motivations driving consumer interest in natural products, namely the feeling that consumption of natural products sourced locally provides consumers with a broad range of health benefits. In the Q&A session that followed, a member of the audience asked the blogger the following question:*

> *"Your presentations are interesting, but it seems to me that much of what you believe is based on observation with little scientific data to back your assertions that consuming natural, organic, locally produced food leads to healthier and safer eating."*

> *In response to the question, the blogger responded, "F*** science! As soon as someone brings up science in this context, all I hear is that you are telling me that I'm wrong. I am not interested in what you have to say about science. We don't need science to know that what we're doing is right."*

There's no way to put a percentage on how much food hype occurs on both sides of the ledger. However, science has shown that chemicals, pesticides, and processing aren't inherently bad, just as no single food will save your life.

Chapter 27:
GODZILLA FOOD

ONE OF THE GREAT THINGS about growing up in the 1950s was the horror movies. Most of the ones I remember were about beasts created by nuclear radiation. For example, in *The Beast from 20,000 Fathoms* (1953), US nuclear weapons wake a hundred-million-year-old "rhedosaurus" and kill it with a nuclear isotope. In 1954, giant ants in *Them!*, mutated by the Alamogordo atomic tests, closed with this warning, "We haven't seen the end of them. We've only had a close view of the beginning of what may be the end of us. It's still with us."

GODZILLA

In Japan, the 1954 movie was called *Gojira*. Some claim it was "one of the boldest political statements put to film masquerading as a creature feature." When US producers acquired rights to the film, they edited it heavily because Americans weren't ready to see a film about the atom bomb from the eyes of the victims. Raymond Burr was added to the film and it was renamed *Godzilla, King of the Monsters!* For American audiences, Godzilla was no longer a creation of the atomic bomb but a prehistoric dinosaur. The original film, *Gojira,* wasn't shown in the US until fifty years later.

James Grebey, "Godzilla Might Have Dropped Nuclear Horror, but Chernobyl More Than Makes up for It," Polygon, June 4, 2019, https://www.polygon.com/2019/6/4/18647374/godzilla-king-of-monsters-chernobyl-hbo-nuclear-horror.

The horrors that emerged after Hiroshima and Nagasaki frightened the entire world. People remained nervous about a nuclear war between Russia and the United States. President Kennedy encouraged people to build private "fallout" shelters, and Americans built hundreds of thousands of them in the '50s and '60s. Meanwhile, Japanese citizens that lived beyond the immediate effects of the bombings were developing leukemia and other cancers.[44]

During the Cuban missile crisis in 1962, I was a teenager living on the Norfolk Naval Base and watched a marine fire his weapon over the car of an admiral's wife to get her to stop. She had expected to be saluted as she drove through the gate and didn't realize they were checking everyone's ID. The Russians had placed nukes in Cuba that were within striking distance of the US. It was a fearful time, a tense time, and those fears have never left, nor should they.

Who would want to eat irradiated food after all that?

Even though I'd learned about the difference between high and low doses of chemicals, most of what I knew about radiation came from Godzilla and his brethren.

The FDA wasn't the first government organization to think about irradiating food. In 1943, two years before World War II was over, the Army Quartermaster Corps considered providing irradiated meat to provide frontline troops with shelf-stable rations. The war ended before it became necessary.

By 1954, the National Academy of Sciences put together six committees called the Biological Effects of Atomic Radiation (BEAR) to determine what we understood about the effects of atomic radiation on living organisms. In 1958, partially resulting from the committee's reports, Congress called irradiation a food additive to ensure that no one could use this dangerous technology without FDA oversight.

What Congress didn't know then was that the head of one of those committees, Hermann J. Muller, had been lying for years about the dangers of radiation.[216] Muller, a biologist, received the Nobel Prize in 1946 for work on the effect of radiation on fruit flies. After giving fruit flies cancer

---

44 Not everyone. More recent studies show that some people benefited from exposure to low-dose radiation. See Edward J. Calabrese, "LNT and Cancer Risk Assessment: Its Flawed Foundations Part 1: Radiation and Leukemia: Where LNT Began," *Environmental Research* 197 (2021).

by exposing them to high doses of X-rays, Muller theorized that any level of radiation could give humans cancer. This has come to be called the "one-hit" theory that says it only takes one small dose of radiation to cause cancer. Meanwhile, another scientist, Charlotte Auerbach, was advancing the same theory for chemicals and cancer. Rachel Carson, in her groundbreaking work *Silent Spring* (1962), also subscribed to the one-hit theory.

During the thirties and forties, Muller's theory came under attack by scientists who discovered that radiation has a "threshold," a level of exposure below which there is no harm. At one point, with the threshold challenges disproving Muller's theories growing, one of his colleagues, Milislav Demerec, asked, "What can be done to save the one-hit model?"[217]

Muller lied about the studies and what people were saying about them in his 1946 Nobel Prize speech.[45] In fact, he lied about his critics. He and his like-minded colleagues accused anyone who disagreed with them of being biased. The BEAR panel was composed mostly of Muller fans, and not one panel member ever mentioned the many papers that disputed Muller's findings.

Thus, for radiation, the one-hit model, or what's now called the linear no-threshold (LNT) dose-response curve, was set in concrete.[46] The theory implied that tiny amounts of radiation can cause cancer, so all exposure to radiation must be avoided.[47]

---

45 Muller had been shown a huge study beforehand that demonstrated that low doses of radiation had a threshold beneath which there was no harm, but he chose not to mention it in his speech. Edward J. Calabrese, "Ethical Failings: The Problematic History of Cancer Risk Assessment," *Environmental Research* 193 (2021).

46 The one-hit or linear no-threshold (LNT) dose-response model implies that no matter how small the exposure, or dose, there is always some harm, at least to some people who may be highly sensitive. Today, it is routinely applied to both radiation and chemicals so as to be protective where there is uncertainty about a threshold. It is much in dispute.

47 Additionally, there are two main classes of radiation: ionizing and non-ionizing. Radio waves are non-ionizing and are ubiquitous. These include sunshine, radio, and television broadcast signals going through the walls you're sheltered behind at this very moment. You are also immersed in the non-ionizing radiation of WiFi generated by your computer's modem, the cell phone signals burning out your brain, and the microwaves frying your poodle. However, in the case of your poodle, his cells will be rearranged not by the microwaves, but by the water in his cells being overheated by microwaves. Ionizing radiation includes x-rays and gamma rays generated in huge quantities in nuclear explosions, and to a smaller extent by your doctor's x-ray machines and some older televisions with cathode ray tubes (CRTs).

Oddly enough, this "finding" contradicted the founding principle of the science of poisons, toxicology. That principle, articulated in the sixteenth century by a physician named Paracelsus, says, "Poison is in everything and no thing is without poison. The dosage makes it either a poison or a remedy."[218]

Put simply, the dose makes the poison.

Although Paracelsus didn't know it, evolutionary biologists are discovering that no life on earth would have been possible if exposure to even high levels of radiation or chemicals killed them. Life evolved in a highly stressful environment where there were much higher levels of ionizing radiation and toxic chemicals; evolution favored organisms that could adapt. Today, we and all life forms are still adapting.[219]

Irradiating food was invented in the 1920s by a French scientist but, by the time the FDA got around to announcing it for wheat and wheat flour in 1963 to get rid of insects, food activists were getting better at their jobs.[220] They were becoming adept at stoking food fears about new technologies used for foods.

But I was shocked when the FDA first announced that we would allow pork, fruits, and vegetables to be purposely irradiated in 1985.[221]

The FDA's announcement to allow irradiated foods was immediately followed by the creation of the National Coalition to Stop Food Irradiation in California. They weren't the only ones. Mike Jacobson of the CSPI said, "While irradiation does kill bacteria, it involves the use of inherently dangerous materials and poses its own risks to workers, the environment, and consumers."[222] At the time, I thought they were right.

New technologies have always scared people. When they first heard about it, some people thought pasteurization (heating) might induce scurvy.[223] In fact, nothing else has ever made such difference in food safety and it is still one of our best methods for protecting food.

Our consumer studies staff was responsible for studying the knowledge, attitudes, and behavior of consumers, and they were tasked with investigating how people felt about irradiation. In 1986 they hired Harold Sharlin, an electrical engineer, to do the studies. I knew Harold when he was older, a kindly looking man with slightly shaggy white hair. After he

These CRTs are dangerous, having the potential of creating boobs.

retired, he formed a volunteer group to educate kids about science.[224] Late in life, he also looked at non-military uses of nuclear energy.[225] I wonder if his experiences working for the FDA had anything to do with that.

His report on irradiating foods found that a large percentage of the population hadn't heard of it. In his report, he said, "A common reaction to a new technology is caution or fear. It conjured up visions of Hiroshima and Three Mile Island."[226] But Harold found that "FDA scientists were firm in their conviction that the overwhelming mass of research data left no doubt that irradiation of food was safe and wholesome at the approved dose level."[227]

Had people been aware of what the FDA scientists found, and accepted those findings, it would have prevented hundreds of thousands of cases of foodborne diseases and thousands of deaths from food poisoning by eliminating organisms like salmonella and E. coli. We know a lot about irradiation now, but no one has figured out how to get people to stop being afraid of it. Most spices, herbs, and dry vegetable seasonings in the US are treated with ionizing radiations, but very few people are aware of it.

For me, the turning point in my beliefs came when I visited one of our food labs. I met a young scientist who, because of the regulations allowing irradiation, had created a new regulatory tool. He had multiple computers, test tubes, and all sorts of equipment in his lab that I didn't recognize. He was about twenty-five years old and dressed in a white lab coat.

He thought irradiating foods was a great idea, but expensive, so that food companies might lie about having irradiated their food. Accordingly, he developed a test to check if the food had been irradiated.

I asked him, "Does irradiated food give off radiation?"

"Yes," he said, "and I can measure it."

I asked, "How much radiation is left in the food?"

He laughed.

"Think of sitting on a chair in the sun. When you stand up, you are that much closer to the sun. That's the additional amount of radiation you would be exposed to."

Just as it was with the discovery of pasteurization, most gains in food safety will come from better technology. The CDC has estimated that "irradiation of high-risk foods could prevent up to a million cases of bacterial foodborne disease that result in the hospitalization of more than 50,000 persons and kill many hundreds each year in North America."[228]

This won't happen automatically, particularly if we use the "precautionary principle" regarding new technologies.[48] This principle says we should avoid doing something, particularly with respect to new technologies, if we're not sure whether or not there will be harm. But irradiation works and it doesn't leave enough residual radiation to be of concern.

Biotechnology and nanotechnology hold tremendous promise for both food safety and nutrition. But, as Marchant puts it, "The exotic nature of these emerging technologies, media sensationalism, and activist campaigns create 'risk cascades' that sensationalize and amplify the risk of some technologies to the point of stigmatization."[229]

Perhaps the FDA can play just as big a role in letting people know what is safe as letting them know what is risky.

I thought for the longest time that irradiation was *the answer* for food safety. If we could safely irradiate things like oysters that contain nasty pathogens, that would solve a huge part of our food safety problems. It is currently approved for fruits, vegetables, spices, raw poultry, and red meat.[230] However, we shouldn't indiscriminately irradiate foods that supply us with healthy microbes.

---

48 The precautionary principle has multiple meanings, but it "generally is regarded as implementing the concept of 'better safe than sorry' by requiring proponents of a technology to demonstrate its safety before it can be marketed." Gary Marchant, "Lessons for New Technologies," *Mercatus* working paper, August 26, 2008.

Chapter 28:
NICE TO MEAT YOU

NATURE EVOLVES AT A glacial pace relative to science. We have been improving on nature by using "artificial selection"—Charles Darwin's word for breeding. But now, humans are poised to not just assist Mother Nature, but to take the pro wrestling tag from her. Hacking nature—plants, animals, and humans—is the next global revolution.

Although we have been editing genes since about 10,000 years ago, beginning after the last Ice Age, we're now going into overdrive. For centuries, these practices created the characteristics we wanted in plants and animals—orchestrating plants to grow larger vegetables and fruits or producing pigs that don't get sick.[231] That's still happening, but now we are manipulating genes in laboratories that will never see dirt. Why would we ever want to do that?

Among other reasons, farms are, well, dirty. They are host to wild and domesticated birds and animals, not to mention insects, and all of them are defecating on our food. Crops also need water, which may be contaminated. Sure, farms are beautiful to look at, but they're also pathogen refuges.

Similar to the food-safety problems with fruits and vegetables, over one in four bacterial, chemical, parasitical, and viral illnesses come from beef, game, pork, or poultry. They are responsible for nearly half of all food-borne hospitalizations.[232]

While we are getting ill from eating farm animals, not eating them produces a different problem. Peg Coleman is an expert in the microbiome[49] as well as in risk analysis. I called her one night to talk about the microbiome and the new types of protein.

> PC: Well, I have a problem, particularly with cell-based protein and the precision fermentation products. I'm concerned they will be missing the microbes we normally consume in meats, poultry, and shellfish.

> Me: But presumably we could add the right microbes to those products?

> PC: Maybe when we know more, but we don't know enough now. The other problem is that when we talk about "meat," we're talking about lots of different kinds raised in different environments. I mean there's phylum, class, species. There's just too much we don't know. Anyway, I'm concerned about all of the ways we've destroyed our microbiome, including pasteurizing milk. My data shows that we should be drinking raw milk.

> Me: But pasteurizing milk is one of the great public health victories for us beginning around the 1920s.

> PC: Maybe, but the data now shows that, on-balance, at least today, people would be better off drinking raw milk for the beneficial microbes.

> Me: OK, but other than drinking raw milk what else can we do?

---

49 Microbiomes are places in and on our bodies where huge numbers of microbes work in concert with our mammalian cells (or any animal) and help to protect and nourish us.

PC: First, I like the idea proposed by an Irish microbiologist of a recommended daily allowance (RDA) for microbes, although it might make more sense to have recommendations for individuals.[233] Either way, it draws attention to the problem and helps to steer us away from thinking all microbes are dangerous germs. Second, I think some probiotics make sense, and I particularly like the idea of kefir.

I'm still not sure about drinking raw milk, but the new meats and other proteins appear to me to be a big improvement over the traditional ones. Start with the environment. Environmental concerns associated with raising animals range from methane-containing cow burps into the atmosphere, to the tremendous amounts of water and land it takes to grow them. It takes 1,800 gallons of water to produce a pound of beef and 458 gallons to produce a pound of chicken, whereas it only takes about 200 gallons to produce a pound of lab-grown meat.[234]

Some of these concerns have been around for nearly fifty years, as argued by Frances Moore Lappé's bestselling book, *Diet for a Small Planet*. She argued that we need a vegetarian diet to feed the planet:

For every 16 pounds of grain and soy fed to beef cattle in the United States, we only get 1 pound back in meat on our plates. The other 15 pounds are inaccessible to us, either used by the animal to produce energy or to make some part of its own body that we do not eat (like hair or bones) or excreted.[235]

Today, some farm animals are treated as another piece of capital, often raised in painful, confined cages for their entire lives. Yuval Noah Harari, a bestselling author, historian, and philosopher, writes that, "Domesticated chickens and cattle may well be an evolutionary success story, but they are also among the most miserable creatures that ever lived. The domestication of animals was founded on a series of brutal practices that only became crueler with the passing[236] of the centuries."[237] He believes that "industrial farming is one of the worst crimes in history." [238] Why should we continue this practice when there are new technologies being developed that will not subject farm animals to poor living conditions and early death?[239]

Percy Bysshe Shelley, one of the major English Romantic poets and the husband of *Frankenstein* author Mary Shelley, was an animal activist in the early nineteenth century. He wrote:

> *Let the advocate of animal food, force himself to a decisive experiment on its fitness, and as Plutarch recommends, tear a living lamb with his teeth, and plunging his head into its vitals, slake his thirst with the steaming blood; when fresh from the deed of horror let him revert to the irresistible instincts of nature that would rise in judgment against it, and say, Nature formed me for such work as this. Then, and then only, would he be consistent.*[240]

Whether or not you agree with those sentiments, they are fodder for those who believe that we need to move beyond farms. The beef industry is fighting back. For example, one author notes that, "In sub-Saharan Africa, manure is a nutrient resource which maintains soil health and crop productivity."[241]

Some meat facilities advertise that they raise their meat "regeneratively," "free-range, no antibiotics, no hormones, grass-fed and pasture-finished with a carbon impact negative."[242]

Meat advocates also say:

> *Traditional beef repeatedly provides a nutritious protein source. A 3-ounce serving of lean beef offers 25 grams of protein or half of the recommended daily value. Simultaneously it is packed with B6, B12, zinc, phosphorous, niacin, riboflavin, iron, choline and selenium. Lean cuts have less than 10 grams of total fat, 4.5 grams of saturated fat, and less than 95 milligrams of cholesterol, and can be as lean as a 3-ounce skinless chicken thigh, according to the Beef Checkoff.*[243]

Nevertheless, conventional meats, fowl, and seafood increasingly have major challenges confronting them. So do the new proteins.

While traditional proteins have to contend with Percy Bysshe Shelley, farmless proteins have to contend with Mary Shelley's fans. Critics of any form of tampering with what they falsely believe to be natural apply the prefix "Franken" to these foods as easily as they apply "gate" as a suffix to a scandal. As we saw earlier, this kind of alarmism has been effective at keeping foods from being irradiated.

And yet, produce has been grown without farms for centuries.

One of the seven wonders of the ancient world was the famous Hanging Gardens of Babylon, reputed to be the first attempt to grow plants hydroponically.[244] Similarly, the Aztecs, having no land of their own, build *Chinampas,* water rafts that were up to 200 feet long, growing vegetables and even trees whose roots reached through mud and vines to the water below.[245]

Today, our most interesting non-farm technology is precision-fermentation tanks. Enter the Impossible Burger.

Impossible Burgers start with DNA from the roots of soy plants and use CRISPR technology to insert the DNA into special yeasts.[50] They then grow the yeasts in fermentation tanks. Fermentation is the centuries-old technology used to make yogurt, cheese, and beer. But it is the DNA-cutting technology (CRISPR) that allowed us to take the heme from the soy root and genetically insert it into the yeast that makes the resultant burgers taste just like real meat.

The benefits of this technology are extensive.[51]

There are *no* zoonotic diseases transmitted, *no* animal hormones, *no* antibiotics, *no* concern about weather or droughts, and *no* animal suffering. In addition, there is much *less* land and water needed, much *less* greenhouse gas emissions, and much *less* agricultural runoff.[52] These products may also be necessary to feed a growing world population.

---

50 CRISPR stands for "clustered regulatory interspersed short palindromic repeats."

51 See my recently published paper on this: Richard A. Williams, "Opportunities and Challenges for the Introduction of New Food Proteins," *Annual Review of Food Science and Technology* 12:75-91 (March 2021), http://www.annualreviews.org/eprint/MEUIQW-G8I9THRDUV2USE/full/10.1146/annurev-food-061220-012838.

52 "Animal products such as meat, fish, eggs, and milk, required about 83 percent of the

The same "no's" and "less's" apply to cell-based meats, otherwise known as "cultured" meat. These products start with actual animal cells that are grown in laboratories. When the process concludes, the result won't just look and taste like meat, poultry, or seafood; it will be actual flesh. We have used the same technology for decades to grow drugs, vaccines, antibodies, and flesh for burn victims. Just like HACCP, now mandated for all foods, cell-based meat was first investigated by NASA for use by astronauts in the early 1990s.[246]

At least some people felt these products were inevitable. In 1931, Winston Churchill said that in fifty years, "We shall escape the absurdity of growing a whole chicken in order to eat the breast or wing, by growing these parts separately under a suitable medium."[247]

PRECISION FERMENTATION

Precision fermentation (PF) is growing much more rapidly than plant or cell-based meats and seafood. Currently, fermentation is used for drugs, fuel, clothing, dietary supplements, and recyclable bottles, with food being the new, hot area. Instead of starting with a single cell and growing a plant or animal in months or years, PF uses microbes that can double their biomass in hours.

There are different ways of using microbes to grow food. One way is to use synthetic biology, which is like computer programming except it uses DNA code (extracted from plants, animals, or made up). The code is inserted into a yeast (a mold) or a bacterium, and then it tells the yeast what to make.

These products are made in laboratories, which can be small or the size of a football field. They start with a cell or microorganism specifically selected to grow an ingredient or a food. If genetically engineered, the cell is programmed

---

total farmland to produce only 18 percent of our calories and 37 percent of our protein. If everyone on the planet switched to an exclusively plant-based diet, there would be enormous benefits including a 76 percent reduction in land use for food production, a 49 percent reduction in greenhouse gas emissions, a 50 percent reduction in soil pollution due to acidification and a 49 percent reduction in water pollution to due to eutrophication." From David McClements, *Future Foods: How Modern Science is Transforming the Way We Eat*, Springer Nature Switzerland, 2019, p. 10.

grow an ingredient or a food. If genetically engineered, the cell is programmed with a DNA sequence. In some cases, the cell will excrete what is needed but in others, it grows what is needed inside the cell.

The cells (a seed stock) are then placed in a broth to feed them while they grow into millions more cells. They move to larger tanks when the food is gone and, finally, when there is enough mass, they go into a production vessel called a bioreactor or fermenter.

At this point, growth is tightly controlled for temperature, pressure, pH, and other factors as it becomes the final product. The last two stages are harvesting the product (in some cases eliminating the genetically engineered cells) and purifying it.

Can there be food safety problems in lab-grown meats? Yes. But they can be grown in relatively sterile environments compared to farms. But, critics wonder, are they really healthy from a nutritional perspective?

First, in terms of calories, fats, sodium, and other nutrition issues, they are probably a little better for you now, but they will be much better in the future. The reason is, unlike conventional meats and seafood, they can be dramatically reengineered quickly as nutrition science progresses. Ultimately, perhaps they will be manufactured to meet individual nutrition needs.

The clean-label folks have also weighed in and said, "But what about all of those 'ingredients?'" Look at the ingredient labels in the chart below.

IMPOSSIBLE BURGER[a]	BEYOND MEAT BURGER[a]	BEEF BURGER
Water, soy protein concentrate, coconut oil, sunflower oil, natural flavors; 2 percent or less of: potato protein, methylcellulose, yeast extract, cultured dextrose, food starch modified, soy leghemoglobin, salt, soy protein isolate, mixed tocopherols (vitamin E), zinc gluconate, thiamine hydrochloride (vitamin B1), sodium ascorbate (vitamin C), niacin, pyridoxine hydrochloride (vitamin B6), riboflavin (vitamin B2), vitamin B12.	Water, pea protein isolate, expeller-pressed canola oil, refined coconut oil; 2 percent or less of the following: cellulose from bamboo, methylcellulose, potato starch, natural flavor, maltodextrin, yeast extract, salt, sunflower oil, vegetable glycerin, dried yeast, gum arabic, citrus extract (to protect quality), ascorbic acid (to maintain color), beet juice extract (for color), acetic acid, succinic acid, modified food starch, annatto (for color).	Water (63 percent). Additives allowed in meat (and poultry): BHA, BHT, tocopherols, carrageenan, whey protein concentrate, food starch, cellulose, bromelain, citric acid, corn syrup, lecithin, mono- and di-glycerides, ficin, gelatin, glycerine, hydrolyzed protein, modified food starch, monosodium glutamate, papain, sodium or potassium salts of tripolyphosphate, hexametaphosphate, acid pyrophosphate or orthophosphates, BHA, BHT, sodium caseinate, sodium erythorbate, sodium nitrate, sugar, dried whey.[b] Some contaminants and residues in meat: polychlorinated dibenzo-p-dioxins and dibenzofurans (PCDD/Fs), polychlorinated biphenyls (PCBs), polybrominated diphenyl ethers (PBDEs), perfluorooctane sulfonate (PFOS), perfluorooctanoic acid (PFOA), pesticides, toxic metals, and veterinary drugs.[c]

a. Amanda Capritto, "Impossible Burger vs. Beyond Meat Burger: Taste, Ingredients, and Availability, Compared," CNET, October 25, 2019, https://www.cnet.com/health/nutrition/beyond-meat-vs-impossible-burger-whats-the-difference/.
b. "Additives in Meat and Poultry Products," USDA, https://www.fsis.usda.gov/food-safety/safe-food-handling-and-preparation/food-safety-basics/additives-meat-and-poultry.
c. MeeKyung Kim, Chemical Contaminants and Residues in Food, Dieter Schrenk and Alexander Cartus (eds.), Woodhead Publishing Series in Food Science, Technology and Nutrition, p. 447–468.

As mentioned above, a 2018 article in *Science* found that eliminating traditional animal products and replacing them with alternative proteins could:

- Reduce food's use of land by 76 percent (including a 19 percent reduction in arable land).
- Cut greenhouse gas emissions by 49 percent.
- Reduce acidification by 50 percent.
- Reduce eutrophication (oxygen deprivation in water) by 49 percent.
- Reduce withdrawals of fresh water by 19 percent.[248]

The FDA, of course, doesn't care about these things because these aren't listed in its charter. But inventors aren't bound by regulatory stovepipes; they can try to address as many problems as possible. By inventing alternatives to animal proteins, they can address food safety, nutrition, the environment, and animal welfare issues all at once.

These new foods won't just be confined to meat, poultry, and seafood. They will improve on the Hanging Gardens of Babylon and grow produce that would be "orders of magnitude more energy, water and space-efficient than current farming practices."[249]

Hopefully, the FDA won't use old food-standard rules (for everything but cell-based meats that USDA controls) to call new meats "Counterfeit Chicken" or "Frankenstein Franks." Food standards that freeze recipes in time or require distasteful names should be remnants of the Great Depression. In addition, if the FDA decides that every new protein needs to be precleared before it goes on the market, each product will cost millions and take many more years to come to market. In those instances, the new technologies will be suppressed as they barely start.

We *don't* have to "get them somewhere."

Chapter 29:
BETTER FOODS

"If I had asked people what they wanted, they would have said 'faster horses.'"
—Henry Ford

THAT'S THE THING about inventors: they invent what you need, even if you don't know you need it. People thought they didn't need telephones when they were invented.[53] A spokesman for the telegraph company Western Union who was offered the patent for the telephone said, "The idea is idiotic on the face of it."[250]

We've already talked about precision fermentation and vegetable- and cell-based proteins, but there are numerous new foods and food components coming that will make food safer, more nutritious, and add diversity to our food supply. Approximately 75 percent of the entire world's food supply comes from only twelve plant and animal species.[251] The genetic diversity of plants has been declining since 1900, and any new virus or pest could cause a catastrophe such as the Irish Potato Famine.[54]

---

53 Farm families in the isolated West were perhaps the first people to really want telephones. Often living in isolation, they connected phones to barbed wire that allowed them to connect with everyone on the line.

54 The Irish Potato Famine began in 1845 and wiped out three-quarters of the crop for seven years, resulting in one million Irish people dying from starvation and related causes.

One of the most interesting new food technologies, but the scariest for many people, is genetic engineering. It's not always clear to me why people are afraid of a technology that's trying to make a safer or more nutritious food but don't object as violently when Disney World puts out a donut grilled cheese (four slices of American cheese sandwiched between two glazed doughnuts). [252]

Even though people are afraid of genetically modified foods, the science community has concluded that the fears are not warranted.

> *To date, the totality of institutional, governmental, and international organizations, as well as the scientific literature analyzing the safety of GM foods, has concluded that consuming GM-derived foodstuff poses no more a threat to human health than foodstuff derived from conventional breeding methods.*[253]

CRISPR-CAS9

Most people by now have heard of CRISPR-Cas9. This term is used for a system that can pick out a specific stretch of DNA (the hereditary material that consists of long chemical chains) and "edit" it by chopping out a section of those chains and leave it blank to repair itself, improve it, or replace it entirely. If it is replaced, the replacement may come with DNA from the same or a different species, or even with a specially designed synthetic gene.

By doing so, in a food, or a human, or any other living thing, we can change the function of the DNA. This can, for example, make a plant or human resistant to disease. For plants or animals, it can make them grow faster or increase yields. These systems improve on crossbreeding, a slow and uncertain method for achieving improved plants and animals.

The fixes can be limited to a certain time period, for the life of the organism or to extend to future generations.

Walter Isaacson says of CRISPR that it "could someday be used to fix genetic problems, defeat cancers, enhance our children, and allow us to hack evolution so that we can steer the future of the human race." [a]

a Walter Isaacson, *The Code Breaker: Jennifer Doudna, Gene Editing, and the Future of the Human Race* (New York: Simon and Schuster, 2021), p. 477.

There are multiple ways of genetically editing a plant or animal, and one of the least precise methods is moving genes from one species to another—that is, genetically modified organism (GMO) technology.[254] Gene editing, on the other hand, is a "small, controlled tweak to a living organism's existing DNA," versus inserting a foreign gene (i.e., GMO).[255]

The gene-editing work of CRISPR-Cas9 is exactly what has been done through conventional breeding for thousands of years, except that it's easier, cheaper, faster, and more precise. In fact, selecting plants and animals for desirable traits was the earliest form of genetic engineering. Later on, we engaged in crossbreeding, which was still primitive. Even more primitive is mutation breeding that exposes seeds to "X-rays, UV light, neutrons-alpha-beta particles, fast and gamma rays" to generate mutant seeds.[256]

What should give most people comfort is that the new plant varieties we are creating now are indistinguishable from the traditional breeding methods.[257] We didn't invent CRISPR; we were just lucky enough to watch our microbes doing it and learn how to do it ourselves.[55]

Since they end up being the same types of products produced by the more primitive methods like traditional breeding, labeling them in a way that makes sense produces a challenge. Here's at least an honest way:

---

55 Our bacteria and archaea are constantly being attacked by nasty viruses called bacteriophages. Unlike our mammalian immune system, they don't have specialized cells to attack them. What they do have is enzymes to attack the viruses, break them up, capture pieces of virus DNA, store those pieces, and replicate them. They make RNA out those pieces to identify them the next time they attack, and then mutilate them next time they try it. They only attack invading viruses, not surrounding cells. What the researchers found was that if our bacteria can do it, we can do it ourselves. Using the same system to identify DNA that we don't like (that produces disease or makes a plant less drought tolerant), we can find the offending DNA, cut it out, and replace it.

Genetically engineering foods is one of the new technologies that will enable us to eat safer and more nutritious foods in a way that no regulatory program ever could. For a start, we will be able to control the amount of saturated fat or fiber in foods. We'll also be able to add higher amounts of antioxidant carotenoids (to fight cancer) or take out natural trans fatty acids. To feed a growing world population, we can produce crops that have higher yields, use less water and pesticides, and are resistant to disease.[258] We can also give foods a longer shelf life. Our ability to improve foods to meet our needs will be limited only by the constraints we place on it.

One report describes the future of gene-edited foods this way:

> *By moving production to the molecular level, the number of nutrients we can produce is no longer constrained by the plant or animal kingdoms. While nature provides us with millions of unique proteins, for example, we consume just a fraction of these because they are too difficult or too expensive to extract from macro-organisms. In the new system of production, not only do these proteins become instantly accessible, but millions more that do not even exist today. Free to design molecules to any specification we desire, the only constraint will be the confines of the human imagination. Each ingredient will serve a specific purpose, allowing us to create foods with the exact attributes we desire in terms of nutritional profile, structure, taste, texture, and*

functional qualities. Virtually limitless inputs will, therefore, spawn virtually limitless outputs.[259]

But just putting the right foods and ingredients into our mouths isn't sufficient; we also have to deliver them in a form our bodies can use more efficiently. David McClements calls the structures we need to do this "submarines." Just like CRISPR, nature has its own submarines.[56] Submarines encase things like nutraceuticals, probiotics, glucose, or salt so that they are made available in the right places at the right times in our digestive system. For example, if you continually have blood sugar rapidly rising and falling—that is, a glucose spike—it can lead to type 2 diabetes. But if the release of glucose is evened out with submarines, you can avoid this complication. Another example is encasing probiotics to get past the stomach into the large intestine where they can do the most good.

New foods may also be created with nanotechnologies. Nano particles are so small that you can't see them unless you have a powerful microscope. At that scale, they perform what appears to be magic. The magic is this: take any of the 118 elements from the periodic table (iron, gold, copper, carbon, and all those initials you had to memorize in high school chemistry class), and their properties change when they isolate them at the nano scale.

For example, carbon nanotubes become one hundred times stronger than steel, with one-fourth the density. A nano-scale glass can absorb water and become so strong it can lift 50,000 times its weight.[260] In medicine, a tiny nanoparticle is used to insert gene fragments into cells to kill cancers. Another medical product uses nanoparticles for an influenza vaccine.[261]

Some researchers are injecting nano-sized fat droplets with water to reduce fat content. Others have created nano-sized salt, which increases the exposure to taste buds, giving the impression of more salt that is in the food.[262]

Nano technology is also going to help to keep food safe with nano-sized sensors in food packaging, letting you know when the food inside is spoiled.[263] Some newer packaging is also helpful in extending the shelf life of the contents by retarding spoilage. This type of intelligent packaging will ultimately allow us to do away with "sell by" or "use by" dates that are

56 For example, some natural nutraceuticals are inside cells that have biological compartments to protect them.

not good indicators of when a food has gone bad (the indicators usually are telling us to throw the food out too soon).

Nano filters can be used to desalinize water as well as screen out pesticides, drugs, metals, and pathogens.[264] Scientists are also creating edible, antimicrobial nanoparticles made of thyme, garlic, cloves, and peppermint that can penetrate microbes or insects and kill them.[265]

I remember a conversation I had with a food-company executive years ago about how I thought food companies would react to the new food labels.

> *Me: I think what's going to happen is that, as consumers react to what they see in their foods, food companies are going to have to change the formulations in their foods to make them healthier.*

> *Executive: Why should we have to do that? We now give consumers exactly what they want for taste, price, convenience, and health. They have everything they need, and they can make the choices they want.*

Consumers may not know which new products or new technologies that they want, but it is clear that people are asking those who sell us food to do more for us, workers, the environment, farm animals and a growing population. As they demand more, we are creating a whole new class of food entrepreneurs that will satisfy those demands.

Chapter 30:
BETTER PROCESSES

THE FDA FACES food-safety and nutrition problems in the home, restaurants, and food plants. The approach taken in each is to regulate and educate. Let's start with the home.

For nutrition we have the food label, and for food safety we have "Fight Bac."[266] Fight Bac stands for "fight bacteria" and is a program designed during the 1997 campaign to stop consumers from poisoning themselves with pathogenic bacteria. Bac is an ugly little monster that was pointed mostly at consumers but also at restaurants.

The program told consumers to wash their hands, prevent cross contamination, cook foods to proper temperatures, and refrigerate properly. Are consumers misinformed? Sure, some people cut onions and leave them on the counter and think, because they turn brown, they are sucking up germs (actually it's enzymatic browning). While most consumers follow the four recommendations, less than half use a thermometer to measure internal temperatures.[267] In a recent survey, nearly two out of three consumers said they were looking to technology to help keep foods safe.[268]

That is exactly what's happening and, in a sense, we're going to return to the nineteenth century to do so. We're going to start making our own food at home again. As with HACCP, 3D printers were originally conceived to help the space program.[269] Already widely used in manufacturing, 3D printers make things by adding layers incrementally through computer-controlled nozzles. They are already present in some restaurants and food manufacturers and, ultimately, may be just as common as personal computers in homes.

At home there are a number of 3D food printers like the Sushi Singularity that uses a customer's biological samples to make sushi that meets their nutritional needs.[270] Restaurants use 3D printers to create pizzas, crackers, spaghetti, and fancy chocolates but, ultimately, they will be able to create any kind of dish imaginable. Beyond creating interesting dishes, 3D printers will eventually make personalized food for each member of the household to meet personal nutritional needs. They can be programmed to only produce what each person needs, as well as recycle unused food that will help avoid the 27 million tons of food waste in our kitchens each year.[271]

Another tremendous advantage of these printers is that the food is made on the spot with packaged ingredients, and, as long as the printer is clean, we'll have no problems with unsafe leftovers, dirty cutting boards, or insufficient cooking times.

But won't the same problems that Fight Bac goes after still plague us? In a talk I gave a few years ago, I suggested that we won't be going to the store to buy the fats, proteins, carbohydrates, and flavors for our 3D printers. In fact, the most likely scenario is what French chef Hervé This calls "note-by-note cooking using shelf-stable powders and liquids."[272] Instead of trucks and cars, perhaps 3D ingredients will be delivered by flying drones to pipes in our roofs.

Although the FDA has jurisdiction over restaurants, it's mostly state and local agencies that regulate and inspect them. About 40 percent of all meals come from restaurants, coffee shops, hot dog stands, convenience stores, and delicatessens. From 1998 to 2004, 52 percent of all reported foodborne disease outbreaks came from those sources.[273]

The FDA has the voluntary Food Code that's supposed to be a model for how smaller governments should regulate restaurants. In 2019, the FDA published a guide to "navigate" their food code.[274] It included:

- Identify Chapter, Part, Sub-part, Section, Paragraph, and Sub-paragraph and how these delineations are used.

- Describe the purpose of debitable and nondebitable provisions.

- Define the terms "shall," "may," "may not," and "means," and understand their action, provide examples."

Needless to say, many states don't find the Food Code that helpful. But restaurateurs know that food safety is important, and one of their biggest issues is workers. Over one million people work in food services, including waiters and waitresses, cooks, managers, and food preparation workers.[275] Their average annual salary is about $21,000, and most cannot afford to miss work. That means, no matter what rules are in place, some are going to come to work with communicable diseases. What's more, they speak over thirty languages, and 75 percent of them change jobs every year (making supervision and training difficult).[276]

Innovators are responding with robots. In San Francisco, a restaurant is making a burger with CREATOR, which they claim is "one of the most precise culinary tools on earth" that grinds, slices, grates, toasts, seasons, grills, and customizes burgers—with no human hands.[277] Another robot, "Penny," delivers foods to tables.[278] Second-generation Penny can bring food and drinks and doesn't have dirty hands.

Finally, the FDA, along with CDC and USDA, is responsible for recalling and tracing contaminated foods back to their source. In May 2008, the FDA and CDC tried to track down an outbreak from a rare form of salmonella.[279] They decided the culprit was tomatoes and warned the public against consuming them. Tomato farmers recalled and destroyed tomatoes (spending as much as $250 million) only to have the feds finally trace the problem back to a pepper farmer in Mexico.

Not only is there a financial cost to misidentifying the culprit or lumping in all products together because the farm or producer can't be identified, consumers continue to get ill and die when trace-backs are slow.

Enter entrepreneurs with blockchain. Most people familiar with blockchain think about how it is used to make Bitcoin work.

BLOCKCHAIN

Blockchain records transaction details and, once recorded, the shared records cannot be erased, changed, or hacked. The records are stored on multiple computers and there is no central entity that oversees them. For foods, it can track where the food is, who has it, and what has been done to it along the way from seed to table. All or parts of it can be shared with anyone selectively. There have been two major issues that have prevented its incorporation in tracking foods. First, different companies use different systems. Standardization would help but to fix technology in place making it difficult to improve. The second problem is that it is not cheap.

Using blockchain with tracking chips (like radio-frequency identification tags [RFID] or universal product codes) attached to individual foods will allow everyone in the system to know where food is at any given moment and how long it has been there. One innovation that couples with blockchain is a spray-on DNA barcode that can be added to fruits and vegetables.[280] Originally a biodefense tool for the Department of Defense, this technology takes small snippets of organisms not found in supermarkets, like some seaweeds, and puts them on foods.

Because the records stay in the system, trace-back is comparatively instantaneous. One exercise in tracking by Walmart showed that using blockchain to trace contaminated mangoes back to their source took 2.2 seconds, whereas without it, it took over six days.[281]

The FDA's role for these new innovations will be to ensure they are safe.

Chapter 31:
DEVISING DEVICES FOR OUR DAILY DIET

The biggest threat to progress is that the use of data by health-care professionals to diagnose illnesses and recommend treatment could cause health and wellness wearables to cross into the realm of "medical devices," which would put them under the regulatory thumb of the Food and Drug Administration.
—Joe DeSantis[282]

JUDITH BROWN, A CHICAGO pediatrician and working mom, is routinely asked by parents, "What should I focus on? Fat? Calories? Sugar? Sodium?" Her answer is, "You need to look at everything."[283] That's right, but hardly a day goes by when I don't read that some individual food will make us healthier or sicker. The problem with Brown's advice, and the advice coming out of the FDA, is that most of us don't have enough time in the day to learn nutrition, much less be able to sort out the good from the bad research.

There is help coming. It won't be from a book, a federal health agency, a doctor who claims to be a food guru, a friend, or your family. It's also not going to be a complicated math panel like the NFP, or a food plate divided into equal portions of macronutrients that may have no relevance to your needs. It will be what the FDA will call a "medical device," and it will know everything the FDA and USDA have been trying to get you to learn—in fact, much more than that. It will also tell you what you need to know, meal by meal.

If you were driving your car back in the 1980s listening to Bon Jovi sing "Livin' on a Prayer," and you didn't know where you were going, you had to reach over into the glove compartment and pull out a paper map. If no one else was in the car, you might have had to pull over and try to first figure out where you were, then how to get where you were going. In 1990, Mazda introduced the first GPS in automobiles and quickly ended the need for paper maps.

Suppose you couldn't remember who sung "Livin' on a Prayer." You could ask friends, call a local DJ, or go to the library and see if you could find books about rock 'n' roll. Today, you can just punch it into your phone and get the author, the lyrics, and even play the song. You also don't have to keep big filing cabinets with yellowed, musty documents anymore, hoping your filing system will allow you to find those receipts for your taxes. I had to order all of my journal articles from our library in the early '80s.

Technology has helped us in countless ways, saving time, money, and hassle. Today, it is poised to help you eat better so we can jettison all the complex labels, plates, junk nutrition science, and contradictory expert advice.

Let's get rid of this FDA advice on how to understand the "new" nutrition-facts panel:

> *Look at the amount of sodium in one serving listed on the sample nutrition label. Is percent DV of 37 percent contributing a lot or a little to your diet? Check the General Guide to percent DV. This product contains 37 percent DV for sodium, which shows that this is a HIGH sodium product (it has more than 20 percent DV for sodium). If you consumed 2 servings, that would provide 74 percent of the DV for sodium—nearly three-quarters of an entire day's worth of sodium.*[284]

It's almost as much fun to read as an essay on dirt (actually, dirt versus soil is interesting).

The next sentence in that advice is:

Are you paying attention to how much you eat during the entire day, so that the total amount of saturated fat, as well as other nutrients you want to limit, stays below 100 percent DV?

Most people don't pay attention; it would be time consuming. Just like learning everything about your computer, or how your car works, or everything about your house or apartment, you don't spend hours everyday learning about them. You have other things to worry about.

That's where today's technology is coming in. We'll see devices that will record everything you eat, including all the important ingredients, nutrients, and calories, and add them up each day.

Ultimately, to help direct our health, our devices will need to know not only our persistent health conditions but also monitor biomarkers.[57]

I started with an online program, Habit, and found out immediately that I handle carbohydrates well but should cut back on my saturated fat intake.[285] It wasn't a pleasant experience because I had to prick my finger several times to submit blood samples, but the results were interesting.

Here are my highlights:

- I'm a carb champion.

- Fats are challenging—my blood fat level is elevated.

- I need a normal amount of protein.

- Triglycerides are up.

- My genotype says I'm not prone to weight gain, but I'm a little heavy.

- I don't have problems with lactose, caffeine, or vitamin D.

I still have a lot to learn about this. For example, am I also a "Fast Carb" champion, using the term my former boss (Commissioner Kessler)

---

57 A biomarker is something we can measure that shows that a person (or any organism) is progressing toward a disease, or if they already have it, how severe it is. Blood pressure, for example, is a biomarker.

uses for Fritos?[286] OutSense is another online product. It's an Israeli device that attaches to your toilet and optically scans urine and stool.[287] But what I really want is a device like a smart watch, and one interesting one is coming from Australia.

Peter Vranes is the cofounder of Nutromics. Instead of blood or waste, he believes a good place to look for health biomarkers is sweat.

I read about his new device, a wearable smart patch, and called him.[288]

We agreed on a time, 8:00 p.m. Eastern Standard Time, which is 2:00 p.m. the next day in Australia. As agreed, he called me. I'd been to Australia several years before to speak to the government about risk analysis and was looking forward to the accent.

I asked him how he got into the idea of Nutromics.

> *Peter Vranes: I was in the cosmetics industry and I just felt I wanted to do more for health.*

> *Me: I read online that instead of monitoring blood, you monitor sweat. I thought sweat was just water and salt?*

> *PV: Oh no. Sweat is actually your interstitial fluid, the fluid that surrounds your body's cells.*

> *Me: OK, why is that important?*

> *PV: Because we can easily monitor sweat, and sweat contains biomarkers of disease that can tell us about the effects of food you have just eaten. Those biomarkers include glucose, important for diabetes, but also other markers for cancer and heart disease. It's better to monitor sweat because it's less than one millimeter under the skin and the nerve endings aren't affected by the tiny needles in the skin patch. With blood, you have to prick your finger five times a day. It hurts, so people don't do it.*

He says we're living in a reactive world. Rather than preventing disease, we just wait until people get ill and then turn them over to doctors. He doesn't want his device to be used by doctors; he wants to give consumers real-time information to change their diets immediately.

> *PV: We spend a lot of time looking at diabetics but it's also for people with pre-diabetes. Most people who are pre-diabetic don't even know it. Here's what's important [he pauses]: one in two. That's the number of adults in the US who are diabetic or pre-diabetic. This is really about precision nutrition. Population advice doesn't really help anyone. For example, the USDA MyPlate is bunk.*

I agreed with him and told him I'm really looking forward to his device.

Suggestic is different. Unlike the others, it is a nutrition *platform*. A platform is like your phone; it allows apps that others develop to operate on it. It works for different types of data, like biomarkers, genetics, health characteristics, diet, or exercise, and points you to foods that are good for you.[289] Some apps make recommendations for restaurants taking information about where you live or shop. Others use information on how much you run or EKG readings from your smartphone. Finally, some apps use your preferences for foods you like or what you are trying to accomplish—for example, to lose weight or beat diabetes.

One app that plugs into Suggestic uses research to suggest foods you can eat that will help you live longer. For example, what you eat affects your gut microbe mix, which in turn affects how your genes control your cells' longevity.[290]

It was created by an Israeli engineer, Shai Rozen. He is currently located in Mexico, and I got him on the phone to talk to him about his product.

As with others, I asked him, "So why did you decide to do this?"

He responded, "In my last company, it was just about making money. But this is about doing something good. I know it sounds corny, but it makes me feel good about what we're doing. Hopefully, it will make a lot of us feel good."

From my conversations with these inventors and other research, I tried to envision what the products will ultimately do.

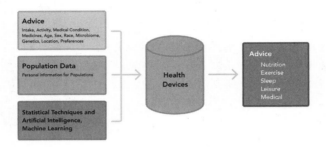

Personalized Health Devices

Something like the above will build on personal devices. We already have personal devices that monitor heart rhythms (including atrial fibrillation), blood pressure, electrocardiograms (ECGs), EKGs, temperature, respiratory rate, sleep, alcohol consumption, fertility tracking, and an electronic pain reliever.[291]

Future devices will know everything about you, and others like you, to make recommendations for your health. Of course, you will have to decide what information you want to share based on how much you trust the company to de-identify your information. "De-identification" is what's done under HIPAA rules with the information you give your doctor.

One thing that will differ completely from a lot of the advice you get now is that the device will know what you like to eat and will adjust advice accordingly. Unlike people trying to advise former President Bush to eat broccoli, if you don't like it, it won't tell you to eat it.

Note that the advice won't stop with nutrition. Because they're linked, they will also include medical recommendations.

Here's the way one author put it:

> *From bacteria in our poo, to metabolites in blood, or even the genes we have inherited from our parents, digital health brands need to ensure that we understand the person as a whole, as a system, in order to fine-tune nutrition and health advice. For this we need to track individual response*

to an intervention whether that comes from following specific dietary changes, to exercise, nutritional supplements or drugs, for instance.[292]

The interactions between our bodies, the environment, and our actions are complicated and lead to some conclusions:

1. Most population-based advice may turn out to be largely useless. There is variation in our genetics, our microbiome, and our environment. For example, in 1972, Richard Lewontin noted, "The original question of how much variation there is within populations has now been resolved. In a variety of species including Drosophila, mice, birds, plants, and man, it is the rule, rather than the exception, that there is more genetic variation between individuals than within populations." In fact, there is more variation within groups of people than between them.

2. Most deterministic studies done to date have probably not accounted sufficiently for confounders. An example is the conclusion that eating red meat causes cancer. Cancer is a "multi-factorial process" and red meat, at best, is a contributing factor.

3. In the future, deterministic studies will be done using new statistical techniques that can vary multiple factors at once. Even so, many, if not most, of the recommendations will be probabilistic; that is, "For you, eating red meat increases your chance of getting a specific type of cancer by 14 percent."

Richard C. Lewontin, "The Apportionment of Human Diversity," *Evolutionary Biology* (1972), p. 382.

These devices are needed right now. We know that the data used in the memory-based recall studies are horribly flawed. We also know that the science, particularly the epidemiology, that underlies diet/disease studies is flawed by a lot more than just bad input data. We also don't want to have to add up every calorie or gram of saturated fat we consume each day. Bad and uncertain science leads to the cornucopia of flawed advice, usually contradictory, from self-styled experts on what to eat.

The result: a recent study by the Rand Corporation found that 60 percent of American adults now live with at least one chronic condition like high cholesterol, high blood pressure, anxiety, arthritis, heart disease, or diabetes.[293] Women are more likely to have multiple conditions, but that may be only because they go to doctors more often than men to find that out.

Health devices are being rapidly developed, but there are two road-blocks. The first, as we talked about above, is monitoring the necessary biomarkers related to your food and drug intakes. Because this is such an urgent problem, inventors around the world are working hard to solve this.

The second is overregulation.

Even though these devices will be primarily about food in the begin-ning, they will ultimately be broadly about health and as a result will be regulated by the Center for Devices and Radiological Health (CDRH) in the FDA. Just as with food additives and prescription drugs, they will require premarket approval.

As the makers of 23andMe (home genetic-information test) found out, that is a problem. Although allowed to operate in the United Kingdom, the FDA ordered them to stop production in the US because it was a medical device that alerted people to a possible future disease based on their genetic profile.[294] They were only allowed back on the market when they stopped making medical recommendations.

It takes an average of nine months and $75 million dollars for a new device to be approved, unless there is already something like it on the mar-ket.[295] The time, money, and hassle are all factors that will slow innova-tion that could make us healthier and prevent heart disease, diabetes, and many illnesses.

The FDA initially said that some of the devices would not need to be so tightly controlled as long as they don't "diagnose, cure, mitigate, treat, or prevent disease, or affect the structure or function of humans (or other animals)."[296]

But if they don't do any of those things, then they won't be very help-ful either.[297] If you're predisposed to becoming a diabetic, a device could tell you that. But if it does, the FDA is going to put a stop to it until it goes through lengthy and expensive trials.

Obviously, we know there are always people who want to take short-cuts and some who won't get it right. But we're in the midst of an obesity epidemic that is leading us to more diabetes, heart disease, and other health problems, so we must carefully weigh keeping poor products off with the threat of unnecessarily inhibiting innovation.

Chapter 32:
TAKING CARE OF THE LITTLE THINGS

"CHANGE YOUR BACTERIA, change your life."[298]

The oldest living life forms on earth, beginning 3.7 billion years ago, are microbes. We, on the other hand, have only been around for 300,000 years. We were born in a sea of microbes and have had to learn to live with them. Our microbiomes are composed of 100 trillion tiny microbes like bacteria and protozoa that live on and in our bodies (mostly in the gut) and can weigh up to five pounds. Microbes make up between 50 to 90 percent of our cells, which means we share the human structure with them.[299] With every gram you swallow, you eat around one million microbes.[300] Every hour, we breathe out 37 million bacteria.[301]

Even though we're a new microbial mix every day, they are such a huge part of us that some believe that we are just one superorganism consisting of human and microbial cells.[302] In fact, they are intermixed. Our microbial cells are often telling our mammalian cells what to do, when to perform some function, and when to stop. As one author says, "Exactly who is in charge, mammalian cells or microbes, is an open question."[303]

Just as microbes depend on us as their host hotel, we depend on them—a lot. They help to shape our organs from birth; they protect us from poisons and disease; when we eat, they break down our food into nutrients and energy (calories); they work with our immune system to make sure it functions properly; and they do some of immune work themselves. They also affect our moods. Among themselves, they fight each other to tell us what we should eat, and the winners can either be microbes making us fat or thin.[304] Microbes seem to be the ones that control our statins that reduce cholesterol levels and, concomitantly, the risk of heart attacks and strokes.[305]

Perhaps one of the more exciting finds is that, around midlife (forty to fifty years), the composition of our microbes changes and they become oracles predicting the length of our lives. It may also be the case that we will be able to adjust the microbial mix to help us live longer.[306]

Our actions may be controlled more by microbes than we can possibly imagine. As one author puts it:

> *Our darkest fiction is full of Orwellian dystopias, shadowy cabals, and mind-controlling supervillains. But it turns out that the brainless, microscopic, single-celled organisms that live inside us have been pulling our strings all along.*[307]

But our understanding of the value that they provide to us is only recent. For the last one hundred years, we've been trying to kill them all. One big microbe killer has been the indiscriminate use of antibiotics, found both in the animals we eat and the drugs we use to treat infections.[58] While antibiotics have been lifesavers, they have also helped to kill our microbiome.

The second big microbe killer was illustrated by the movie producer of *Scarface* and the subject of *Aviator*, Howard Hughes. To live a germ-free life, he wore tissue boxes on his feet and wrote a manual on how to open a can of peaches in a sanitized way so that germs couldn't get into the bowl.[308]

In the United States, 90,000 people die every year in hospitals from microbial infections, as patients stew in their own microbial juices.[309] One researcher found an easy answer; open a window to allow more microbes in, particularly beneficial ones that could compete with the pathogenic types.[310]

In 1969, the "grandfather of modern oral microbiology," Theodor Rosebury, said, "We are becoming a nation of tubbed, scrubbed, deodorized neurotics." He wrote that in 1969. Things are worse now with antibacterial

---

58　While antibiotics are useful for farm animals, some of it is because of the conditions they are raised in, but it also contributes to antibiotic resistance.

wipes, "soaps, shampoos, toothbrushes, hairbrushes detergents, crockery, bedding—even socks."[311]

That was before the hand-hygiene craze, but now things have gotten crazier with COVID-19. It also hasn't helped that we've moved away from the country into sanitized cities and mothers have become petrified if they see their children putting dirty hands into their mouths. We have everything from cell phone sanitizers to hermetically sealed houses. And, of course, we have the FDA's war on bacteria, as mentioned earlier.

By destroying our microbiomes, we have traded one health risk for another. "We reduced the risk of death from infectious diseases. However, we increased the risk of lifelong disability and premature death due to non-communicable diseases."[312]

Noncommunicable diseases include diabetes, cancer, and heart disease, among many others. Obviously, these are also food-related, and we now know that food and the health of our microbial communities are closely linked. There is a tremendous amount of research on foods that contain *prebiotics* that feed microbes and help us to have a healthy diversity. These include, for example, fermented foods, like yogurt and sauerkraut. Vegetables like broccoli and onions are *probiotics*, foods that contain combinations of helpful live bacteria and yeasts. Of course, vegetables can also harbor pathogenic bacteria as well.

MICROBIAL WAR

Every second, there are never-ending battles between antagonists and alliances between bacteria in your body. Helpful bacteria, called *commensals*, fight malignant bacteria, called *pathogens*. Some of the bacteria have been with you since you slid down the birth canal, but others are picked up every day from air, food, water, pets, sex, dirt, and other environmental influences. Because we change the mix of our microbes (including bacteria, algae, and fungi)—our so-called microbiome—every day, we are a different person every day. In *The War of the Worlds*, the microbes killed the aliens, but we are dependent on ours just as they are dependent on us.

One of the things we have come to understand about microbes is that there is a two-way communication channel between our gut microbes and our brain. Part of that communication is telling us what it wants to eat. It may be telling us to eat helpful or less helpful food, depending on who is winning the battle at the moment.

Good microbes are aided in the fight against pathogens by our own cells' immune system. Over time, the mammalian immune system is trained to recognize the difference between commensals and pathogens. Both commensals and the antibodies in our immune system kill pathogens. To get past those two systems, pathogens, just like chemicals, need a pretty heavy dose to make us sick.

Since their discovery, we have treated all microbes as though they were the enemy and needed to be destroyed. The first true antibiotic (killer of microbes) was penicillin (a fungal metabolite) and is estimated to have saved 200 million lives. That's true, but in 2016, five out six Americans got prescriptions for antibiotics. Excessive use of antibiotics and excessive hygiene kill microbes, both commensals and pathogens. As a result, we appear to have been weakening our microbiome for generations.

We are only just beginning to understand microbiomes. A too small or insufficiently diverse microbiome has been linked to mental illnesses and conditions such as anxiety, depression, autism, and obesity, as well as diseases like dementia, Parkinson's, Alzheimer's, type 2 diabetes, heart disease, multiple sclerosis, chronic inflammation, cancer, schizophrenia, irritable and inflammatory bowel syndrome, and leaky gut.

Eating the right foods for our microbial health is becoming a big business. There are numerous products and plans that offer you prebiotic and probiotic supplements. There are two problems with much of this advice: first, just like with medicine, we all have different needs for our microbiome. Second, as David McClements admitted in 2020, "Currently, it is not possible to define what a good microbiome should look like."[313]

One interesting finding is that soluble fiber, a prebiotic, appears to be important for a healthy microbiome. I discovered this talking to a nutritionist from the Institute for the Advancement of Food and Nutrition Sciences (IAFNS). Marie Latulippe, besides having a name that sounds like Paris in the spring, is both stylish and intellectually fascinating at the same time. She is in charge of organizing and leading IAFNS research activities into the microbiome. One of the many food components that seems to affect the microbiome has to do with potatoes.

I had a Zoom call with Marie in late February 2021.

Marie Latulippe: One of the things researchers are looking at is something called "resistant starch." That's fiber that your own body can't digest but the microbes in your large intestine can use for food.[59]

Me: Where do you find it?

ML: In potatoes, for example. If you cook a potato in any form, after it cools, it forms a type of resistant starch.

Me: What does it do?

ML: The research is ongoing, so we don't know for sure, but it seems to help with insulin sensitivity that helps people keep their blood glucose levels stable. It may also help people control their weight; we just don't know yet.

Me: Of course, it was only recently that USDA was saying that potatoes weren't allowed in the WIC program because they were associated with increases in obesity.

ML: This was later reversed, one reason being that potatoes were a good source of a nutrient most people need more of—potassium.

---

59 That is the definition of prebiotic.

From the beginning of 2020 to February 2021, there have been 57,100 articles about the microbiome in Google Scholar. We are also beginning to see supplements and medical treatments to fix unhealthy microbiomes. One treatment is to transfer microbe-containing feces from a healthy person to a sick one either by using a frozen poop pill or by injecting it into the anus.

This prompted the TV comedy show *South Park* to speculate on Super Bowl Champion Tom Brady.

> *Tom Brady: All right, all right, uhm, I'm proud of our team today. It was ah, I thought the defense did a great job keeping us in the game and, again, I think that the offense has a lot of room for improvement and all that starts with me. Questions? Yeah.*
>
> *Reporter 1: Can we have your poop?*
>
> *TB: No, guys, I'm not gonna take any requests for my microbiome. I just wanna focus on the team. We're ten and one now you know but we can't let up. Yeah.*
>
> *Reporter 2: Please, can we have your poop?*
>
> *TB: Okay, I'm not, I'm not gonna stand here you guys and just, does anyone have a real question?*
>
> *Reporter 3: Tom, after you leave here, are you gonna go eat somewhere, or go right home and have a...?*
>
> *TB: No, no. See, I'm not gonna tell you guys where I'm going because then you're all gonna try and follow me into the bathroom. You're not taking my feces so unless you have a football question, we're done here.*

Reporter 4: Can we buy your poop?

If our microbiome is constantly changing, it may mean we will have to find the means to constantly monitor it and change it. There are several possibilities for monitoring. One way is by smell. Our own microbes communicate by smell in a cell-to-cell process called "quorum sensing."[314] Using biosensors, we may be able to detect these smells to alert us of coming imbalances in our microbiomes or alert us to treatment possibilities.[315]

Ensuring we have a healthy microbiome may be a better way to prevent noncommunicable diseases than trying to use our current information/diet/disease model. It might also affect how and when we take antibiotics, how much exercise we need, or how we approach hygiene.

For food safety, we are beginning to realize that, like all microbes, pathogens have to fight other microbes for their survival. We may be able to help the bacteria that fight pathogens get the upper hand to prevent food poisoning.

This research is happening now. For example, at MIT, Jim Collins is programming gut bacteria to destroy pathogens like *Shigella* and *Vibrio cholerae*.[316] Synthetic biologists are not only delivering therapeutic bacteria to the gut but are also using them to "monitor and respond to conditions inside the body."[317] In 2018, a team in Singapore created gut bacteria engineered to stick to colon cancer cells and secrete an enzyme that converts a natural substance found in broccoli and other vegetables into a molecule that inhibits tumor growth.[318]

What is the FDA's role in all of this? In 2013, the FDA decided to regulate stools used in fecal transfers as drugs after finding out they had been successfully used to completely cure people affected by the pathogen *Clostridium difficile*.[319] This caused doctors to have to fill out lengthy forms for preapproval, causing dangerous delays in treatment. The FDA backed down, but only for that pathogen.

Instead of requiring premarket approval, the FDA can create and validate biomarkers for microbes or their metabolites to monitor their activities.[320] This will help to make the market function more smoothly by allowing consumers to evaluate what is working for them and to choose among the different products.

Some have become concerned about synthesizing microbes that may have unexpected impacts. To control such an issue, scientists have been looking at kill switches that would stop them in that eventuality. That might also be a useful role for the FDA, to require kill switches with post-market monitoring when there is the possibility of unexpected impacts.

There is still a great deal to learn about the microbiome, especially in monitoring it and its ability to treat diseases, but the science is advancing rapidly. How fast it goes may depend largely on how the FDA, with congressional oversight, allows the science to proceed.

ENGINEERING HUMANS

Adjusting our microbial partners is one way to prevent or treat disease, but there is another way to avoid getting sick—we can remake ourselves. We can genetically modify our own biology to cure or prevent diseases, and even to extend our lives by perhaps centuries. It may start from something as simple as Metformin, a drug designed in the '50s to treat diabetes, which is now undergoing clinical trials as an anti-aging drug. It seems to ward off numerous noncommunicable diseases.

Genetically engineering ourselves has already started with a bone-marrow transplant from a healthy patient to one with a defective immune system.[1] We can also knock out or change a mutated gene, replace a gene with a healthier copy, or add a brand new gene, perhaps synthetic, to fight or avoid a disease.[2] We will find genetic sequences that exist in other living things that are useful implants to ward off disease. Importantly, there is the possibility of synthesizing entirely new genomes. Finally, we will be "reengineering the human genome itself for the purpose of preventing diseases from occurring in the first place[3]

We can expect to see nanobots scouring our bodies and fixing what's broken or diseased.[4] We'll soon be 3D printing synthetic organs to fix bad ones or just to improve them.

Ultimately, the goal is to extend life, like the *Artica islandica* (quahog clam) that can live up to 400 years old[5]Or, we may decide that we want to be more than human—trans-human, or post-human—perhaps digitizing and disembodying our brain.[6] No matter what we do, we are set to replace nearly 400 billion years of evolution. Some will liken it to eugenics, while others will see us winning the fight against cruel nature.

[1] George Church and Ed Regis, *Regenesis: How Synthetic Biology Will Reinvent Nature and Ourselves*, p. 216.
[2] Jamie Metzl, *Hacking Darwin: Genetic Engineering and the Future of Humanity*, p. 98.
[3] Metzl, p. 115.
[4] Church and Regis, p. 160.
[5] Church and Regis, p. 219.
[6] Metzl, p. 162.

Chapter 33:
PREVENTIVE INCENTIVES

"BUT, RICHARD, THEY'LL already be *daid*!"

That was Diane Rehm castigating me during one of the pauses in her WAMU radio show in Washington, DC. It was 2016, and the title of her show was *Delays in New Food Safety Regulations*.[321]

Diane is still considered a Washington fixture in policy circles, and I was honored to be on her show for the second time. Even though I was a vice president at the nonprofit Mercatus Center at George Mason University, I continued to write about food issues. Following up on a lengthy paper I'd written on food safety in 2010, I'd testified in the Senate a month before the Diane Rehm show on federal regulation of food safety.[322] [323]

My testimony emphasized how the old system of anticipatory regulations and inspections had failed in the three previous HACCP programs: seafood, juice, and meat and poultry HACCP (USDA rule). In my paper, I'd quoted Matt Ridley: "Empires, indeed governments generally, tend to be good things at first and bad things the longer they last."[324] In 2010, the FDA was 104 years old. I asked: If most firms become inefficient and die out before turning forty, can the FDA still be efficient?

The Seafood HACCP program had failed, and it wasn't just because we didn't reduce illnesses from oysters. A 2001 General Accounting Office study of the FDA's HACCP program found that it "does not sufficiently protect consumers." Even an internal FDA study (never released) in 2004 showed that it had accomplished nothing.[325]

Many of the 48 million illnesses that happen every year are because of outbreaks, which is when two or more people get the same illness from contaminated food or drinks.[60] When there is an outbreak, the CDC in Atlanta coordinates the efforts between the FDA or USDA and state investigators to find which food was responsible and tries to locate the source. They also tell consumers what's happening.

The new Food Safety Modernization Act (FSMA) was intended to address the problem of those illnesses. It was what brought me onto the Diane Rehm radio program, along with Erik Olson of the Pew Research Center.

Diane Rehm: And, Erik Olson, the law has yet to go into effect. How come?

Erik Olson: Well, officially the law went into effect in January when the president signed it, but the real problem is to make any law like this work, you have to have an agency that has rules to implement it, and that's where we got stuck. Basically, for the last year and a half, we have been waiting and waiting for these rules to come out. Frankly they have been over at the White House's Office of Management and Budget for over eight months. The major rules to actually give this law some teeth and so what we have now is essentially a paper tiger.

DR: Richard Williams, a paper tiger?

Me: No, the FDA is hardly a paper tiger. The FDA has been trying to pass regulations that anticipate problems for over one hundred years. I was at the FDA for over twenty-sev-

---

60 Most cases are "sporadic," meaning they are not linked to an outbreak although they could affect multiple people but just not be detected by public health authorities. Part of the problem is that symptoms of some types of pathogen poisoning are similar to flu.

en years and worked on many of those regulations. We did have things like good manufacturing practices and things like hazard analysis and critical-control-point rules, and we've been trying to pass these regulations to make food safe for a long, long time.

DR: I think the original law goes back to 1906, isn't that correct, and then amended in 1936. I think that my concern would be how much preventive investigation there is actually going on. We've got hundreds of growers out there. The question is how many inspectors does the FDA have? And, by the way, just let me point out, we did invite the FDA on the program. We also invited the Office of Management and Budget and neither desired to come on. So, how do you cover that range of growers, for example, with just a very few inspectors?

Me: I actually think it is extremely difficult to cover a large number of growers not only in this country but from a number of countries that export fruits and vegetables to us. We also have thousands and thousands of manufacturers, and we will never have enough inspectors to adequately inspect people. In the long run, I don't think that's going to be the solution. Adding more and more inspectors to the FDA to get to plants in some sort of reasonable time so that we create an incentive for them to produce safer food is not going to work. The answer, I think, lies in making sure that, when they do have a problem, we can trace the problem back to the farm or manufacturer that caused it, and that creates an incentive for them to inspect each other and to exercise due diligence.[326]

The problem with regulations is that the FDA, and governments generally, can find problems but rarely have workable solutions. Once a problem is identified, just as with seafood, they feel compelled to pass a regulation. As my old boss Leo had once told me, you just have to show that you are doing something.

Enforcement through inspections is a problem because there are never enough resources to provide sufficient compliance incentives. For the FDA to be effective, they might have to inspect once a week, requiring a jump in inspections from 5,700 per year to 2.5 million.[327] Currently, the FDA inspects food plants an average of once every six years. In my classes, I compared it to a parent telling their child to keep their room clean and they would check on them every six years to make sure they were doing it.

And so, on the Diane Rehm show, I suggested, as I did to the Senate, that we think about better incentives. Every time a company is identified with an outbreak, it makes other companies look at their own processes because of the massive costs to the firm of a recall. But one other thing has changed as well: with the existence of the World Wide Web, consumers are now much more aware of food-safety outbreaks. Both the CDC and the FDA have websites announcing them, but there are also many private companies that do the same, such as Foodsafetynews.com.[328]

A 2008 Google search for "food recall" netted 18,000 stories. In 2020, the same search returned 439 million hits. If you're a victim, you can also subscribe to FindLaw, which will help you find a product-liability attorney.[329]

In fact, even old Harvey Wiley, the founder of the FDA, realized the power that comes from putting this kind of information into the hands of consumers. After he left government, he went to work for *Good Housekeeping* magazine, exposing poor food-safety practices to American housewives.[330]

Hence, the incentives for food company executives to exercise due diligence. Food recalls are so expensive that a paper in *Food Safety* magazine called them the "biggest threat to profitability," costing an average of $10 million in direct costs, damage to the brand, and lost sales.[331] In fact, 15 percent of consumers say that they would never again purchase from a manufacturer with a recalled product.

Just ask the Peanut Corporation of America. Their executives got twenty-eight years in jail[332] but they got off easy compared to the dairy farmer and milk salesman that sold melamine-tainted milk in China. They were executed.[333]

Diane screamed at me, though, during the break. "What good does it do to trace back problems and go after firms *after* people have been poisoned? They'll already be *daid.*"

It might have helped if she listened to *Freakonomics Radio* on her own station, a program that started back in 2010 with economists talking about incentives.[334] They talk about material incentives, social incentives (desire to be accepted and liked), and moral incentives, and frequently confound listeners with the reasoning behind certain phenomena.

Years before I went into the FDA, I managed a Jack in the Box and a Wendy's. Jack in the Box was easy to manage for food safety because everything was frozen, but Wendy's specializes in fresh burgers. That means you need to be careful not to over-order, or the meat will go bad. Managing Wendy's taught me my first lesson about food safety: it's difficult to tie an outbreak to any food. That's exactly why we need to get better at it.

For some pathogens, like *Staphylococcus aureus*, you can get sick within a few hours of eating. For Hepatitis A, it can take twenty-eight days. For Listeria, it can take only a few days to get sick, but two months later it can affect an unborn child.[335] Because of the time lags and because food-borne poisoning shares many of the same symptoms as flu, illnesses are often difficult to trace back.

In 2017, there were 841 foodborne disease outbreaks (bacteria, viruses, and parasites) with about 15,000 illnesses reported.[336] CDC revised its estimate from 76 million cases of foodborne diseases per year down to 48 million using better data and methods.[337] They didn't say there were fewer illnesses, just that the old method wasn't so great. In fact, the old method was created by two FDA scientists who, in 1985, said that if you make enough ridiculous assumptions about underestimation, you come up with 76 million cases of food poisoning. The joke was lost, as this became the official number of cases of foodborne disease for years.[338]

Robert Scharff, former CFSAN economist and risk analyst, is now a professor at Ohio State University. He is tall with full head of jet-black hair and an easy smile. In one of his many papers on food safety, Bob calculated that one out of four cases of foodborne poisoning come from fruits and vegetables.

When the Food Safety Initiative was getting underway, one of our regulation writers told me he was trying to write a rule that would fence off every single farm in America (and I suppose foreign farms that exported to us).[61] He wanted to keep not just farm animals out of the fields but also deer, raccoons, and other critters that would come in and poop in the fields. I asked him what he would do about birds flying over, rodents digging under, and insects flying and crawling in, but he didn't have an answer for that.

As if that wasn't enough, we sent our epidemiologists down to Mexico because a lot of produce coming up in the trucks was contaminated. They came back with an interesting story. They told me that the farmers installed portable potties in the fields, but that the Mexican workers wouldn't always use them. Instead, they pooped on the lettuce. When the epidemiologists were able to conduct interviews with the workers alone, they confessed that the owners were beating them. They wanted to get even. Beyond the horrors associated with this work environment, this could be valuable information for local produce marketers. Imagine little stickers on cantaloupes advertising, "Beatings-Free Produce."

A more serious way to bring down the number of cases of foodborne diseases is to have a quicker way to trace problems back to their source. New technologies are already being used, like radio frequency identification (RFID) tags and blockchain, coupled with artificial intelligence that can trace foods from an infected person back to a farm or fisherman. The tags contain fixed information on the source, while blockchain tracks where the product has been. Once tracked, whole genome sequencing compares the harmful microbe in the stool of an infected person to the pathogen obtained from a contaminated food so that the source of the contamination is confirmed.

I knew about these technologies, but it was the epidemiology branch that accidentally showed me a much better way to incentivize industry to keep foods safe. Shortly before I left the FDA, the epidemiologists on my staff got creative: they went back through old food-safety recalls and examined the data. From the data they identified likely causes of contamination in the plants or on farms. They did their best to identify the root causes (like

---

61 About 40 percent of all land in the US is farmland, using up 915 million acres. With 2.1 million farms, I get an average of about 435 acres per farm, which would take 764 billion linear feet of fencing.

temperature failures or infected workers) and then put all the data together in an electronic file.

One of the epidemiologists asked for a meeting to show me their results.

Epidemiologist: As you see, by digging through the data, we got some pretty specific problems that aren't that hard to fix.

Me: What you do you plan to do with this report?

Epidemiologist: We're planning to give it to the field [FDA's] inspectors.

Me: Why not put it up on our website? I'll bet a lot of people would be interested.

They did, and we forgot about it.

About six months later, an executive at a food-safety conference and I were talking and, when I brought up the epi database, he knew all about it.

He said, "I've never seen something go around the industry so fast. Everyone that had a similar practice has taken steps to fix them to make sure that they will never have that problem."

"Was that more of an incentive than a regulation?" This was truly exciting for me.

"Oh yeah."

Since then, partly because of the Food Safety Modernization Act, FDA has now held a series of meetings about blockchain and other ways to trace outbreaks back to the source of the problem.[339] They have finally laid out a plan that acknowledges the need to find trace problems back, investigate root causes, and publicize them.[340] That is a preventive incentive.

Chapter 34:
CHANGE FOR LIFE

THE KOBAYASHI Maru Simulation[62]

"He cheated," scoffs David.

"I changed the conditions of the test," Kirk retorts. "Got a commendation for original thinking. I don't like to lose."

"Then you never faced that situation," Saavik says. "Faced death."

"I don't believe in the no-win scenario," Kirk says. "As your teacher, Mr. Spock, is fond of saying, I like to think there always are…possibilities."

This was from *Star Trek*, when Captain Kirk explains how he beat an impossible simulation test as a candidate The simulation was set up to see how a starship captain could deal with a no-win situation. Kirk went into the program, changed it, and won.

That is precisely what the FDA is facing with food safety and nutrition—a no-win problem unless they change the program, *their* program.

A regulation has three steps:

1. Define the problem—This is normally done by scientists and risk assessors to identify the problem, how serious it is, and how widespread.

---

62 The opening scene of *Star Trek II: The Wrath of Khan*, "I Don't Believe in the No-Win Scenario," https://unwinnable.com/2012/07/03/kobayashi-maru/.

2. Identify potential solutions—This is where science sometimes plays a role, but more often it is lawyers and economists trying to figure out the different ways to "skin a cat."

3. Decide on the solution—This is left for attorneys, economists, and ultimately politicians.

The problem for the FDA has always been how the FDA can make existing foods safer and educate consumers to make healthier choices. There are limited potential solutions to problems framed this way, and the solutions, which have almost universally failed, are governed by the FDA's culture, laws, and legal precedents.

But entrepreneurs are moving outside of the FDA's program and they are solving safety and nutrition problems using technology and new science to create better foods and processes.

When I came to the FDA, I wanted to believe that I was going to be helping to solve problems. Unlike Captain Kirk, I understood neither the culture nor the constraints. Even though the FDA wasn't my first choice after graduate school, once I got there and realized the scope of what we were dealing with, I was excited. I knew I was going to learn firsthand how the government worked and was going to get into some of the most serious issues that people care about—food safety and nutrition. It didn't take long for me to be told I was fired for refusing to change an analysis, but I loved the issues and stayed.

One of our former commissioners, Herbert Ley, said in 1970, "The thing that bugs me is that the people think the FDA is protecting them. It isn't. What the FDA is doing and what the public thinks it's doing are as different as night and day."[341] He was talking about FDA's relationship with drug companies. I came to believe the same thing, but not about protecting drug companies—rather, about what FDA does in the food arena. It's about manipulating the science and economics to "get those guys," keeping the money flowing and the power growing, and keeping Congress, the courts, the regulated firms, and everyone else at bay.

That's why I don't believe the politicians and commissioners who talk about "nothing good in foods will come without the FDA," and that only the

FDA can ensure "that the foods we eat are safe and don't cause us harm." Just recently, the deputy commissioner for the FDA also said, "The FDA is the most prestigious regulatory agency on earth."[342] Maybe it was true at the beginning, but the FDA is now in danger of being left behind. They are the boulder in the middle of the stream, and the innovative stream is going around them. For me, when I had completed my thirty years in government, I had gotten to the point where I was part of decision-making, but I was completely disillusioned with the little progress we had made during my tenure.

As I approached my thirtieth year in government and was trying to decide whether or not to leave, I was thinking about all of the good I could continue to do if I stayed and was trying to compare that to a job offer I had at George Mason University. Around this time, because every manager in CFSAN was so nasty to each other, the center director hired several industrial psychologists to talk to us. I reluctantly agreed to go along with this.

On my third and last session with the psychologist, we were discussing whether I was going to leave or stay. She had asked about how I felt about the nasty the atmosphere in FDA and why I was so discouraged about my twenty-seven-year career there. Then she asked me about the Mercatus Center at GMU.

"It seems like a really good place," I said. "The people are friendly, all seem to work together, and if I went there, I would be given a free hand to run the regulatory shop any way I wanted to."

"Stop!" she said. "You don't need to talk about it anymore. When you talked about the FDA, your body language was closed down; you were miserable. But the moment you started talking about Mercatus, you opened up. It's where you want to go, where you want to be. You owe it to yourself to go there."

And that, as they say, was that.

The approach of trying to anticipate food-safety problems and passing regulations to prevent those problems worked for early twentieth century issues. In Harvey Wiley's day, plants were filthy and overrun with rats and operators were deliberately adding poisons to foods. The problems were obvious and so were the solutions.

Now, because of we are still using an outmoded approach, including mandating fifty-year-old process rules (HACCP), we continue to have one out of six people (48 million) getting sick from food poisoning, resulting in 3,000 deaths every year.

Today, when there is a food-safety outbreak, everyone knows about it with the web. Consumers find out about the outbreaks and hold manufacturers to account, often refusing to buy food from them again. Food manufacturers find regulations almost a distraction. As one told me at a food safety meeting in DC when I asked him what he would be doing if he weren't complying with regulations, he said:

> *Where should I start? The ingredients [from farms or other manufacturers] can be contaminated; the overall plant cleanliness; worrying about how clean we are getting the machines; the employees may come to work sick or not be motivated; there are rats and flies; cooking temperatures and times; cooling policies, transportation, and warehouse issues; and packaging. I have a full-time job. I actually know how to do my job. Honestly, I don't hate you guys, but you can't do my job from your desk in DC.*

Food standards made sense when the problem was to keep fillers like sawdust and more dangerous substances out of food, but today they are anachronisms. Food additive rules handle the poisons and there are more important jobs to do than protecting incumbent manufacturers from competing with newer, better products.

Our approach to nutrition has also been shown to be defective and outdated. Food labels have been with us nearly fifty years and people still do not understand them or the underlying science and, as a result, they still don't know how to decide what to eat. One study predicts that half of the US population will be obese within a decade with the accompanying comorbidities of heart disease and diabetes.[343] For these, the FDA has run out of solutions.

FDA uses bad science, both from without and within. Outside of FDA, nutrition science relies on poor eating intake data and biased epidemiology. Inside, FDA uses poor science, like dunking oranges in colored water to prove rainwater can contaminate them and overly conservative risk assessments that would find drinking over eight ounces of water in a day dangerous. Such science serves as a rationale to regulate more industries with more severe regulatory limits than necessary. On the other hand, FDA insists that industries only use high quality science with "significant scientific agreement."

In some cases, the result of poor science isn't just excessive cost due to overregulation; some regulations can actually increase risk—such as we found with infant formula. FDA economics is also problematic. FDA managers ensure that economists will produce analyses that support their decisions. The losers are small businesses and consumers, who don't have much of a voice in all of this. But soon, some consumers are going to take charge of their own food-related health. As more information emerges, consumers are likely to learn that trying to eat naturally, with clean labels, isn't making them safer or healthier. This will particularly apply to younger consumers that are more open to new food technologies.[344] Unlike in years past, they are more likely to ask questions about where food comes from, how it is made, and the risks and benefits.

Because of the vast gulf left by the FDA, inventors are redefining the problem, which is leading to innovative solutions. They don't recognize that there *is* a program—basically, a box. Regulators, both because of legal requirements and FDA's culture, cannot see anything outside of the box, and when they do, they appear to resent it.[63]

The technologies and sciences behind new food innovations include robotics, 3D printing, genetic engineering, precision fermentation, artificial intelligence (with machine learning), consumer monitoring technologies, nanotechnology, microbiome research, big data, augmented reality, and blockchain. These new technologies will help us not just to solve public health problems with food, but private health more generally.

It is impossible for the FDA to have experts in all the new technologies. Thus, it has two roles to play in this new world. One is to do what it has always done—to act as "cops." When firms are guilty of either intentional or negligent behavior (knowingly negligent) resulting in disease, the

---

63 Within the international food-standards organization, Codex, when confronted with private standards, had "significant anxiety…that the rapid pervasion of private food safety standards is serving to undermine the Commission's role," Henson and Humphrey, "The Impacts of Private Food Safety Standards on the Food Chain and on Public Standard-Setting Processes," paper prepared for *FAO/WHO*, May 2009, p. 1.

FDA must continue to act to take dangerous products off the market. This includes tracing back problems and identifying the root causes. This role is important, but getting new technologies into the market is more important.

The second role that the FDA can play is in the technological space, such as ensuring that obvious problems with new technologies do not stay on the market, creating biomarkers to allow consumers to monitor their health as their devices counsel them, and, in rare instances, using premarket review to approve products. What they should not do is to be a dam holding up technology. That can set public health on a slow slog upward that puts people's lives at risk. They can be heroes, but not by being autocratic.

I was compelled to write this book because no one seems to ever talk about it. Instead, we constantly hear how necessary the FDA is to keep our food safe. Maybe, but not in the way they are doing it now. The hope is that more people will begin to discuss this in the neighborhoods, in the media, and in Congress.

For me, after getting out, I would tell my students I am in step ten of the Twelve-Step Program of Bureaucrats Anonymous, but I am definitely getting better every day.

REFERENCES

1   Sinclair Lewis, *The Jungle,* (Digireads.com Publishing, 2015).

2   Robert Crunden, *Ministers of Reform* (University of Illinois Press, 1985), p. 188; William H. Harbaugh, *Power and Responsibility: The Life and Times of Theodore Roosevelt* (New York: Octagon Books, 1975), p. 247; Harvey Wiley, *An Autobiography* (The Bobbs-Merrill Company, 1930), p. 189.

3   Harbaugh, *The Life and Times of Theodore Roosevelt*, p. 189.

4   Harbaugh, *The Life and Times of Theodore Roosevelt*, p. 103–109.

5   Eleanor Foa Dienstag, *In Good Company: 125 Years at the Heinz Table* (New York: Warner Books, 1994).

6   Callan O'Laughlin, "Roosevelt Stirs House to Action," *Chicago Daily Tribune,* June 5, 1906.

7   Alex Ferguson, "Who Benefits From Raw Milk?," *Food Safety News,* February 15, 2010.

8   "Lawn Darts Are Banned," CPSC Publication 5053, https://www.cpsc.gov/s3fs-public/5053.pdf.

9   Richard J. Ronk, "History of the US Food and Drug Administration," interview by Robert Tucker and Ronald Ottes, May 10, 1995, https://wayback.archive-it.org/7993/20170723171932/https://www.fda.gov/downloads/AboutFDA/WhatWeDo/History/OralHistories/SelectedOralHistoryTranscripts/UCM328758.pdf.

10 Maggie Fox, "Get Lead out of Hair Dyes, FDA Orders," NBC News, October 30, 2018, https://www.nbcnews.com/health/health-news/get-lead-out-hair-dyes-fda-orders-n926186.

11 Allison Aubrey, "FDA Bans Use of 7 Synthetic Food Additives after Environmental Groups Sue," *The Salt,* October 6, 2018, https://www.npr.org/sections/thesalt/2018/10/06/655135633/fda-bans-use-of-7-synthetic-food-additives-after-environmental-groups-sue.

12 Farah Shaikh, "4 Advantages of Food Additives," Foods For Better Health, https://www.foodsforbetterhealth.com/advantages-of-food-additives-34825.

13   Sabin Russell, "Nixon's War on Cancer: Why It Mattered," Fred Hutch News Service, Sept 21, 2016.

14   Malcolm Gladwell, "Citing Law, FDA Bans Many Uses of Red Dye No. 3," *Washington Post,* January 30, 1990.

15   Edward J. Calabrese, "The Additive to Background Assumption in Cancer Risk Assessment: A Reappraisal," *Environmental Research* (2018), p. 175–204.

iii   Aimee Picchi, "Cheerios, Nature Valley Cereals Contain Roundup Ingredient, Study Finds," CBS News, June 13, 2019.

iv   Clark Carrington, *The Science-Policy Shell Game: The Probability of Truth* (Amazon Digital Services, 2016), Kindle.

16   Compound Interest, "Cosmetic Chemistry—The Compounds in Red Lipstick," *Cosmetic Chemistry*, August 18, 2014.

17   Bruce N. Ames et al., "Dietary Pesticides (99.99 Percent All Natural)," *Proceedings of the National Academy of Sciences* 87 pp. 7777-7781, October 1990.

18   Randal D. Shields, "Food and Drug Law: The Infant Formula Act of 1980," *Akron Law Review*, July 2015.

19   Shang-Yu Lin, "Infant Formula: A Comparison of Legislation in the United States and Taiwan," March 18, 2012.

20   Emily E. Stevens, "A History of Infant Feeding," *Journal of Perinatal Education* 18, no. 2 (Spring 2009), 32–39.

21   "Institute of Medicine Committee on Nutritional Status During Pregnancy and Lactation," *Nutrition During Lactation*, IOM, Washington, DC, 1991.

22   Barry Meier, "What Prompted Investigations into Pricing of Baby Formula," *New York Times*, January 19, 1991.

23   "Current Good Manufacturing Practices, Quality Control Procedures, Quality Factors, Notification Requirements, and Records and Reports, for Infant Formula," *Federal Register*, June 10, 2014.

24   Barbara W. Tuchman, *The March of Folly: From Troy to Vietnam"* (New York: Ballantine Books, 1984).

25   Todd Kliman, "How Michael Pollan, Alice Waters, and Slow Food Theorists Got It All Wrong: A Conversation with Food Historian (and Contrarian) Rachel Laudan," *Washingtonian,* May 29, 2015.

26   Jasmine Wiggins, "How Was Ketchup Invented," *National Geographic,* April 21, 2014.

27   Matt Blitz, "The Momentous Peanut Butter Hearings," *Today I Found Out,* December 18, 2014.

28   Federal Register / vol. 44, no. 247 / Friday, December 21, 1979 / Proposed Rules, p. 76997.

29   Federal Register / vol. 44, no. 247 / Friday, December 21, 1979 / Proposed Rules, p. 75993.

30   Mike Chase, *How to Become a Federal Criminal* (New York: Atria Books), p. 57.

31   Chase, *How to Become a Federal Criminal,* p. 98.

32   Michael R. Taylor, "Reforming Food Safety: A Model for the Future," Resources for the Future, February 2002.

33   Carl Sagan, *The Demon-Haunted World: Science as a Candle in the Dark* (New York: Ballantine Books, 1997).

34   "Ensuring Safe Food: From Production to Consumption," NCBI, https://www.ncbi.nlm.nih.gov/books/NBK209113.

35   "President Clinton Announces Food Safety Initiative," White House Archives, October 2, 1997, https://clintonwhitehouse4.archives.gov/WH/New/html/19971002-8886.html.

36   Mark Powell, "Trends in Reported Foodborne Illness in the United States, 1996–2013," *Risk Analysis* (2015), p. 9.

37   Tomohide Yasuda, "Food Safety Regulation in the United States: An Empirical and Theoretical Examination," *The Independent Review* 15, no.2 (Fall 2010), p. 203.

38   Tomohide, "Food Safety Regulation in the United States," p. 201–226.

39   Jerry Ellig, *Government Performance and Results* (New York: CRC Press, 2012).

40   Charles Seife, "How the FDA Manipulates the Media," *Scientific American*, October 1, 2016, https://www.scientificamerican.com/article/how-the-fda-manipulates-the-media/.

41   "Justification of Estimates for Appropriations Committees," FDA, DHHS, 2019.

42   James Q. Wilson, *Bureaucracy: What Government Agencies Do and Why They Do It* (New York: Basic Books Inc., 1989), p. 179.

43   Daniel Carpenter, *Reputation and Power* (Princeton: Princeton University Press, 2010), p. 18.

44   "Procedures for the Safe and Sanitary Processing and Importing of Fish and Fishery Products: Final Rule," *Federal Register* 60, no. 242 (December 18, 1995), https://www.govinfo.gov/content/pkg/FR-1995-12-18/html/95-30332.htm.

45   *Federal Register* 60, no. 242, p. 65107.

46   Richard Williams, "Guidance on Guidance," *Regulation* (Winter 2018–2019), p. 64.

47   William E. Gibson, "Mandatory Inspection of Fish Sought," *Sun Sentinel*, September 6, 1991.

48   Ron Nixon, "Catfish Farmers, Seeking Regulation to Fight Foreign Competition, Face Higher Bills," *New York Times,* March 20, 2015.

49   Amy Evans, "The Oysterman," *The Bitter Southerner*, https://bittersoutherner.com/the-oysterman#.XpDERohKiV8.

50   George McGovern, "George McGovern in the Journal," *Wall Street Journal,* October 21, 2012.

51   George McGovern, "A Politician's Dream Is a Businessman's Nightmare: A 1992 Column on the Realities of Running a Business" *Wall Street Journal,* October 21, 2012.

52   "Processing Parameters Needed to Control Pathogens in Cold-Smoked Fish," FDA, March 29, 2001, https://www.fda.gov/media/103624/download.

53   "Final Rule: Procedures for the Safe and Sanitary Processing and Importing of Fish and Fishery Products," *Federal Register* 60, no. 242 (December 18, 1995), p. 65906.

54   "Final Rule: Procedures for the Safe and Sanitary Processing."

55   "Joseph A. Levitt," Hogan Lovells, https://www.hoganlovells.com/en/joseph-levitt.

56   Gerardo Raminez, "An FDA Update on Egg Safety," *Food Safety Magazine,* April/May 2004.

57   Denise Powell, "Health Effects of Eggs: Where Do We Stand?," CNN Health, March 27, 2019.

58   Franziska Spritzler, "Are Whole Eggs and Egg Yolks Bad For You, or Good?," *Healthline,* July 12, 2016.

59   Joseph Lamour, "Americans Eat on Average Almost 300 Eggs a Year," Kitchn, April 30, 2019, https://www.thekitchn.com/americans-eat-on-average-almost-300-eggs-a-year-267411.

60   Thomas Sullivan, "A Tough Road: Cost to Develop One New Drug Is $2.6 Billion: Approval Rate for Drugs Entering Clinical Development is Less Than 12%," *Policy and Medicine*, March 21, 2019.

61   "Drug Approvals—From Invention to Market…A 12-Year Trip," MedicineNet, July 14, 1999.

62   "Dietary Supplement Health and Education Act (DSHEA)—20 Years Later—The Good, the Bad and the Ugly," *National Law Review*, June 7, 2014.

63   "Current Good Manufacturing Practice in Manufacturing, Packaging, Labeling, or Holding Operations for Dietary Supplements: Final Rule," Federal Register 72, no. 121 (June 25, 2007), p. 34766.

64   "Current Good Manufacturing Practice in Manufacturing," p. 34767.

65   "Current Good Manufacturing Practice in Manufacturing."

66   38 Fed. Reg. 2125 Jan. 19, 1973.

67   "Larry Groce—Junk Food Junkie (1976)," YouTube video, https://www.you-tube.com/watch?v=jQnIL-XPerQ.

68   W. Robbins, "Nutrition Study Finds US Lacks a Goal," *New York Times*, June 22, 1974, p. 21.

69   "CBS Documentary Hunger in America (1968)," YouTube video, https://www.youtube.com/watch?v=h94bq4JfMAA.

70   "Dietary Goals for the United States," S. Rep., at p. 52 (1978), https://thescienceofnutrition.files.wordpress.com/2014/03/dietary-goals-for-the-united-states.pdf.

71   "Dietary Goals for the United States."

72   38 Fed. Reg. 2125 Jan. 19, 1973.

73   "Larry Groce—Junk Food Junkie (1976)."

74   "ARGS Residency," https://www.argsresidency.com/.

75   "George McGovern's Legacy: The Dietary Goals for the United States," the McDougal Newsletter 11, no. 10 (October 2012), https://www.drmcdougall.com/misc/2012nl/oct/mcgovern.htm.

76   Phillip J. Hilts, "U.S. Plans to make Sweeping Changes in Labels on Food," *The New York Times,* March 8, 1990.

77   Nutrition Labeling and Education Act, Pub. L. No. 101-535, 104 Stat. 2356, 21 USC, Sec. 2. Nutrition Labeling (F)(b) ((1)(A).

78   This was also cited in Jerry Ellig and Richard Williams, "David versus Godzilla: Bigger Stones," working paper 19-23 in the C. Boyden Gray Center for the Study of the Administrative State, September 13, 2019.

79   *Federal Register* 44, no. 247 (December 21, 1979), proposed rules, 75992.

80   "Nutrition Labeling: Small Business, Exemption Public Forums," *Federal Register* 57, no. 88 (May 6, 1992).

81   Donald R. Arbuckle, "The Role of Analysis on the 17 Most Political Acres on the Face of the Earth," *Risk Analysis,* June 2017.

82   Richard Belzer, "Areas of Concern about FDA's Seafood HACCP Rule RIA," November 9, 1995.

83   "Regulatory Program of the United States Government, April 1, 1990–March 31, 1991," p. 26.

84   "Michael R. Taylor," interview by Suzanne White Junod and Ronald T. Ottes, December 23, 1992, p. 17.

85   "Regulatory Impact Analysis of the Proposed Rules to Amend the Food labeling Regulations," *Federal Register* 56, no. 229 (November 27, 1991), p. 60870.

86   Cristin E. Kearns et al., "Sugar Industry and Coronary Heart Disease Research," *JAMA Intern Med* 176, no. 11 (2016).

87 R.B. McGandy, D.M. Hegsted, and F.J. Stare, "Dietary Fats, Carbohydrates and Atherosclerotic Vascular Disease," *New England Journal of Medicine*, August 3, 1967.

88 Melissa Bailey, "Sugar Industry Secretly Paid for Favorable Harvard Research," StatNews, September 12, 2016, https://www.statnews.com/2016/09/12/sugar-industry-harvard-research/.

89 "Williams Hubbard," interview by Michael R. Taylor, Suzanne White Junod, and Ronald T. Ottes, December 23, 1992, p. 13.

90 (Lewis and Yetley, 1990; NFPA, 1990),

91 Alan S. Levy et al., "Nutrition Labeling Formats: Performance and Preference," *Food Technology*, July 1991, p. 121.

92 Regulatory Impact Analysis of the Proposed Rules to Amend the Food labeling Regulations," *Federal Register* 56, no. 229 (November 27, 1991), https://www.foodrisk.org/files/NLEA-Proposed-60856-60877.pdf.

93 Regulatory Impact Analysis of the Proposed Rules to Amend the Food labeling Regulations," *Federal Register* 58, no. 3, January 6, 1993, http://foodrisk.org/files/NLEA-2927-2941.pdf.

94 "Michael R. Taylor," interview by Suzanne White Junod and Ronald T. Ottes, p. 58.

95 Bonnie Taub-Dix, *Read It Before You Eat It: Taking You from Label to Table* (CreateSpace Independent Publishing Platform, 2017).

96 "Oral History Interview with David A. Kessler, M.D. Commissioner of Food and Drugs US Food and Drug Administration November 1990–February 1997," https://www.fda.gov/media/129170/download.

97 Omri Ben-Shahar and Carl Schneider, *More Than You Wanted to Know: The Failure of Mandated Disclosure* (Princeton: Princeton University Press, 2014), p. 8.

98 Alexander Persoskie et al., "US Consumers' Understanding of Nutrition Labels in 2013: The Importance of Health Literacy," Prev Chronic Diks 2017, 14:17006.

99 "Fat Menus Don't Guarantee Skinny Customers," Center for Consumer Freedom, 2007, reprinted from chapter 9: "What Role Does Food Away from Home Play in the Diets of Food Assistance Recipients," Charlotte Tuttle et al., in "USDA America's Eating Habits: Food Away from Home?," September 2018, p. 143.

100 "Nutrition Facts Food Labels Are Too Confusing for Most People, FDA Researchers Say," Reuters, January 24, 2013.

101 "Food Labeling Survey," International Food Information Council Foundation and the American Heart Association, January 2019.

102   Jania Matthews, "Americans Find Doing Their Own Taxes Simpler Than Improving Diet and Health," IFIC, May 23, 2012.

103   Jayachandran Variyam, "Do Nutrition Labels Improve Dietary Outcomes?," *Health Economics* 17 (2008), p. 704.

104   "Long-Term Trends in Diabetes," CDC's Division of Diabetes Translation, April 2017, https://www.cdc.gov/diabetes/statistics/slides/long_term_trends.pdf.

105   "Type 2 Diabetes in Children," Healthline, https://www.healthline.com/health/type-2-diabetes-children.

106   Anicka Slachta, "Total heart disease deaths rise in US," *Cardiovascular Business,* August 27, 2019.

107   Christopher Wanjek, "New 'Smart Choices' Food Labels Are Deceptive," *LiveScience*, September 9, 2009.

108   https://www.youtube.com/watch?v=MYIAdd2Z9Mc.

109   "Remarks by the First Lady on a Nutrition Facts Label Announcement," Obama White House Archives website, https://obamawhitehouse.archives.gov/the-press-office/2014/02/27/remarks-first-lady-nutrition-facts-label-announcement.

110   Daniel S. Putler and Elizabeth Frazao, "Assessing the effects of Diet/Health Awareness on the Consumption and Composition of Fat Intake," *Economics of Food Safety* (Amsterdam: Elsevier Sciences Publishing Co.), p. 248.

111   Denise Minger, *Death by Food Pyramid* (Malibu: Primal Blueprint Publishing, 2013), p. 155.

112   Minger, "Death by Food Pyramid," p. 157.

113   Olga Khazan, "When Trans Fats Were Healthy," *The Atlantic*, November 8, 2013.

114   Olga Khazan, "When Trans Fats Were Healthy," *The Atlantic,* November 8, 2013.

115   Radley Balko, "Stop Doing What I Said," Cato Institute, June 23, 2006.

116   IBID.

117   John D. Graham and Jonathan Baert Wiener, *Risk vs. Risk: Tradeoffs in Protecting Health and the Environment* (Cambridge: Harvard University Press, 1997).

118   "Small Entity Compliance Guide: Trans Fatty Acids in Nutrition Labeling, Nutrient Content Claims, and Health Claims," US Food and Drug Administration, August, 2003.

119   Harvard Center for Risk Analysis, https://www.hsph.harvard.edu/hcra/.

120   "Final Determination Regarding Partially Hydrogenated Oils (Removing Trans Fat)," *Federal Register* (May 18, 2018).

121 Subrata Thakar, "FDA Bans the Use of Artificial Trans Fats in Foods," *Cardiovascular Business*, June 21, 2018.

122 Goran Blazeski and Thomas Nast, "The Man Who Invented Santa Claus," Vintage News, December 9, 2016.

123 Tom Standage, *An Edible History of Humanity* (New York: Bloomsbury, 2009).

124 "Childhood Obesity Facts: Prevalence of Childhood Obesity in the United States," CDC website, https://www.cdc.gov/obesity/data/childhood.html.

125 "Percentage of Children (Ages 10–17) Who Are Overweight or Obese," KFF.org, https://www.kff.org/other/state-indicator/overweightobese-children/?currentTimeframe=0&sortModel=%7B%22colId%22:%22Location%22,%22sort%22:%22asc%22%7D.

126 "Overweight and Obesity Statistics," NIH website, https://www.niddk.nih.gov/health-information/health-statistics/overweight-obesity.

127 Nicole Rura, "Close to half of U.S. population projected to have obesity by 2030," *The Harvard Gazette,* December 18, 2019.

128 K. Flegal, M. Carroll, R. Kuczmarski, and C. Johnson, "Overweight and Obesity in the United States: Prevalence and Trends, 1960–1994," *International Journal of Obesity* 22 (1998), p. 39–47.

129 Susan K. Boyer, ed., "Calories Count: Report of the Working Group on Obesity," *Vidyya Medical News Service* 6, no. 74 (March 2004), http://www.vidyya.com/vol6/v6i74_3.htm.

130 "White House Takes Aim at Obesity," CNN, November 19, 2004, https://www.cnn.com/2004/HEALTH/diet.fitness/03/12/obesity.campaign/.

131 "The $72 Billion Weight Loss & Diet Control Market in the United States, 2019–2023: Why Meal Replacements Are Still Booming, but Not OTC Diet Pills—ResearchAndMarkets.com," Business Wire, February 25, 2019.

132 "CFR—Code of Federal Regulations Title 21," US Food and Drug Administration, https://www.accessdata.fda.gov/scripts/cdrh/cfdocs/cfcfr/CFRSearch.cfm?fr=101.9&SearchTerm=nutrition%20label.

133 Mitra Toosi and Teresa L. Morisi, "Women in the Workforce Before, During, and After the Great Recession," US Bureau of Labor Statistics, July 2017.

134 Michelle J. Saksena et al., "America's Eating Habits: Food Away from Home," USDA Economic Research Service, September 2018.

135 Cheryl D. Fryar et al., "Fast Food Consumption Among Adults in the United States, 2013–2016," NCHS Data Brief, no. 322, October 2018.

136 "Menu Labeling Rule: Key Facts for Industry," FDA website, https://www.fda.gov/media/116000/download.

137 Joshua Petimar et al., "Estimating the Effect of Calorie Menu Labeling on Calories Purchased in a Large Restaurant Franchise in the Southern United States: Quasi-Experimental Study," BMJ, October 30, 2019.

138 Anthelme Brillat-Savarin wrote in *Physiologie du gout, ou meditations de gastronomie transcendante, 1826*: "*Dis-moi ce que tu manges, je te dirai ce que tu es.*" [Tell me what you eat, and I will tell you what you are].

139 John P. A. Ioannidis, "Why Most Published Research Findings are False," PLOS Medicine, August 30, 2005.

140 Marcia Angell, "Drug Companies and Doctors: A Story of Corruption," the *New York Review*, January 15 2009, http://www.nybooks.com/articles/archives/2009/jan/15/drug-companies-doctorsa-story-of-corruption/.

141 Quoted in Bill Sacks et al., "Epidemiology Without Biology: False Paradigms, Unfounded Assumptions, and Specious Statistics in Radiation Science (with Commentaries by Inge Schmitz-Feuerhake and Christopher Busby and a Reply by the Authors)," *Biological Theory* (2016).

142 "Bush Mocks Bush," BBC News, March 25, 2001, http://news.bbc.co.uk/2/hi/americas/1241240.stm.

143 "How to Understand and Use the Nutrition Facts Label," FDA website, https://www.fda.gov/food/nutrition-education-resources-materials/how-understand-and-use-nutrition-facts-label.

144 "Dietary Guidelines for Americans," USDA Food Nutrition Service website, https://www.fns.usda.gov/cnpp/dietary-guidelines-americans.

145 "Food & Nutrition," Health.gov, http://health.gov/dietaryguidelines/.

146 https://health.gov/sites/default/files/2019-10/1980thin.pdf.

147 https://www.ahajournals.org/doi/full/10.1161/01.cir.94.7.1795

148 N.D. Kohatsu, J.G. Robinson, J.C. Torner, "Evidence-Based Public Health: An Evolving Concept," *American Journal of Preventive Medicine* 27 (2004), p. 417–21.

149 Minger, "Death by Food Pyramid," p. 7.

150 Misti K. Gueron et al., "What Are the Flaws of MyPlate," *Everyday Health*, https://www.everydayhealth.com/diet-nutrition/experts-what-are-the-flaws-of-myplate.aspx.

151 F.O. Uruakpa et al., "Awareness and Use of MyPlate Guidelines in Making Food Choices," *Procedia Food Science* 2 (2013), p. 180–186.

152 Karen Siegel et al., "Association of Higher Consumption of Foods Derived from Subsidized Commodities with Adverse Cardiometabolic Risk Among US Adults," *JAMA Internal Medicine,* August 1, 2016.

153 "2015–2020 Dietary Guidelines," Health.gov, https://health.gov/our-work/food-nutrition/2015-2020-dietary-guidelines/guidelines/chapter-2/current-eating-patterns-in-the-united-states/#figure-2-1-desc-toggle.

154 Jailen Johnson, "Fad Diets are Bad Diets," American Council on Science and Health, July 2, 2018, https://www.acsh.org/news/2018/07/02/fad-diets-are-bad-diets-13134.

155 Stacey Colino, "How Much Do Doctors Learn About Nutrition," *US News & World Report*, December 7, 2016.

156 Elizabeth Narins, "The 21 Craziest Diets Ever—Debunked," *Cosmopolitan*, January 21, 2015.

157 "The $72 Billion Weight Loss & Diet Control Market in the United States."

158 Quote from Sharon M. Donovan of the University of Illinois at Urbana Champaign in Andrea Petersen, "Do Babies Need to Eat Meat," *Wall Street Journal,* October 12, 2020.

159 Nina Teicholz, *The Big Fat Surprise: Why Butter, Meat and Cheese Belong in a Healthy Diet* (New York: Simon and Schuster, 2014).

160 Nina Teicholz, *Wall Street Journal*, September 11, 2018.

161 Debbie Koenig, "Controversial Studies Say It's Ok to Eat Red Meat," WebMd, September 30, 2019, https://www.webmd.com/diet/news/20190930/controversial-studies-say-its-ok-to-eat-red-meat.

162 David L. Katz, "Meat Eating and Your Health: Is There, Really, News?," LinkedIn, September 30, 2019, https://www.linkedin.com/pulse/meat-eating-your-health-really-news-david/.

163 Gina Kolata, "Eat Less Red Meat, Scientists Said. Now Some Believe That Was Bad Advice," *New York Times*, September 30, 2019, https://www.nytimes.com/2019/09/30/health/red-meat-heart-cancer.html.

164 Katz, "Meat Eating and Your Health."

165 "Research Involving Prisoners," University of Pittsburg Human Research Protection Office website, https://www.irb.pitt.edu/content/research-involving-prisoners.

166 "The Rooster Who Crowed Too Soon (A Fable)," FrumpyHausFrau (blog), January 4, 2012, http://frumpyhausfrau.com/farm/the-rooster-who-crowed-too-soon-a-fable/.

167 "How Science Goes Wrong," *The Economist*, October 21, 2013, https://www.economist.com/leaders/2013/10/21/how-science-goes-wrong. p://calteches.library.caltech.edu/51/2/CargoCult.pdf.

168 Laura Eggerston, "Lancet Retracts 12-Year-Old Article Linking Autism to MMR Vaccines," *CMAJ*, March 9, 2010.

169 Karin Roberts, "When It Comes to Vaccines, Celebrities Often Call the Shots," NBC News, October 28, 2018, https://www.nbcnews.com/health/health-care/when-it-comes-vaccines-celebrities-often-call-shots-n925156.

170 "From Arvind Suresh, "Autism Increase Mystery Solved? No, It's Not Vaccines, GMOs, Glyphosate—Or Organic Foods," September 22, 2019, re-

printed from the Geneticliteracyproject.org, https://geneticliteracyproject.org/2016/09/22/autism-increase-mystery-solved-no-its-not-vaccines-gmos-glyphosate-or-organic-foods/.

171 https://www.pbs.org/wgbh/frontline/article/jenny-mccarthy-were-not-an-anti-vaccine-movement-were-pro-safe-vaccine/.

172 Brett Dahlberg, "Cornell Food Researcher's Downfall Raises Larger Questions for Science," NPR, September 26, 2018.

173 "How Science Goes Wrong."

174 Requoted in Kabat, p. 39, from G. Taubes, "Epidemiology Faces Its Limits," *Science* 269 (1995), p. 164–69.

175 Michelle Minton, "Heads in the Sand: How Politics Created the Salt-Hypertension Myth," *Scientocracy,* edited by Patrick J Michaels, and Terence Kealey, CATO Institute, Washington DC, 2019, p. 105.

176 Minton, "Heads in the Sand," p. 116.

177 Minton, "Heads in the Sand," p. 117.

178 Gary Taubes, "The (Political) Science of Salt," *Science* (1998), p. 898.

179 https://www.cdc.gov/nchs/nhanes/wweia.htm .

180 Edward Archer et al., "Government Dietary Guidelines," Mercatus working paper, 2017, https://www.mercatus.org/system/files/mercatus-archer-gov27t-dietary-guidelines-v1.pdf.

181 "Meet the Faces behind FDA Science," FDA website, https://www.fda.gov/science-research/fda-science-jobs-and-scientific-professional-development/meet-faces-behind-fda-science.

182 "FDA's Key Principles of Scientific Integrity," FDA website, https://www.fda.gov/science-research/about-science-research-fda/fdas-key-principles-scientific-integrity.

183 Brian Roe et al., "The Impact of Health Claims on Consumer Search and Product Evaluation Outcomes: Results from FDA Experimental Data," *Journal of Public Policy and Marketing* 18, no. 1 (Spring 1999), p. 89–105.

184 Vicki S. Freimuth et al., "Health Advertising: Prevention for Profit," *AJPH* 78, no. 5 (May 1988).

185 See *Pearson*, 164 F.3d at 659.

186 "Letter Regarding Dietary Supplement Health Claim for Vitamin E and Heart Disease (Docket No 99P-4375)," FDA, February 9, 2001.

187 The denial letter was to Jonathan Emord, Esq., http://wayback.archive-it.org/7993/20171115122059/https://www.fda.gov/Food/IngredientsPackagingLabeling/LabelingNutrition/ucm073251.htm.

188 "Health Claims," Emford and Associates website, http://emord.com/firm-profile/health-claims/.

189 "Standards for Produce Safety," FDA website, https://www.fda.gov/media/94332/download.

190 Richard Williams, "Regulatory Reform Is a Start, but We Need New Ways of Making Laws," Real Clear Policy, July 1, 2019, https://www.realclearpolicy.com/articles/2019/07/01/regulatory_reform_is_a_start_but_we_need_new_ways_of_making_laws_111229.html.

191 "About Risk," JIFSAN, https://jifsan.umd.edu/training/risk/about.

192 Adam Thierer, "Reconsidering Technology During the COVID-19 Crisis," *Discourse,* March 24, 2020.

193 Kabat, p. 116.

194 Kavin Senapathy, "If you Can't Pronounce It, Don't Eat It' and Other Food Mantras That Don't Hold Water," *Forbes,* June 26, 2017.

195 Mark Hyman, *Food Fix* (New York: Little, Brown Spark, 2020), p. 260.

196 Cynthia R. Greenlee, "People Used to Be so Scared of Coffee That Bach Wrote a Cantata about It," *Bon Appetit*, June 14, 2017.

197 Hemraj Sharma, "A Detail Chemistry of Coffee and Its Analysis," *Coffee,* March 20, 2020.

198 Raghavendra Gupta, "How Many Chemicals Present in a Cup of Coffee?," Research Gate, https://www.researchgate.net/post/How-many-chemicals-present-in-a-cup-of-coffee.

199 Bee Wilson, "Why We Fell for Clean Eating," *The Guardian*, August 11, 2017.

200 Wilson, "Why We Fell for Clean Eating."

201 Hyman, *Food Fix*, p. 190.

202 Hyman, *Food Fix*, p. 226–27.

203 Tim Crowe, "Broccoli Is Bad for You, Like Really Toxic Bad," *Thinking Nutrition*, June 4, 2015.

204 Marion Nestle, "Superfoods Are a Marketing Ploy," *The Atlantic*," October 23, 2018.

205 Ed Yong, *I Contain Multitudes: The Microbes within Us and a Grander View of Life* (New York: Harper Collins, 2015), p. 183.

206 "Dirty Dozen: EWG's 2021 Shopper's Guide to Pesticides in Produce," EWG, https://www.ewg.org/foodnews/dirty-dozen.php.

207 Bruce Ames and L.S. Gold, "Dietary Pesticides (99.99% All Natural)," *Proceedings of the National Academy of Sciences* 87, no. 1 (1990), p. 7777–81.

208 "Pesticide Residues," USDA National Agricultural Library website, https://www.nal.usda.gov/fsrio/pesticide-residues.

209 Claudia Reinhardt and Bill Ganzel, "The Science of Hybrids," *Wessels: Living History Farm,* 2003 https://livinghistoryfarm.org/farminginthe30s/crops_03.html.

210 Tom Standage, *An Edible History of Humanity* (New York: Bloomsbury, 2009), p. 26–27.

211 Standage, *An Edible History of Humanity*, p. 26.

212 David Julian McClements, *Future Foods: How Modern Science is Transforming the Way We Eat* (Switzerland: Springer Nature, 2019), p. 54.

213 McClements, *Future Foods*, p. 284.

214 Colin Hill, "RDA for Microbes, Are You Getting Your Daily Dose?," *The Biochemist* 40 (August 2018).

215 "FTC Complaint Charges Deceptive Advertising by POM Wonderful," Federal Trade Commission website, September 27, 2010, https://www.ftc.gov/news-events/press-releases/2010/09/ftc-complaint-charges-deceptive-advertising-pom-wonderful.

216 This discussion is taken from Edward J. Calabrese, "From Muller to Mechanism: How LNT Became the Default Model for Cancer Risk Assessment," in *Environmental Pollution* 241 (May 22, 2018).

217 Edward J. Calabrese, "From Muller to Mechanism," p. 293.

218 https://www.asmalldoseoftoxicology.org/paracelsus.

219 Robert Golden et al., "Assessing the Scientific Basis of the Linear No Threshold (LNT) Model with Threshold Models for Cancer Risk Assessment of Radiation and Chemicals," *Chemico-Biological Interactions* 301 (March 1, 2019), p 2–5.

220 Doris Stanley, "Backgrounder: Food Irradiation," USDA Agricultural Research Service, December 10, 1997.

221 Stanley, "Backgrounder."

222 Adam Lieberman and Simona Kwon, "Facts Versus Fears: A Review of the Greatest Unfounded Health Scares of Recent Times," *American Council on Science and Health*, September 2004.

223 Joseph H. Hotchkiss, "Lambasting Louis: Lessons from Pasteurization," in Allan Eaglesham, Steven G. Pueppke, and Ralph W.F. Hardy, eds., *Genetically Modified Food and the Consumer*, National Agricultural Biotechnology Council, 2001.

224 Grace Klonski, "Retired Engineers Work to Enhance Science Education," LaserFocusWorld, January 15, 2007.

225 "Annual Report 2016," Reset, https://resetonline.org/wp-content/uploads/2014/09/2016annualreport.pdf.

226 Harold I. Sharlin, "Prototype Study in Conveying Health Risk Issues," *Irradiation of Foods* 20 (June 3, 1986), p. 4–20.

227 Sharlin, "Prototype Study," p. 8.

228 Dennis G. Maki, "Don't Eat the Spinach—Controlling Foodborne Infectious Disease," NEJM, November 9, 2006.

229 Gary Marchant, "Lesson for New Technologies," Mercatus working paper, August 26, 2008.

230 USDA "Irradiation and Food Safety FAQ https://www.fsis.usda.gov/food-safety/safe-food-handling-and-preparation/food-safety-basics/irradiation-and-food-safety-faq faq#:~:text=To%20date%2C%20the%20FDA%20and,raw%20poultry%2C%20and%20red%20meats.

231 Huaqiang Yang et al., "Genome Editing of Pigs for Agriculture and Biomedicine," *Frontiers in Genetics,* September 4, 2018.

232 Colin G. Scanes, "Animals and Human Disease: Zoonosis, Vectors, Food-Borne Diseases, and Allergies," in *Animals and Human Society* (Cambridge, MA: Academic Press, 2018), p. 4332–4354.

233 Colin Hill, "RDA for Microbes—Are You Getting Your Daily Dose?," *Food Production*, August 2018.

234 Donovan Alexander, "Here Are 5 Things You Should Know About Lab-Grown Meat," *Interesting Engineering*, December 12, 2018.

235 Francis Moore Lappé, *Diet for a Small Planet* (New York: Ballantine Books, 1971).

236 Yuval Noah Harari, "Industrial Farming Is One of the Worst Crimes in History," *The Guardian*, September 25, 2015.

237 Harari, *Sapiens* (New York: HarperCollins Publishers, 2018).

238 Harari, "Industrial Farming."

239 Alex Tekip, "Data and Technology Offer Ways to Improve Quality of Life for Farmers and Animals," *Michigan State University AgBio Research*, September 23, 2019.

240 Percy Bysshe Shelley, *A Vindication of Natural Diet,* Smith and Davy, Queen Street, Seven Dials, 1813.

241 An Notenbaert, quoted in "Livestock Scientists, No Your Meat-Free Diet Will Not Save the Planet," Fast Company, December 18, 2020.

242 Fortune, Aidan,"Belcampo Meat Co: 'We want to be an agent of change in the meat industry" - PODCAST," *Food navigator-usa.com*, May 1, 2020.

243 Megan Webb, "Studies Favor Diets Containing Meat but Consumers Have Alternatives," *University of Minnesota Extension,* September 2018.

244 Evan Folds, "The History of Hydroponics," March 10, 2018. https://medium.com/@evanfolds/the-history-of-hydroponics-99eb6628d205

245 "Aztec Agriculture: Floating Farms Fed the People," History on the Net , January 8, 2021, https://www.historyonthenet.com/aztec-agriculture-floating-farms-fed-the-people.

246 McClements, *Future* Foods, p. 10.

247 Winston Churchill, "Fifty Years Hence," *Strand Magazine*.

248 J. Poore and T. Nemecek, "Reducing Food's Environmental Impacts through Producers and Consumers," *360 Science* (2018), p. 987–92.

249 Ed Gent, "Precision Fermentation: What It Is, and How It Could Make Farming Obsolete," Singularity Hub, January 19, 2020.

250 Jay Yarrow, "This Apocryphal Story about the Telephone Should Be an Inspiration to Every Young Company," *Business Insider,* January 2, 2014.

251 "What Is Happening to Agrobiodiversity?," FAO, http://www.fao.org/3/y5609e/y5609e02.htm#TopOfPage.

252 Dillon Thompson, "Disney World Fans Are Divided over the Park's 'Disgusting' New Food Item: 'Does Not Sound Appetizing," Yahoo! News, January 25, 2021, https://www.yahoo.com/news/disney-world-fans-freaking-park-175803420.html.

253 Paul Enriquez, "CRISPR GMOs," *North Carolina Journal of Law and Technology* 18, no. 4 (May 2017), p. 473.

254 "GMO vs Gene Editing vs Genetic Engineering," Nanalyze, June 22, 2017, https://www.nanalyze.com/2017/06/gmo-vs-gene-editing-vs-genetic-engineering/.

255 Courtney Schmidt and Lon Swanson, "Genetically Modified vs. Gene Editing," Wells Fargo website, https://global.wf.com/hub_article/genetically-modified-vs-gene-editing/.

256 Ramazon Beyaz and Mustafa Yildiz, "The Use of Gamma Irradiation in Plant Mutation Breeding," IntechOpen, November 17, 2017, https://www.intechopen.com/books/plant-engineering/the-use-of-gamma-irradiation-in-plant-mutation-breeding.

257 Scott Haskell, "CRISPR and Our Food Supply: What's Next in Feeding the World?," Michigan State University, October 13, 2020.

258 Jennifer Kuzma, "Regulating Gene-Edited Crops," *Issues in Science and Technology* (Fall 2018).

259 Catherine Tubb and Tony Seba, "Rethinking Food and Agriculture 2020–2030," RethinkX sector disruption report, September 2019, p. 14.

260 Rebecca Boyle, "7 Amazing Ways Nanotechnology is Changing the World," *Popular Science*, November 14, 2012.

261 Nathan Donahue, "What Was the Most Important Breakthrough in Nanotechnology In 2018?," *Forbes*, January 3, 2019.

262 Katharine Sanderson, "What You Need to Know about Nano-Food," *The Guardian*, April 26, 2013.

263 P. Müller and M. Schmid, "Intelligent Packaging in the Food Sector: A Brief Overview," *Foods* 8, no. 1 (2019), p. 16.

264 McClements, *Future Foods*, p. 301.

265 McClements, *Future Foods*, p. 308.

266 "Fight Bac Campaigns," FDA website, https://www.fda.gov/food/buy-store-serve-safe-food/fight-bacr-campaigns.

267 "Food Safety Survey," Office of Disease Prevention and Health Promotion website, https://health.gov/healthypeople/objectives-and-data/data-sources-and-methods/data-sources/food-safety-survey.

268 "Emerson Survey: New Food Safety Technologies Rising in Importance for Consumers," December 1, 2020.

269 Carolota V., "A Guide to 3D Printed Food—Revolution in the Kitchen?," 3Dnatives, February 4, 2019, https://www.3dnatives.com/en/3d-printing-food-a-new-revolution-in-cooking/#!.

270 Donovan Alexander, "3D Printing Will Change the Way You Eat in 2020 and Beyond," *Interesting Engineering*, March 27, 2020.

271 "About Food Waste," Move for Hunger, https://moveforhunger.org/food-waste.

272 Niamh Michail, "Top of Form Cooking with 'Pure Chemical Compounds' Is the Future of Food, Says Hervé This," Food navigator.com, February 27, 2018.

273 Frederick J. Angulo et al., "Eating in Restaurants: A Risk Factor for Foodborne Disease," *Clinical Infectious Diseases* (November 15, 2006).

274 "FDA Releases Decoding the Food Code: Information to Assist the User, an Online Based Training Module," FDA, June 14, 2019.

275 "FDA Report on the Occurrence of Foodborne Illness Risk Factors in Fast Food and Full Service Restaurants, 2013–2014."

276 Lana Bandoim, "Mass Production of a Self-Driving Restaurant Robot Is Coming," *Forbes,* January 24, 2020.

277 "Imagining a New Culinary Possibility," Creator, https://www.creator.rest/.

278 Bandoim, "Mass Production of a Self-Driving Restaurant Robot."

279 Jane McGrath, "10 Costly Food Recalls," How Stuff Works, https://money.howstuffworks.com/10-food-recalls.htm#pt9.

280 James Andrews, "DNA Spray-on Technology Could Revolutionize Food Traceability," *Food Safety News*, November 17, 2014.

281 Bridget Hayden et al., "Blockchain: Intersections with Food Safety and Intellectual Property," *Food Safety Magazine,* November 5, 2019.

282 Joe Desantis, "Hey FDA, Hands off My Fitness Tracker," *The Hill*, September 17, 2020.

283 Judith Brown, "Food Nutrition Labels," *PediaTrust,* 1/2/2018. https://pediatrust.com/Blog/January-2018/FOOD-NUTRITION-LABELS-ARE-YOU-CONFUSED.

284 "How to Understand and Use the Nutrition Facts Label."

285 Habit.com.

286   David Kessler, *Fast Carbs, Slow Carbs: The Simple Truth about Food, Weight, and Disease* (New York: HarperCollins, 2020).

287   Shoshanna Solomon, "Startup's 'Smart Toilet Bowl' Scans Poop and Urine for Medical Insights," the *Times of Israel*, November 9, 2020.

288   "Personalised Nutrition Smart Patch to Be Developed in Australia," RMIT University, April 27, 2020.

289   McClements, *Future Foods*, p. 249.

290   Michael Daniel and Tollefsbol Trygve, "Epigenetic Linkage of Aging, Cancer and Nutrition," *Journal of Experimental Biology* (January 1, 2015), p. 59–70.

291   "18 Portable Health Gadgets That Can Change Your Life," *Travel Away*, April 17, 2020. https://travelaway.me/portable-health-gadgets/.

292   Mariëtte Abrahams, "The Personalized Nutrition Trend—How Digital Health Brands Can Revolutionize Healthcare," MedTech Engine, May 16, 2017, https://medtechengine.com/article/personalised-nutrition/.

293   RAND Corporation, "Chronic Conditions in America: Price and Prevalence," *RAND REVIEW*, July 12, 2017.

294   Richard Williams et al., "Health Options Foreclosed: How the FDA Denies Americans the Benefits of Medical Research," Mercatus working paper, September 2016.

295   Richard Williams et al., "US Medical Devices, Choices and Consequences," *Mercatus Research*, October 2015.

296   "Food Labeling," *Code of Federal Regulations* 21, no. 2 (April 1, 2020), https://www.accessdata.fda.gov/scripts/cdrh/cfdocs/cfcfr/CFRsearch.cfm?-fr=101.93.

297   Williams et al., "US Medical Devices: Choices and Consequences."

298   Rodney Dietert, *The Human Superorganism: How the Microbiome is Revolutionizing the Pursuit of a Healthy Life* (New York: Dutton, 2016), p. 46.

299   Yong, *I Contain Multitudes*, p. 10.

300   Yong, *I Contain Multitudes*, p. 145.

301   Yong, *I Contain Multitudes*, p. 251.

302   See Dietert, *The Human Superorganism*.

303   Dietert, *The Human Superorganism*, p. 65.

304   Yong, *I Contain Multitudes*, p. 264.

305   Dietert, *The Human Superorganism*, p. 139.

306   Joe Myxter, "Gut Microbiome Implicated in Healthy Aging and Longevity," *ISB,* February 18, 2021.

307   Yong, *I Contain Multitudes*, p. 71.

308   M. Dittman, "Hughes's Germ Phobia Revealed in Psychological Autopsy," *American Psychological Association* 36, no. 7 (July/August, 2005), p. 102.

309   Yong, *I Contain Multitudes*, p. 256–57.

310 Yong, *I Contain Multitudes*.

311 Yong, *I Contain Multitudes*, p. 129.

312 Dietert, *The Human Superorganism*, p. 27.

313 McClements, *Future Foods*, p. 217.

314 Dietert, *The Human Superorganism*, p. 235.

315 Craig Miller and Jordan Gilmore, "Detection of Quorum-Sensing Molecules for Pathogenic Molecules Using Cell-Based and Cell-Free Biosensors," *Antibiotics,* May 16, 2020.

316 Yong, *I Contain Multitudes*, p. 239.

317 Claire Ainsworth, "Therapeutic Microbes to Tackle Disease," *Nature*, January 20, 2020.

318 Ainsworth, "Therapeutic Microbes."

319 Yong, *I Contain Multitudes*, p. 233.

320 Williams, Richard A. and Kathryn Ghani, "A New Role for the FDA in Medical Device Regulation," Center for Growth and Opportunity at Utah State University policy paper," June 2019, https://www.thecgo.org/wp-content/uploads/2020/07/A-New-Role-for-the-FDA-in-Medical-Device-Regulation.pdf.

321 https://www.mercatus.org/sites/default/files/RichardWilliams-Rehm.mp3.

322 Richard Williams, "A New Role for the FDA in Food Safety," Mercatus Center working paper, November 15, 2010, https://www.mercatus.org/publications/regulation/new-role-fda-food-safety.

323 Richard Williams, "Federal Regulation of Food Safety," testimony before the US Senate Committee on Homeland Security and Governmental Affairs, August 17, 2016.

324 Matt Ridley, *The Rational Optimist: How Prosperity Evolves* (New York: Harper Collins, 2010), 182.

325 "Food Safety: Federal Oversight of Seafood Does Not Sufficiently Protect Consumers," Government Accountability Office, January 2001.

326 https://www.mercatus.org/sites/default/files/RichardWilliamsRehm.mp3

327 Williams, "A New Role for the FDA in Food Safety,"

328 "Foodborne Illness Outbreaks," Food Safety News, May 15, 2021, https://www.foodsafetynews.com/foodborne-illness-outbreaks/.

329 "Food Recalls," Find Law, https://injury.findlaw.com/product-liability/food-recalls.html.

330 https://www.goodhousekeeping.com/institute/about-the-institute/a17940/good-housekeeping-institute-timeline/.

331 "Recall: The Food Industry's Biggest Threat to Profitability," *Food Safety Magazine*, October 2012.

332 "Former Peanut Company President Receives Largest Criminal Sentence in Food Safety Case: Two Others also Sentenced for Their Roles in Salmonella-Tainted Peanut Product Outbreak," US Department of Justice, September 21, 2015.

333 "China Executes Two for Tainted Milk Scandal," *The Guardian*, November 2009.

334 "On the Radio," Freakonomics, http://freakonomics.com/hours/.

335 "Foodborne Illness-Causing Organisms in the US: What You Need to Know," FDA website, https://www.fda.gov/media/77727/download.

336 "Surveillance for Foodborne Disease Outbreaks United States, 2017: Annual Report," CDC website, https://www.cdc.gov/fdoss/pdf/2017_FoodBorneOutbreaks_508.pdf.

337 Robert Roos, "New Study Puts Cost of US Foodborne Illness at $77 Billion," CIDRAP, January 3, 2012.

338 Douglas L. Archer and John E. Kvenberg, "Incidence and Cost of Foodborne Diarrheal Disease in the United States," *Journal of Food Protection*, October 1, 1985.

339 FDA, "A NEW ERA OF SMARTER FOOD SAFETY," Docket No. FDA-2019-N-4187, Hilton Washington DC/Rockville Hotel, Oct 21, 2019.

340 "New Era of Smarter Food Safety: FDA's Blueprint for the Future," FDA website, https://www.fda.gov/media/139868/download.

341 "Citation Cold Case," The Millennium Project, http://www.ratbags.com/rsoles/comment/ausscience1207_lies.htm.

342 Frank Yannis, "FDA Blueprint for Food Safety," February 11, 2021.

343 Nicole Rura, "Close to Half of U.S. Population Projected to Have Obesity by 2030," Harvard T. H. Chan School of Public Health, December 19, 2019.

344 Krista Garver, "Research Shows Younger Consumers Open to New Food Technology, and They'll Probably Talk About It," *Food Industry Executive*, November 6, 2019.